Suzuki
DR-Z400, DR-Z400E, DR-Z400S & DR-Z400SM
Service and Repair Manual

by Alan Ahlstrand

Models covered

Suzuki DR-Z400 (kick start), 2000 through 2005
Suzuki DR-Z400E (electric start), 2000 through 2009
Suzuki DR-Z400S, 2000 through 2010
Suzuki DR-Z400SM, 2005 through 2010

ABCDE
FGHIJ
KLMNO
PQRST

ISBN-13: **978-1-56392-933-5**
ISBN-10: **1-56392-933-3**

Library of Congress Control Number: 2011945023
Printed in the USA

Haynes Publishing
Sparkford, Nr Yeovil, Somerset BA22 7JJ, England

Haynes North America, Inc
861 Lawrence Drive, Newbury Park, California 91320, USA

12-208

Contents

LIVING WITH YOUR SUZUKI

Introduction

Pre-ride checks

MAINTENANCE

Routine maintenance and servicing

Contents

REPAIRS AND OVERHAUL

Engine, transmission and associated systems

Chassis components

Wiring diagrams

REFERENCE

Index

Suzuki
Every Which Way

by Julian Ryder

From Textile Machinery to Motorcycles

Suzuki were the second of Japan's Big Four motorcycle manufacturers to enter the business, and like Honda they started by bolting small two-stroke motors to bicycles. Unlike Honda, they had manufactured other products before turning to transportation in the aftermath of World War II.

In fact Suzuki has been in business since the first decade of the 20th-Century when Michio Suzuki manufactured textile machinery.

The desperate need for transport in post-war Japan saw Suzuki make their first motorised bicycle in 1952, and the fact that by 1954 the company had changed its name to Suzuki Motor Company shows how quickly the sideline took over the whole company's activities. In their first full manufacturing year,

Suzuki made nearly 4500 bikes and rapidly expanded into the world markets with a range of two-strokes.

Suzuki didn't make a four-stroke until 1977 when the GS750 double-overhead-cam across-the-frame four arrived. This was several years after Honda and Kawasaki had established the air-cooled four as the industry standard, but no motorcycle epitomises the era of what came to be known as the Universal

The T500 two-stroke twin

One of the later GT750 'kettle' models with front disc brakes

50 cc racer won six of the eight world titles chalked up by Suzuki during the 1960s as well as providing Mitsuo Itoh with the distinction of being the only Japanese rider to win an Isle of Man TT. Mr Itoh still works for Suzuki, he's in charge of their racing program.

Europe got the benefit of Suzuki's two-stroke expertise in a succession of air-cooled twins, the six-speed 250 cc Super Six being the most memorable, but the arrival in 1968 of the first of a series of 500 cc twins which were good looking, robust and versatile marked the start of mainstream success.

So confident were Suzuki of their two-stroke expertise that they even applied it to the burgeoning Superbike sector. The GT750 water-cooled triple arrived in 1972. It was big, fast and comfortable although the handling and stopping power did draw some comment. Whatever the drawbacks of the road bike, the engine was immensely successful in Superbike and Formula 750 racing. The roadster has its devotees, though, and is now a sought-after bike on the classic Japanese scene. Do not refer to it as the Water Buffalo in such company. Joking aside, the later disc-braked versions were quite civilised, but the audacious idea of using a big two-stroke motor in what was essentially a touring bike was a surprising success until the fuel crisis of the mid-'70s effectively killed off big strokers.

The same could be said of Suzuki's only real lemon, the RE5. This is still the only mass-produced bike to use the rotary (or Wankel) engine but never sold well. Fuel consumption in the mid-teens allied to frightening complexity and excess weight meant the RE5 was a non-starter in the sales race.

Japanese motorcycle better than the GS. So well engineered were the original fours that you can clearly see their genes in the GS500 twins that are still going strong in the mid-1990s. Suzuki's ability to prolong the life of their products this way means that they are often thought of as a conservative company. This is hardly fair if you look at some of their landmark designs, most of which have been commercial as well as critical successes.

Two-stroke Success

Early racing efforts were bolstered by the arrival of Ernst Degner who defected from the East German MZ team at the Swedish GP of 1961, bringing with him the rotary-valve secrets of design genius Walter Kaaden. The new Suzuki 50 cc racer won its first GP on the Isle of Man the following year and winning the title easily. Only Honda and Ralph Bryans interrupted Suzuki's run of 50 cc titles from 1962 to 1968.

The arrival of the twin-cylinder 125 racer in 1963 enabled Hugh Anderson to win both 50 and 125 world titles. You may not think 50 cc racing would be exciting - until you learn that the final incarnation of the thing had 14 gears and could do well over 100 mph on fast circuits. Before pulling out of GPs in 1967 the

Suzuki's GT250X7 was an instant hit in the popular 250 cc 'learner' sector

The GS400 was the first in a line of four-stroke twins

Development of the Four-stroke range

When Suzuki got round to building a four-stroke they did a very good job of it. The GS fours were built in 550, 650, 750, 850, 1000 and 1100 cc sizes in sports, custom, roadster and even shaft-driven touring forms over many years. The GS1000 was in on the start of Superbike racing in the early 1970s and the GS850 shaft-driven tourer was around nearly 15 years later. The fours spawned a line of 400, 425, 450 and 500 cc GS twins that were essentially the middle half of the four with all their reliability. If there was ever a criticism of the GS models it was that with the exception of the GS1000S of 1980, colloquially known as the ice-cream van, the range was visually uninspiring.

They nearly made the same mistake when they launched the four-valve-head GSX750 in 1979. Fortunately, the original twin-shock version was soon replaced by the 'E'-model with Full-Floater rear suspension and a full set of all the gadgets the Japanese industry was then keen on and has since forgotten about, like 16-inch front wheels and anti-dive forks. The air-cooled GSX was like the GS built in 550, 750 and 1100 cc versions with a variety of half, full and touring fairings, but the GSX that is best remembered is the Katana that first appeared in 1981. The power was provided by an 1000 or 1100 cc GSX motor, but wrapped around it was the most outrageous styling package to come out of Japan. Designed by Hans Muth of Target Design, the Katana looked like nothing seen before or since. At the time there was as much anti feeling as praise,

but now it is rightly regarded as a classic, a true milestone in motorcycle design. The factory have even started making 250 and 400 cc fours for the home market with the same styling as the 1981 bike.

Just to remind us that they'd still been building two-strokes for the likes of Barry Sheene, in 1986 Suzuki marketed a road-going version of their RG500 square-four racer which had put an end to the era of the four-stroke in 500 GPs when it appeared in 1974. In 1976 Suzuki not only won their first 500 title with Sheene, they sold RG500s over the counter and won every GP with them - with the exception of the Isle of Man TT which the works riders boycotted. Ten years on, the RG500 Gamma gave road riders the nearest experience they'd ever get to riding a GP bike. The fearsome beast could top 140 mph and only weighed 340 lb - the other alleged GP replicas were pussy cats compared to the Gamma's man-eating tiger.

The RG only lasted a few years and is already firmly in the category of collector's item; its four-stroke equivalent, the GSX-R, is still with us and looks like being so for many years. You have to look back to 1985 and its launch to realise just what a revolutionary step the GSX-R750 was: quite simply it was the first race replica. Not a bike dressed up to look like a race bike, but a genuine racer with lights on, a bike that could be taken straight to the track and win.

The first GSX-R, the 750, had a completely new motor cooled by oil rather than water and an aluminium cradle frame. It was sparse, a little twitchy and very, very fast. This time Suzuki got the looks right, blue and white bodywork based on the factory's racing colours and endurance-racer lookalike twin headlights. And then came the 1100 - the big GSX-R got progressively more brutal as it chased the Yamaha EXUP for the heavyweight championship.

And alongside all these mould-breaking designs, Suzuki were also making the best looking custom bikes to come out of Japan, the Intruders; the first race replica trail bike, the DR350; the sharpest 250 Supersports, the

The GS750 led the way for a series of four cylinder models

Later four-stroke models, like this GSX1100, were fitted with 16v engines

RGV250; and a bargain-basement 600, the Bandit. The Bandit proved so popular they went on to build 1200 and 750 cc versions of it. I suppose that's predictable, a range of four-stroke fours just like the GS and GSXs. It's just like the company really, sometimes predictable, admittedly - but never boring.

It's a V-twin Jim, but not as we know it

The late 1990s was a time when Honda and Suzuki decided it was time to keep up with their Italian neighbours at Ducati and build a V-twin. Both built a softer, road orientated version and a harder-edged model to homologate for Superbike racing. Honda's bike was uncontroversial, and did exactly what it said on the tin. Suzuki's didn't.

Everybody agreed the TL1000S had a great engine that felt just like a big V-twin should and that in the days before the R1 it was as quick as you could want. Then rumours started circulating about some nasty habits. Some reports in specialist magazines said the TL was prone to vicious tank-slappers; others equally vehemently said the rumours were rubbish. It was enough to persuade the British importer to retro-fit steering dampers, and suspicion centred on the rear suspension system and its innovative (or weird, depending on which camp you were in) rotary damper. After some unpleasant accidents and subsequent court cases, things quietened down. The

steering damper certainly helped and fuel-injection tweaks that smoothed out the power delivery on later models helped riders keep the bike under control. However, the model's reputation was seriously damaged and a lot of people fought shy of the TL – which means second-hand examples are satisfyingly cheap for those in the know.

The R-model isn't just a modified version of the S, it's a completely different machine. This was the bike that was supposed to take on Ducati on the tracks and take over

Suzuki's racing efforts from the ageing and now out-gunned GSX-R750. It didn't happen. The R was still high, long and, at nearly 200 kg dry, heavy. They did turn up on race tracks but never made it to the World Superbike grid. The Alstare Corona organisation that ran the works World Superbike effort secretly developed a race-ready TL1000R with multiple World Superbike winner and World Endurance Champion Stephane Mertens of Belgium as the test rider. However, even the team that kept the old 750 competitive well after its sell-by date couldn't get the big twin competitive.

The motor did win a race though, but in a Bimota chassis.

Aussie wild child Anthony Gobert rode a Bimota SB8 with TL1000 motor for the first part of the 2000 season. He scored points in race two of the opening round of the year in South Africa then with an inspired tyre gamble on a drying Phillip Island track at home in Oz he won the first race of round two and followed it up with ninth place in the second race. Next time out in Japan, it blew up spectacularly, flinging Gobert down the track and following him into the barriers. Even the Go-Show admitted it was a crash that scared him severely as well as giving him a collection of minor fractures and burns. The team folded soon afterwards, citing lack of funds. The whole episode summed up the TL's relationship with the race track.

Nothing daunted, Suzuki took another cue from Honda and put their V-twin in a giant trailbike, and again just like Honda they gave it a very strange name, the V-Strom (that is not a misprint). Pushing peak power down to produce more midrange and bottom end made for a very nice motor which suited the chassis brilliantly. The V-Strom, along with its compatriots in the giant trailbike class, is sadly under-rated by those obsessed with sports bikes, but it's the sort of machine on which you can load two people and their luggage and set off to travel on anything from motorways to dirt tracks and enjoy it.

It would be a shame to consign such a great

Suzuki's GSX-R range represented their cutting edge sports bikes

The TL1000S-W

The TL1000R-K1

The DL1000-K2 V-Strom

motor to an early grave so unappreciated, so Suzuki went back to the original TL, the S, and re-invented the bike as a budget sportster in the SV range. It may wear a different designation, but the SV has all the DNA of the TL. With the exception of that strange damper.

Suzuki's first major success in the V-twin cruiser market came with the 750 Intruder in 1985. Using a liquid-cooled engine with a 45-degree angle between the cylinders, twin-shock rear suspension and shaft drive, the bike gave Suzuki a credible entry in the category.

Displacement was reduced to 700cc (and the model designation changed to VS700) for US models in 1986 and 1987. This was in response to a tariff on Japanese bikes over 700cc, which was designed to protect Harley-Davidson, at that time in severe financial peril. The tariff was rescinded at HD's request as their business picked up, and displacement on US models was returned to 750cc in 1988.

The VZ800 Marauder added some styling variety to Suzuki's cruiser line, beginning in 1997. The bike was mechanically almost the same as the Intruder, with chain drive being the most important difference.

The VL800 Volusia, added to the line in 2001, was more of a cruiser than a chopper. It used a single carburetor, rather than the dual carbs of the Intruder and Marauder. The fuel tank was wide, the fenders swoopy, and the front forks made to look plump with the addition of trim covers on the upper fork legs.

The Intruder was renamed the Boulevard S50 (as in 50 cubic inches of piston displacement) for 2005. Mechanically, it's almost unchanged from the Intruder.

The Marauder was renamed the Boulevard M50 for 2005. Its carburetors were replaced by a dual-throttle fuel injection system.

The Volusia was renamed the Boulevard C50 for 2005 and equipped with the same fuel injection system as the M50.

The DR-Z400 was a significant update to Suzuki's off-road bike line, beginning in 2000. It featured a DOHC engine, adjustable front and rear shocks, and disc brakes at front and rear. The DR-Z400 was equipped with a kickstarter, headlight and taillight and didn't have a battery (alternating current is rectified by the regulator/rectifier for use by the headlight and taillight). The DR-Z400E substituted a battery and electric starter for the kickstarter. For nostalgic riders (or cautious ones), Suzuki offered a kickstarter kit for the E model.

The dual-purpose DR-Z400S adds a brake light, mirrors and turn signals to make the bike street legal. A Mikuni CV carburetor replaces the flat-slide Keihin used in most of the off-road models. The DR-Z400SM was added to the line in 2005. Street tires and 17-inch wheels at front and rear, as well as inverted forks, turn the S model into a supermotard.

Acknowledgements

Our thanks to GP Sports of Santa Clara and San Jose, California, for supplying the motorcycles used in the photographs throughout this manual; to David Guy, service manager, for arranging the teardown and fitting the project into his shop's busy schedule; to Tony Correa, service technician, for doing the mechanical work and providing valuable technical information; and to Scott Farstad for lending us his tricked-out DR-Z400SM for the cover.

About this Manual

The aim of this manual is to help you get the best value from your motorcycle. It can do so in several ways. It can help you decide what work must be done, even if you choose to have it done by a dealer; it provides information and procedures for routine maintenance and servicing; and it offers diagnostic and repair procedures to follow when trouble occurs.

We hope you use the manual to tackle the work yourself. For many simpler jobs, doing it yourself may be quicker than arranging an appointment to get the motorcycle into a dealer and making the trips to leave it and pick it up. More importantly, a lot of money can be saved by avoiding the expense the shop must pass on to you to cover its labour and overhead costs. An added benefit is the sense of satisfaction and accomplishment that you feel after doing the job yourself.

References to the left or right side of the motorcycle assume you are sitting on the seat, facing forward.

We take great pride in the accuracy of information given in this manual, but motorcycle manufacturers make alterations and design changes during the production run of a particular motorcycle of which they do not inform us. No liability can be accepted by the authors or publishers for loss, damage or injury caused by any errors in, or omissions from, the information given.

Frame and engine numbers

The vehicle identification number (VIN) is stamped in the right side of the steering head, and is also printed on a plate attached to the steering head. The engine serial number is stamped into a plate on the right side of the crankcase. These numbers should be recorded and kept in a safe place so they can be furnished to law enforcement officials in the event of theft.

The VIN, frame serial number, engine serial number and carburetor identification number should be kept in a handy place (such as your wallet) so they are always available when purchasing or ordering parts for your machine.

The models covered by this manual are as follows:

Suzuki DR-Z400, 2000 through 2005
Suzuki DR-Z400E, 2000 through 2009
Suzuki DR-Z400S, 2000 through 2010
Suzuki DR-Z400SM, 2005 through 2010

Suzuki country and regional codes

Suzuki uses country and regional codes in its model numbers. Those that apply to the DR-Z400/E/S/SM are:

General	E-01
UK	E-02
US	
Except California	E-03
California	E-33
EU	E-19, UE-19
Australia	E-24
Canada	E-28
Brazil	E-37
Israel	E-54

Model codes

Suzuki uses a one- or two-digit code to indicate the model year. Model years and frame numbers are:

Year	Code
2000	Y
2001	K1
2002	K2
2003	K3
2004	K4
2005	K5
2006	K6
2007	K7
2008	K8
2009	K9
2010	L0

Initial frame numbers

DR-Z400	Not available		2008	
DR-Z400E			UK	JS1BC111100 ******
2000 through 2003	Not available		Europe	JS1BC111200 110640
2004/2005			US (including California)	JS1SK43A 82 100001
General	JS1BF111100 105561		Australia	JS1BC111400 100333
US except California	JS1DK433 52 100001		Canada	JS1DK44A 82 100001
California	JS1DK44A 52 100001		Israel	JS1BC111380 100001
Australia	JBS1BB111100 103912		2009	
Canada	JS1DK44A 52 100001		US (including California)	JS1SK43A 92 100001
2006			Australia	JS1BC111400 100421
General	JS1BF111100 106778		Canada	JS1SK43A 92 100001
US except California	JS1DK433 62 100001		2010	
California	JS1DK44A 62 100001		US (including California)	JS1SK43A A2 100001
Australia	JBS1BB111100 ******		Australia	JS1BC111400 100558
Canada	JS1DK44A 62 100001		Canada	JS1SK43A A2 100001
2007			DR-Z400SM	
General	JS1BF111100 100001		2005	
US except California	JS1DK433 62 100001		UK	JS1B8111100 100001
California	JS1DK44A 62 100001		Europe (E-19)	JS1B8111200 100001
Australia	JBS1BB111100 100001		Europe (UE-19)	JS1B82111001 100001
Canada	JS1DK44A 62 100001		US (including California)	JS1SK44A 52 100001
Brazil	Not available		Canada	JS1SK44A 52 100001
2008	Not sold		2006	
2009			UK	JS1B8111100 100618
Australia	JBS1BB111100 109852		Europe	JS1BC111200 103109
DR-Z400S			US (including California)	JS1SK44A 62 100001
2000 through 2004	Not available		Australia	JBS1B8111100 ******
2005			Canada	JS1SK44A 62 100001
UK	JS1BC111100 102810		2007	
Europe	JS1BC111100 108193		UK	JS1B8111100 101217
US (including California)	JS1SK43A 52 100001		Europe	JS1B8111200 106276
Canada	JS1SK43A 52 100001		US (including California)	JS1SK44A 72 100001
Israel	JS1BC111340 100015		Australia	JS1BC111400 100256
2006			Canada	JS1DK44A 72 100001
UK	JS1BC111100 ******		2008	
Europe	JS1BC111200 109106		UK	JS1B8111100 102530
US (including California)	JS1SK43A 62 100001		Europe	JS1B8111200 110838
Australia	JBS1BB111100 ******		US (including California)	JS1SK44A 82 100001
Canada	JS1SK43A 62 100001		Australia	JS1BC111400 100333
Israel	JS1BC111360 100001		Canada	JS1DK44A 82 100001
2007			2009	
UK	JS1BC111100 103534		US (including California)	JS1SK44A 92 100001
Europe	JS1BC111200 110007		Australia	JS1B8111300 100457
US (including California)	JS1SK43A 72 100001		Canada	JS1SK44A 92 100001
Australia	JS1BC111400 100256		2010	
Canada	JS1DK44A 72 100001		US (including California)	JS1SK44A A2 100001
Israel	JS1BC111370 100001		Australia	JS1B8111300 100750
			Canada	JS1SK44A A2 100001

Buying spare parts

Once you have found all the identification numbers, record them for reference when buying parts. Since the manufacturers change specifications, parts and vendors (companies that manufacture various components on the machine), providing the ID numbers is the only way to be reasonably sure that you are buying the correct parts.

Whenever possible, take the worn part to the dealer so direct comparison with the new component can be made. Along the trail from the manufacturer to the parts shelf, there are numerous places that the part can end up with the wrong number or be listed incorrectly.

The two places to purchase new parts for your motorcycle – the accessory store and the franchised dealer – differ in the type of parts they carry. While dealers can obtain virtually every part for your motorcycle, the accessory dealer is usually limited to normal high wear items such as shock absorbers, tune-up parts, various engine gaskets, cables, chains, brake parts, etc. Rarely will an accessory outlet have major suspension components, cylinders, transmission gears, or cases.

Used parts can be obtained for roughly half the price of new ones, but you can't always be sure of what you're getting. Once again, take your worn part to the salvage yard for direct comparison.

Whether buying new, used or rebuilt parts, the best course is to deal directly with someone who specializes in parts for your particular make.

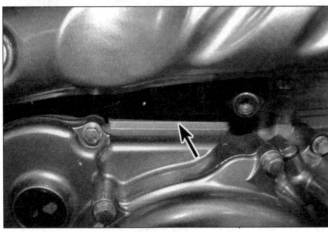

The engine number location

The frame number location

Professional mechanics are trained in safe working procedures. However enthusiastic you may be about getting on with the job at hand, take the time to ensure that your safety is not put at risk. A moment's lack of attention can result in an accident, as can failure to observe simple precautions.

There will always be new ways of having accidents, and the following is not a comprehensive list of all dangers; it is intended rather to make you aware of the risks and to encourage a safe approach to all work you carry out on your bike.

Asbestos

● Certain friction, insulating, sealing and other products - such as brake pads, clutch linings, gaskets, etc. - contain asbestos. Extreme care must be taken to avoid inhalation of dust from such products since it is hazardous to health. If in doubt, assume that they do contain asbestos.

Fire

● Remember at all times that gasoline is highly flammable. Never smoke or have any kind of naked flame around, when working on the vehicle. But the risk does not end there - a spark caused by an electrical short-circuit, by two metal surfaces contacting each other, by careless use of tools, or even by static electricity built up in your body under certain conditions, can ignite gasoline vapor, which in a confined space is highly explosive. Never use gasoline as a cleaning solvent. Use an approved safety solvent.

● Always disconnect the battery ground terminal before working on any part of the fuel or electrical system, and never risk spilling fuel on to a hot engine or exhaust.

● It is recommended that a fire extinguisher of a type suitable for fuel and electrical fires is kept handy in the garage or workplace at all times. Never try to extinguish a fuel or electrical fire with water.

Fumes

● Certain fumes are highly toxic and can quickly cause unconsciousness and even death if inhaled to any extent. Gasoline vapor comes into this category, as do the vapors from certain solvents such as trichloro-ethylene. Any draining or pouring of such volatile fluids should be done in a well ventilated area.

● When using cleaning fluids and solvents, read the instructions carefully. Never use materials from unmarked containers - they may give off poisonous vapors.

● Never run the engine of a motor vehicle in an enclosed space such as a garage. Exhaust fumes contain carbon monoxide which is extremely poisonous; if you need to run the engine, always do so in the open air or at least have the rear of the vehicle outside the workplace.

The battery

● Never cause a spark, or allow a naked light near the vehicle's battery. It will normally be giving off a certain amount of hydrogen gas, which is highly explosive.

● Always disconnect the battery ground terminal before working on the fuel or electrical systems (except where noted).

● If possible, loosen the filler plugs or cover when charging the battery from an external source. Do not charge at an excessive rate or the battery may burst.

● Take care when topping up, cleaning or carrying the battery. The acid electrolyte, even when diluted, is very corrosive and should not be allowed to contact the eyes or skin. Always wear rubber gloves and goggles or a face shield. If you ever need to prepare electrolyte yourself, always add the acid slowly to the water; never add the water to the acid.

Electricity

● When using an electric power tool, inspection light etc., always ensure that the appliance is correctly connected to its plug and that, where necessary, it is properly grounded. Do not use such appliances in damp conditions and, again, beware of creating a spark or applying excessive heat in the vicinity of fuel or fuel vapor. Also ensure that the appliances meet national safety standards.

● A severe electric shock can result from touching certain parts of the electrical system, such as the spark plug wires (HT leads), when the engine is running or being cranked, particularly if components are damp or the insulation is defective. Where an electronic ignition system is used, the secondary (HT) voltage is much higher and could prove fatal.

Remember...

✗ **Don't** start the engine without first ascertaining that the transmission is in neutral.

✗ **Don't** attempt to drain oil until you are sure it has cooled sufficiently to avoid scalding you.

✗ **Don't** grasp any part of the engine or exhaust system without first ascertaining that it is cool enough not to burn you.

✗ **Don't** allow brake fluid or antifreeze to contact the machine's paintwork or plastic components.

✗ **Don't** siphon toxic liquids such as fuel, oil or antifreeze by mouth, or allow them to remain on your skin.

✗ **Don't** inhale dust - it may be injurious to health (see Asbestos heading).

✗ **Don't** allow any spilled oil or grease to remain on the floor - wipe it up right away, before someone slips on it.

✗ **Don't** use ill-fitting wrenches or other tools which may slip and cause injury.

✗ **Don't** lift a heavy component which may be beyond your capability - get assistance.

✗ **Don't** rush to finish a job or take unverified short cuts.

✗ **Don't** allow children or animals in or around an unattended vehicle.

✗ **Don't** inflate a tire above the recommended pressure. Apart from overstressing the carcass, in extreme cases the tire may blow off forcibly.

✔ **Do** ensure that the machine is supported securely at all times. This is especially important when the machine is blocked up to aid wheel or fork removal.

✔ **Do** take care when attempting to loosen a stubborn nut or bolt. It is generally better to pull on a wrench, rather than push, so that if you slip, you fall away from the machine rather than onto it.

✔ **Do** wear eye protection when using power tools such as drill, sander, bench grinder etc.

✔ **Do** use a barrier cream on your hands prior to undertaking dirty jobs - it will protect your skin from infection as well as making the dirt easier to remove afterwards; but make sure your hands aren't left slippery. Note that long-term contact with used engine oil can be a health hazard.

✔ **Do** keep loose clothing (cuffs, ties etc. and long hair) well out of the way of moving mechanical parts.

✔ **Do** remove rings, wristwatch etc., before working on the vehicle - especially the electrical system.

✔ **Do** keep your work area tidy - it is only too easy to fall over articles left lying around.

✔ **Do** exercise caution when compressing springs for removal or installation. Ensure that the tension is applied and released in a controlled manner, using suitable tools which preclude the possibility of the spring escaping violently.

✔ **Do** ensure that any lifting tackle used has a safe working load rating adequate for the job.

✔ **Do** get someone to check periodically that all is well, when working alone on the vehicle.

✔ **Do** carry out work in a logical sequence and check that everything is correctly assembled and tightened afterwards.

✔ **Do** remember that your vehicle's safety affects that of yourself and others. If in doubt on any point, get professional advice.

● If in spite of following these precautions, you are unfortunate enough to injure yourself, seek medical attention as soon as possible.

Note: *The Pre-ride checks outlined in the owner's manual covers those items which should be inspected before riding the motorcycle.*

Engine oil level

Before you start:

Caution: Do not run the engine in an enclosed space such as a garage or workshop.

✔ With the motorcycle held upright, unscrew the dipstick and make sure there's some oil on it. If there's none at all, refer to the oil change procedure in Chapter 1 for additional steps. If there is oil, screw the dipstick back in.

✔ Warm the engine to normal operating temperature and let it idle for a few minutes.

✔ Stop the engine and support the motorcycle in an upright position on level ground, using an auxiliary stand if required.

✔ Leave the motorcycle undisturbed for three minutes to allow the oil level to stabilize.

Bike care:

● If you have to add oil frequently, you should check whether you have any oil leaks. If there is no sign of oil leakage from the joints and gaskets the engine could be burning oil (see *Troubleshooting*).

The correct oil:

● Modern, high-revving engines place great demands on their oil. It is very important that the correct oil for your bike is used.

● Always top up with a good quality oil of the specified type and viscosity and do not overfill the engine.

Oil type	API grade SF/SG or SH/SJ meeting JASO standard MA (the MA standard is required to prevent clutch slippage).
Oil viscosity	SAE 10W-40

1 With the motorcycle held upright, unscrew the filler cap/dipstick from the frame oil tank, wipe it with a clean rag and put it back in the tank (don't screw it in - just let it rest on the threads). Pull the dipstick out and check the oil level on the dipstick scale. If the oil level is low, add oil through the dipstick hole. Add enough oil of the specified grade and type to bring the level on the dipstick up to the upper mark. Do not overfill. Install the filler cap/dipstick.

Coolant level

1 Check coolant level in the radiator behind the right side cover. Loosen the cap stopper screw (if equipped), then turn the cap to its first stop and let any residual pressure escape. Once this is done, remove the cap completely and check the coolant level. It should be up to the bottom of the filler neck. If it's low, add a 50/50 mixture of ethylene glycol-based antifreeze and distilled water, then reinstall the cap.

⚠ *Warning: This procedure requires removal of the radiator cap. Be sure to let the engine cool completely first. If the cap is removed with the engine hot, scalding coolant may shoot out of the radiator and burn you.*

● If the coolant level is frequently low, check the hoses, especially at the connections, for signs of coolant leakage. Also check below the water pump for coolant stains which would indicate leakage from the mechanical seal (refer to the inspection procedures in Chapter 1 if necessary).

● If there no visible leak and the coolant level keeps dropping, the head gasket may be defective. This could allow coolant to leak into the combustion chamber. If you can't find a leak, have the system pressure tested by a dealer service department or other qualified shop.

Suspension, steering and drive chain

Suspension and Steering:
● Check that the front and rear suspension operates smoothly without binding.
● Check that the suspension is adjusted as required.
● Check that the steering moves smoothly from lock-to-lock.

Drive chain:
● Check that the drive chain slack isn't excessive, and adjust it if necessary (see Chapter 1).
● If the chain looks dry, lubricate it (see Chapter 1).

Chain slack	40 to 50 mm (1.6 to 2.0 inches)

1 Place the bike on the sidestand and make sure the transmission is in neutral. Measure slack at the midpoint of the chain's lower run. Repeat the measurement at several points along the chain. If chain slack is not within the specified limit, refer to Chapter 1 and adjust it. There should be a chain slack information decal on the chain guard; if its specifications differ from those in this manual, use the specifications on the decal. If chain slack measurements differ at different points on the chain, it may be binding or kinked. Lubricate the chain as specified in Chapter 1. If this doesn't solve the problem, replace the chain (see Chapter 6). Check the chain for wear or damage and replace it, referring to Chapter 6, if problems are found.

Legal and safety

Lighting and signalling:
● Take a minute to check that the headlight, tail light, brake light, instrument lights and turn signals (if equipped) all work correctly.
● Check that the horn sounds when the switch is operated.

Safety:
● Check that the throttle grip rotates smoothly and snaps shut when released, in all steering positions. Also check for the correct amount of freeplay (see Chapter 1).
● Check that the engine shuts off when the kill switch is operated.
● Check that sidestand return spring holds the stand up securely when it is retracted.

Fuel:
● This may seem obvious, but check that you have enough fuel to complete your journey. If you notice signs of fuel leakage – rectify the cause immediately.
● Ensure you use the correct grade unleaded fuel – see Chapter 4 Specifications.

Brake fluid level

> ⚠️ *Warning: Brake hydraulic fluid can harm your eyes and damage painted surfaces, so use extreme caution when handling and pouring it and cover surrounding surfaces with rag. Do not use fluid that has been standing open for some time, as it absorbs moisture from the air which can cause a dangerous loss of braking effectiveness.*

Before you start:

✔ Sit on the bike and hold it upright. Turn the handlebars until the top of the master cylinder is as level as possible.

✔ Make sure you have the correct hydraulic fluid. DOT 4 is recommended.

✔ Wrap a rag around the reservoir to ensure that any spilled fluid does not come in contact with painted surfaces. If fluid spills, clean it up immediately with soap and water - don't just wipe it off, as the residue may damage paint.

Bike care:

● The fluid in the brake master cylinder reservoir will drop slightly as the brake pads wear down.

● If the fluid reservoir requires repeated topping-up this is an indication of an hydraulic leak somewhere in the system, which should be investigated immediately.

● Check for signs of fluid leakage from the hydraulic hoses and brake system components - if found, rectify immediately (see Chapter 7).

● Check the operation of both brakes before taking the machine on the road; if there is evidence of air in the system (spongy feel to lever or pedal), it must be bled as described in Chapter 7.

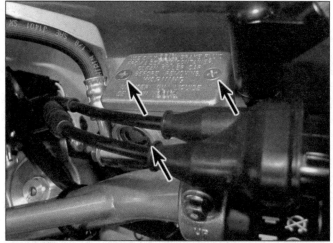

1 The front brake fluid level is visible through the sight glass in the reservoir body - it must be above the LOWER reservoir line.

2 If the fluid is below the line, remove the cap screws and lift off the reservoir cap, diaphragm plate and diaphragm. Top up with new, clean DOT 4 brake fluid, until the level is just below the upper level line cast on the inside of the reservoir. Take care to avoid spills (see WARNING above) and do not overfill. Be sure the diaphragm is correctly seated before installing the plate and cap, then tighten the screws securely.

3 The brake fluid level is visible through the translucent reservoir, located behind the protective cover. It should be between the upper and lower lines. If it's at or below the LOWER line, remove the screws that secure the cap and lift it off. Add the specified brake fluid until the level is up to the upper line on the reservoir, then install the cap and tighten the screws securely.

Tires

The correct pressures:

● The tires must be checked when **cold**, not immediately after riding. Note that low tire pressures may cause the tire to slip on the rim or come off. High tire pressures will cause abnormal tread wear and unsafe handling.

● Use an accurate pressure gauge. Many service station gauges are wildly inaccurate. If you buy your own, spend as much as you can justify on a quality gauge.

● Correct air pressure will increase tire life and provide maximum stability, handling capability and ride comfort.

Tire care:

● Check the tires carefully for cuts, tears, embedded nails or other sharp objects and excessive wear. Operation of the motorcycle with excessively worn tires is extremely hazardous, as traction and handling are directly affected.

● Check the condition of the tire valve and ensure the dust cap is in place.

● Pick out any stones or nails which may have become embedded in the tire tread. If left, they will eventually penetrate through the casing and cause a puncture.

● If tire damage is apparent, or unexplained loss of pressure is experienced, seek the advice of a tire fitting specialist without delay.

Tire tread depth:

● Suzuki recommends a minimum of 4 mm for the front and rear tires on DR-Z400 and DR-Z400E models, and 3mm for the front and rear tires on DR-Z400S and DR-Z400SM models. Many riders consider 2 mm to be a safe minimum for all tires. The tread depth should be measured at the thinnest point, and there should be no bald patches on the tire.

● Many tires now incorporate wear indicators in the tread. Identify the triangular pointer or TWI mark on the tire sidewall to locate the indicator bar and replace the tire if the tread has worn down to the bar.

Tire pressures	
DR-Z400, DR-Z400E	
Australia	18 psi (125 kPa) front and rear
Except Australia	14 psi (100 kPa) front and rear
DR-Z400S	
Front	18 psi (125 kPa)
Rear	
Single rider	22 psi (150 kPa)
Rider and passenger	25 psi (175 kPa)
DR-Z400SM	
Front	25 psi (175 kPa)
Rear	
Single rider	29 psi (200 kPa)
Rider and passenger	33 psi (225 kPa)

1 Check the tire pressures when the tires are cold and keep them properly inflated.

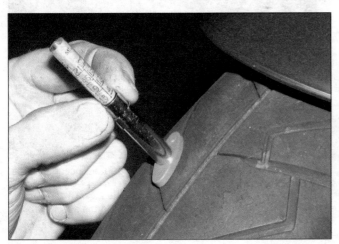

2 Measure tread depth at the center of the tire using a tread depth gauge

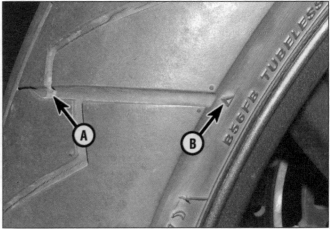

3 Tire tread wear indicator bar (A) and its location marking (B) – usually either an arrow, a triangle or the letters TWI – on the sidewall. Look for the tire information label on the chainguard or swingarm

Chapter 1
Tune-up and routine maintenance

Contents

Degrees of difficulty

| Easy, suitable for novice with little experience | | Fairly easy, suitable for beginner with some experience | | Fairly difficult, suitable for competent DIY mechanic | | Difficult, suitable for experienced DIY mechanic | | Very difficult, suitable for expert DIY or professional | 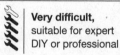 |

Specifications

Engine
Spark plug
  Type
    Standard.. NGK CR8E or Denso U24ESR-N
    Hot type.. NGK CR9E, CR10E or Denso U27ESR-N or U31ESR-N
    Cold type... NGK CR7E or Denso U22ESR-N
  Gap .... 0.7 to 0.8 mm (0.028 to 0.031 inch)
Valve clearance
  Intake .... 0.10 to 0.20 mm (0.004 to 0.008 inch)
  Exhaust .... 0.20 to 0.30 mm (0.008 to 0.012 inch)
Engine idle speed.. 1500 +/- 100 rpm

Chassis

Brake pad thickness (limit)	To wear groove
Front brake lever freeplay	0.1 to 0.3 mm (0.004 to 0.012 inch)
Rear brake pedal height	5 mm (0.4 inch) below footpeg
Throttle lever freeplay	2 to 4 mm (0.08 to 0.16 inch)
Clutch lever freeplay	10 to 15 mm (0.4 to 0.6 inch)
Drive chain slack	40 to 50 mm (1.6 to 2.0 inches)
Minimum tire tread depth	See *Daily (pre-ride) checks*
Tire pressures (cold)	See *Daily (pre-ride) checks*

Torque specifications

Coolant drain bolt	Not specified
Radiator air bleed bolt	5.5 Nm (48 inch-lbs)
Oil drain bolts	
Crankcase	21 Nm (15 ft-lbs)
Oil tank (on frame)	23 Nm (156 inch-lbs)
Oil filter cover bolts	Not specified
Spark plugs	11 Nm (96 inch-lbs)
Spark arrester bolts	11 Nm (96 inch-lbs)

Recommended lubricants and fluids

Engine oil	
Type	API Service SF/SG or SH/SJ, meeting JASO Standard MA*
Viscosity	SAE 10W-40
Capacity	
At oil change (with filter replacement)	1.8 liters (1.9 quarts)
At oil change (without filter replacement)	1.7 liters (1.8 quarts)
After engine overhaul	1.9 liters (2.0 quarts)
Air filter oil	SAE 30 or 10W-40 engine oil
Cooling system	
System capacity	
2008 and earlier (engine and reservoir)	1.25 liters (1.3 quarts)
2009 and later	1.3 liters (1.4 quarts)
Miscellaneous	
Wheel bearings	Medium weight, lithium-based multi-purpose grease
Swingarm pivot bearings	Medium weight, lithium-based multi-purpose grease
Steering shaft bushings	Medium weight, lithium-based multi-purpose grease
Cables and lever pivots	Medium weight, lithium-based multi-purpose grease
Brake pedal/shift lever/throttle lever pivots	Medium weight, lithium-based multi-purpose grease

*The JASO MA standard is required to avoid clutch slippage.

Service record

Date	Mileage	Work performed

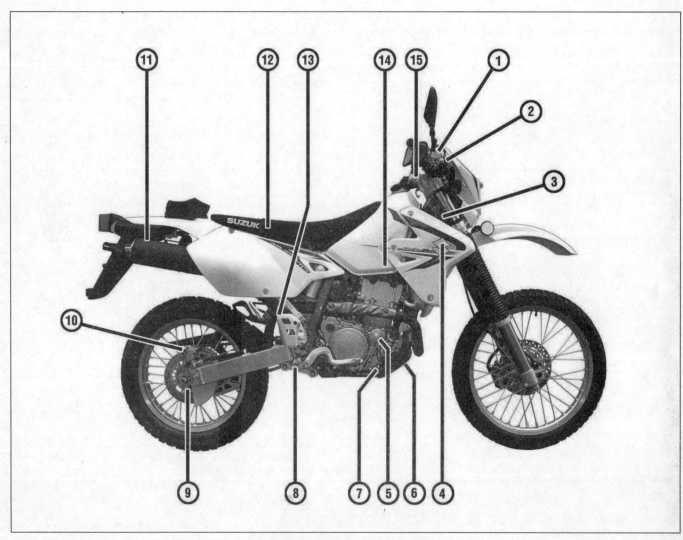

Right side maintenance points

1	Front brake fluid reservoir	7	Coolant drain plug	12	Fuses (under seat)
2	Throttle cable adjuster	8	Rear brake pedal adjuster	13	Rear brake fluid reservoir
3	Engine oil filler cap/dipstick	9	Chain adjuster (right side, DRZ400/	14	Valves (under valve cover)
4	Radiator cap (behind cover)		E/S shown)	15	Steering head adjusting nut
5	Engine oil filter	10	Rear brake pads		
6	Engine oil drain plug (frame oil tank)	11	Spark arrester (inside muffler)		

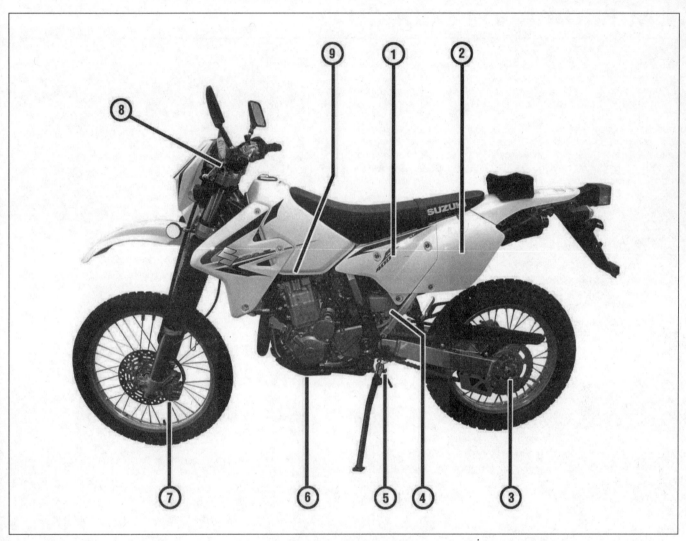

Left side maintenance points

1   Air filter (behind cover)
2   Battery (behind cover)
3   Chain adjuster (left side, DRZ400/E/S shown)
4   Coolant reservoir
5   Sidestand switch
6   Engine oil drain plug (crankcase)
7   Front brake pads
8   Clutch cable adjuster
9   Spark plug

1 Maintenance schedule

Note: *The pre-ride inspection outlined in the owner's manual covers checks and maintenance that should be carried out on a daily basis. It's condensed and included here to remind you of its importance. Always perform the pre-ride inspection at every maintenance interval (in addition to the procedures listed). The intervals listed below are the shortest intervals recommended by the manufacturer for each particular operation during the model years covered in this manual. Your owner's manual may have different intervals for your model. The maintenance schedule for off-road models (DR-Z400, DR-Z400E) is based on hours of operation. The maintenance schedule for road-going models (DR-Z400S, DR-Z400SM) is based on kilometers/miles or months.*

Daily or before riding (all models)
- ☐ Check the operation of both brakes - check the brake lever and pedal for correct freeplay
- ☐ Check the throttle for smooth operation and correct freeplay
- ☐ Make sure the engine kill switch works correctly
- ☐ Check the tires for damage, the presence of foreign objects and correct air pressure
- ☐ Check wheel spoke nipples and tighten if necessary
- ☐ Check the engine oil level
- ☐ Check the engine coolant level*
- ☐ Check the fuel level and inspect for leaks
- ☐ Check the air cleaner filter element (off-road models) and clean it if necessary
- ☐ Inspect the air cleaner drain tube and clean it if necessary
- ☐ Inspect the drive chain - on off-road models, clean and lubricate it
- ☐ Make sure the steering operates smoothly
- ☐ Verify that the headlight and taillight (if equipped) are operating satisfactorily
- ☐ Check all fasteners, including wheel nuts and axle nuts, for tightness
- ☐ Check the underbody for mud or debris that could start a fire or interfere with vehicle operation

Replace the coolant every two years.

Every 30 hours (DR-Z400, DR-Z400SE)
- ☐ Check the exhaust system for leaks and check fastener tightness
- ☐ Clean the spark arrester (US and Canadian models)
- ☐ Check the throttle for smooth operation and correct freeplay

- ☐ Check choke operation
- ☐ Inspect the fuel tap and fuel line (all models) (1)
- ☐ Check idle speed and adjust it if necessary
- ☐ Clean and gap the spark plug and replace it if necessary
- ☐ Inspect the cooling system hoses
- ☐ Inspect the engine oil hoses
- ☐ Check brake operation and brake lever and pedal freeplay
- ☐ Check brake fluid level in the front and rear master cylinders (2)
- ☐ Inspect the brake hoses (3)
- ☐ Check clutch operation and lever freeplay
- ☐ Check all chassis fasteners for tightness
- ☐ Check operation of the decompression lever (DR-Z400)

1. Replace the fuel line every four years.
2. Replace the brake fluid every two years
3. Replace the brake hoses every four years

Every 60 hours (DR-Z400, DR-Z400E)
- ☐ Change the engine oil and filter
- ☐ Replace the spark plug
- ☐ Check the valve clearance and adjust it if necessary
- ☐ Check the wheel bearings for looseness or damage
- ☐ Inspect the front and rear suspension
- ☐ Check steering system operation and freeplay
- ☐ Check the skid plates for looseness or damage

Every 6000 kilometers/4000 miles or 6 months (DR-Z400S, DR-Z400SM)
- ☐ Inspect the air filter element and clean it if necessary (1)
- ☐ Change the engine oil
- ☐ Inspect the engine oil tank and hoses
- ☐ Clean and gap and, if necessary, replace the spark plug
- ☐ Clean the spark arrester (US and Canadian models)
- ☐ Check the throttle for smooth operation and correct freeplay
- ☐ Check choke operation
- ☐ Inspect the carburetor, fuel tap and fuel line (2)

- ☐ Check idle speed and adjust it if necessary
- ☐ Clean and gap the spark plug and replace it if necessary
- ☐ Inspect the cooling system hoses
- ☐ Inspect the engine oil hoses
- ☐ Check brake operation and brake lever and pedal freeplay
- ☐ Check brake fluid level in the front and rear master cylinders (3)
- ☐ Inspect the brake hoses (4)
- ☐ Check the tires for damage, the presence of foreign objects and correct air pressure
- ☐ Check wheel spoke nipples and tighten if necessary
- ☐ Check the clutch for smooth operation and correct lever freeplay
- ☐ Clean and lubricate the drive chain (5)
- ☐ Check all chassis fasteners for tightness

1. More often in dusty or wet conditions.
2. Replace the fuel line every four years.
3. Replace the brake fluid every two years
4. Replace the brake hoses every four years
5. Lubricate the drive chain every 1000 km (600 miles)

Every 12,000 km/7500 miles or 12 months (DR-Z400S, DR-Z400SM)

- ☐ Check the exhaust system for leaks and check fastener tightness

- ☐ Replace the spark plug
- ☐ Check steering system operation and freeplay
- ☐ Inspect the front and rear suspension
- ☐ Inspect the evaporative emission control system (California models)*
- ☐ Inspect the PAIR (secondary air supply) system (UK, Europe, Israel models)

*Replace the system hoses every four years

Every 18,000 km/11,000 miles or 18 months (DR-Z400S, DR-Z400SM)

- ☐ Change the engine oil and filter
- ☐ Replace the air filter element

Every 24,000 km/15,000 miles or 24 months (DR-Z400S, DR-Z400SM)

- ☐ Check the valve clearance and adjust it if necessary
- ☐ Inspect the radiator hoses*
- ☐ Inspect the front and rear brake discs
- ☐ Inspect the wheels and tires
- ☐ Check the wheel bearings for looseness or damage
- ☐ Inspect the front and rear suspension
- ☐ Check the skid plates for looseness or damage

*Replace the radiator hoses every four years.

---

2 Introduction to tune-up and routine maintenance

This Chapter covers in detail the checks and procedures necessary for the tune-up and routine maintenance of your motorcycle. Section 1 includes the routine maintenance schedule, which is designed to keep the machine in proper running condition and prevent possible problems. The remaining Sections contain detailed procedures for carrying out the items listed on the maintenance schedule, as well as additional maintenance information designed to increase reliability. Maintenance information is also printed on decals, which are mounted in various locations on the vehicle (see illustration). Where information on the decals differs from that presented in this Chapter, use the decal information.

Since routine maintenance plays such an important role in the safe and efficient operation of your motorcycle, it is presented here as a comprehensive check list. These lists outline the procedures and checks that should be done on a routine basis.

Deciding where to start or plug into the routine maintenance schedule depends on several factors. If your bike's warranty has recently expired, and if it has been maintained according to the warranty standards, you may want to pick up routine maintenance as it coincides with the next mileage or calendar interval. If you have owned the machine for some time but have never performed any maintenance on it, then you may want to start at the nearest interval and include some

2.1 Decals on the vehicle include maintenance and safety information

4.3 Squeeze the front brake lever to bring the pads out where you can see the wear indicators

4.4 Press the brake pedal to bring the pads out where you can see the wear indicators

additional procedures to ensure that nothing important is overlooked. If you have just had a major engine overhaul, then you may want to start the maintenance routine from the beginning. If you have a used machine and have no knowledge of its history or maintenance record, you may desire to combine all the checks into one large service initially and then settle into the maintenance schedule prescribed.

The Sections that describe the inspection and maintenance procedures are written as step-by-step comprehensive guides to the actual performance of the work. They explain in detail each of the routine inspections and maintenance procedures on the check list. References to additional information in applicable Chapters is also included and should not be overlooked.

Before beginning any actual maintenance or repair, the machine should be cleaned thoroughly, especially around the oil filler plug, spark plug, engine covers, carburetor or throttle body, etc. Cleaning will help ensure that dirt does not contaminate the engine and will allow you to detect wear and damage that could otherwise easily go unnoticed.

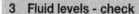

3 Fluid levels - check

Check, and if necessary, top up, the front brake fluid, rear brake fluid, engine oil and coolant as described in *Daily (pre-ride) checks* at the front of this manual.

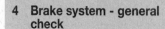

4 Brake system - general check

1   Always inspect the brakes before riding! A routine pre-ride general check will ensure that problems are discovered and remedied before they become dangerous.

2   Inspect the brake lever and pedal for loose pivots, excessive play, bending, cracking and other damage. Replace any damaged parts (see Chapter 7). Make sure all brake fasteners are tight.

3   Squeeze the front brake lever so that the brake pads protrude from the caliper and

look at the wear indicators **(see illustration)**. If the pad material has been worn down so that the wear indicators touch the disc - or are getting close to the disc - it's time for new pads (see Chapter 7).

4   Depress the rear brake pedal so that the pads protrude from the caliper and look at the wear indicators **(see illustration)**. Again, if the pad material is worn down so that the indicators are at or near the disc, install new pads (see Chapter 7).

5   If you have difficulty determining whether the pads are excessively worn because the wear indicator is hard to see (or you have aftermarket pads that don't have any kind of indicator), remove the pads (see Chapter 7), measure the thickness of the pads and compare your measurements to the pad thickness limits listed in this Chapter's Specifications.

6   DR-Z400S and SM models are equipped with a brake light which is activated by a brake light switch at the front brake lever or rear brake pedal. Make sure that the brake light works when the lever or pedal is applied (it should come on just before the brake begins to work). The front brake light switch isn't adjustable. If pressing the brake pedal doesn't cause the brake light to come on, loosen the locknut on the switch adjusting bolt, rotate the bolt as necessary and tighten the locknut **(see illustration)**.

4.6 Loosen the locknut and turn the adjusting bolt to adjust the brake light switch

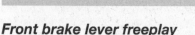

5 Brake levers and pedal - check and adjustment

Front brake lever freeplay

1   Operate the brake lever and measure freeplay at the tip of the lever. On DR-Z400S and SM models, compare it with the value listed in this Chapter's Specifications. If it's incorrect, loosen the locknut and turn the adjusting screw to change it, then tighten

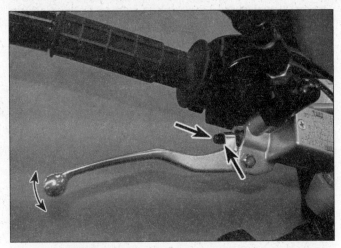

5.1 On S and SM models, loosen the locknut, turn the adjusting screw, then tighten the locknut to change the brake lever freeplay

5.4 Measure brake pedal height from the top of the footpeg to the top of the pedal

the locknut securely **(see illustration)**. On DR-Z400 and DR-Z400E models, there shouldn't be any (zero freeplay). If there is freeplay, bleed the front brakes (see Chapter 7). If this doesn't work, check the master cylinder and calipers for wear and check the brake lines for leaks (see Chapter 7). Front brake freeplay is not adjustable.

2   The position of the front brake lever can be adjusted to suit rider preference. To make the adjustment, loosen the adjuster locknut while pushing the brake lever toward the front of the vehicle. While holding pressure on the lever, turn the adjusting bolt until the lever is where you want it to be.

3   Tighten the adjuster locknut securely and recheck the lever position.

Rear brake pedal height

4   The upper side of the rear brake pedal should be the specified distance (listed in this Chapter's Specifications) below the top of the footpeg **(see illustration)**.

5   If the pedal height is incorrect, loosen the locknut on the adjusting bolt **(see illustration)**. Turn the adjusting bolt to obtain the correct pedal height, then tighten the locknut.

Caution: The distance between the locknut and the hex on the adjusting bolt must not exceed the value listed in this Chapter's Specifications. If it does, check the master cylinder and pedal for wear.

6   After making the adjustment, jack up the rear of the vehicle, spin the rear wheels and check for brake drag. If the brake drags, repeat the height adjustment.

6 Steering system - inspection

1   These motorcycles are equipped with tapered roller bearings at the top and bot-

tom of the steering head. These can become dented, rough or loose during normal use of the machine. In extreme cases, worn or loose steering head bearings can cause steering wobble that is potentially dangerous.

2   To check, support the motorcycle securely and block it so its front tire is off the ground.

3   Point the wheel straight ahead and slowly move the handlebar from side-to-side. Dents or roughness in the bearing will be felt and the bars will not move smoothly. **Note:** *Make sure any hesitation in movement is not being caused by the cables and wiring harnesses that run to the handlebar.*

4   Next, grasp the wheel and try to move it forward and backward. Any looseness in the steering head bearings will be felt as front-to-rear movement of the fork legs. If play is felt in the bearings, they should be adjusted. Refer to Chapter 6 for details.

7 Suspension - check

1   The suspension components must be maintained in top operating condition to ensure rider safety. Loose, worn or damaged suspension parts decrease the vehicle's stability and control.

2   While standing alongside the motorcycle, lock the front brake and push on the handlebars to compress the front forks several times. See if they move up-and-down smoothly without binding. If binding is felt, the front forks should be disassembled and inspected as described in Chapter 6.

3   Carefully check the area around the fork seals for any signs of fork oil leakage. If leakage is evident, the seals must be replaced as described in Chapter 6.

4   Check the tightness of all front suspen-

5.5 Loosen the locknut (lower arrow) and rotate the master cylinder pushrod with the hex (upper arrow)

sion nuts and bolts to be sure none have worked loose.

5   Inspect the rear shock absorber for fluid leakage and tightness of the mounting nuts and bolts. If leakage is found, the shock should be replaced.

6   Raise the rear of the vehicle and support it securely so it can't fall over during this procedure. Grab the swingarm on each side, just ahead of the axle. Rock the swingarm from side to side - there should be no discernible movement at the rear. If there's a little movement or a slight clicking can be heard, make sure the swingarm pivot shaft is tight. If the pivot shaft is tight but movement is still noticeable, the swingarm will have to be removed and the bearings replaced as described in Chapter 6.

7   Inspect the tightness of the rear suspension nuts and bolts.

8.4a If the bike has snail-type chain adjusters, loosen the axle nut and turn the adjusters (one on each side of the swingarm) - use the numbers and dowel to align the adjusters evenly

8.4b If the bike has bolt-type chain adjusters, loosen the axle nut, then loosen the locknut (lower right) and turn the adjusting bolt (lower left) so the indicator lines (top) are at the same point on both sides of the bike

8 Drive chain and sprockets - check, adjustment and lubrication

Check and adjustment

1   A neglected drive chain won't last long and can quickly damage the sprockets. Routine chain adjustment isn't difficult and will ensure maximum chain and sprocket life.

2   To check the chain, support the vehicle securely with the rear wheel off the ground. Place the transmission in neutral.

3   Check the entire length of the chain for damaged rollers or O-rings, loose links and loose pins.

4   Loosen the rear axle locknut (remove the cotter pin first on US and Canadian models) and turn the chain adjusters just enough to remove all slack from the chain (see illustrations). Mark a pin in one of the chain links, then count 20 additional pins and mark the twenty-first pin. Measure the distance between the two marked pins and compare it to the maximum chain length listed in this Chapter's Specifications. If it's beyond the maximum, refer to Chapter 6 and replace the chain and sprockets as a set.

5   Loosen the chain adjusters. Push down and pull up on the bottom run of the chain and measure the slack midway between the two sprockets (see illustration), then compare the measurements to the value listed in this Chapter's Specifications. As wear occurs, the chain will actually stretch, which means adjustment is necessary to remove some slack from the chain. In some cases where lubrication has been neglected, corrosion and galling may cause the links to bind and kink, which effectively shortens the chain's length. If the chain is tight between the sprockets, rusty or kinked, it's time to replace it with a new one. **Note:** *Repeat the chain slack measurement along the length of the chain - ideally, every inch or so. If you find a tight area, mark it with felt pen or paint and repeat the measurement after the machine has been ridden. If the chain's still tight in the same areas, it may be damaged or worn. Because a tight or kinked chain can damage the transmission countershaft bearing, it's a good idea to replace it.*

6   Loosen or tighten the chain adjusters to get the correct amount of slack in the chain, then tighten the rear axle housing locknut (see illustration 8.4a or 8.4b).

7   Unbolt the engine sprocket cover, take it off and inspect the engine sprocket (see illustration). Check the teeth on the engine sprocket and the rear sprocket for wear (see Chapter 6). Refer to Chapter 6 for the sprocket replacement procedure if the sprockets appear to be worn excessively. **Note:** *Never install a new chain on old sprockets and never use the old chain if you install new sprockets - replace the chain and sprockets as a set.*

8.5 Measure drive chain slack along the bottom chain run

8.7 Front sprocket cover bolt locations

8.8a Check the upper and lower contact surfaces of the chain slider . . .

8.8b . . . the upper roller . . .

8   Check the chain rollers and slider **(see illustrations)**. If a roller or slider is worn, replace it (see Chapter 6).

Lubrication

Note: *If the chain is dirty, it should be removed and cleaned before it's lubricated (see Chapter 6).*

9   The best time to lubricate the chain is after the vehicle has been ridden. When the chain is warm, the lubricant will penetrate the joints between the side plates to provide lubrication. The manufacturers of these vehicles specify using heavyweight engine oil only; do not use chain lube, which may contain solvents that can damage the chain's rubber O-rings. Apply the oil to the area where the side plates overlap - not to the middle of the rollers.

 Apply the lubricant along the top of the lower chain run, so that when the machine is ridden, centrifugal force will move the lubricant into the chain, rather than throwing it off.

10   Roll the rear wheels forward to place a new section of chain on the bottom of the run, then lubricate that section. Repeat this until the entire chain has been lubricated.
11   After applying the lubricant, let it soak in a few minutes before wiping off any excess.

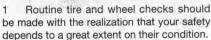
9   Tires/wheels - general check

1   Routine tire and wheel checks should be made with the realization that your safety depends to a great extent on their condition.
2   Check the tires carefully for cuts, tears, embedded nails or other sharp objects and excessive wear. Operation of the motorcycle with excessively worn tires is extremely hazardous, as traction and handling are directly

8.8c . . . and the lower roller for wear or damage

affected. Measure the tread depth at the center of the tire. Replace worn tires with new ones when the tread depth is less than that listed in *Daily (pre-ride) checks* at the front of this manual.
3   Repair or replace punctured tires as soon as damage is noted. Do not try to patch a torn tire, as wheel balance and tire reliability may be impaired.
4   Check the tire pressures when the tires are cold and keep them properly inflated (see *Daily (pre-ride) checks* at the front of this manual). Proper air pressure will increase tire life and provide maximum stability and ride comfort. Keep in mind that low tire pressures may cause the tire to slip on the rim or come off, while high tire pressures will cause abnormal tread wear and unsafe handling.
5   The wire wheels used on these machines should be kept clean and checked periodically for cracks, bending, loose spokes and corrosion. Never attempt to repair damaged wheels; they must be replaced with new ones. Loose spokes can be tightened with a spoke wrench **(see illustration)**, but be careful not

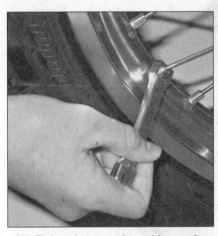

9.5 Tighten loose spokes with a spoke wrench, but don't overtighten them

to overtighten and distort the wheel rim.
6   Check the valve stem locknuts to make sure they're tight. Also, make sure the valve stem caps are in place and tight. If any are missing, install new ones made of metal or hard plastic.

10   Front wheel bearings - check

1   Raise the front of the vehicle and support it securely on jackstands.
2   Spin the front wheels by hand. Listen for noise, which indicates dry or worn wheel bearings.
3   Grasp the top and bottom of the tire and try to rock it back-and-forth. If there's more than a very small amount of play, the wheel bearings are in need of adjustment or replacement. Refer to Chapter 7 for service procedures.

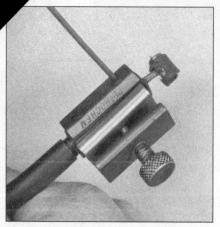

11.3 Lubricating a cable with a pressure lube adapter (make sure the tool seats around the inner cable)

14.2a Unhook the clip and disengage it from the center button

14.2b Remove the filter from the housing

11 Lubrication - general

1   Since the controls, cables and various other components of a motorcycle are exposed to the elements, they should be lubricated periodically to ensure safe and trouble-free operation.

2   The throttle lever, brake lever and brake pedal should be lubricated frequently. Suzuki recommends 10W-30 motor oil inside cables and for the pivot points of levers and pedals. Multi-purpose lithium grease is recommended for cable ends and other lubrication points, such as suspension and steering bushings. In order for the lubricant to be applied where it will do the most good, the component should be disassembled. However, if chain and cable lubricant is being used, it can be applied to the pivot joint gaps and will usually work its way into the areas where friction occurs. If motor oil or

14.3 Carefully pull back the lip of the foam filter element and separate it from the plastic guide inside it

light grease is being used, apply it sparingly as it may attract dirt (which could cause the controls to bind or wear at an accelerated rate). **Note:** *One of the best lubricants for the control lever pivots is a dry-film lubricant (available from many sources by different names).*

3   The throttle and clutch cables should be removed and treated with a commercially available cable lubricant which is specially formulated for use on motorcycle control cables. Small adapters for pressure lubricating the cables with spray can lubricants are available and ensure that the cable is lubricated along its entire length **(see illustration)**. When attaching a cable to its handlebar lever, be sure to lubricate the barrel-shaped fitting at the end with multi-purpose grease.

4   To lubricate the cables, disconnect one end, then lubricate the cable with a pressure lube adapter **(see illustration 11.3)** (clutch cable, see Chapter 2; throttle cable, see Chapter 4).

5   To lubricate the rear suspension linkage, inject grease into the fittings (if equipped) with a grease gun.

6   Refer to Chapter 6 for the following lubrication procedures:

a) *Steering head bearings*
b) *Swingarm bearings and dust seals*

7   Refer to Chapter 7 for the following lubrication procedures:

a) *Rear brake pedal pivot*
b) *Front and rear wheel bearings*

12 Fasteners - check

1   Since vibration of the machine tends to loosen fasteners, all nuts, bolts, screws, etc. should be periodically checked for proper

tightness. Also make sure all cotter pins or other safety fasteners are correctly installed.

2   Pay particular attention to the following:

Spark plug(s)
Engine oil drain plug
Gearshift pedal
Brake pedal
Footpegs
Engine mount bolts
Shock absorber mount bolts
Front axle nut
Rear axle nut
Skid plate bolts

3   If a torque wrench is available, use it along with the torque specifications at the beginning of this, or other, Chapters.

13 Skid plate - check

1   Check the skid plate under the vehicle for damage (see Chapter 8). Have a damaged plate repaired, or replace it.

2   Make sure the skid plate fasteners are all in position and tightly secured.

14 Air filter element and drain tube - cleaning

Element cleaning

1   Remove the left side cover (see Chapter 8).

2   Unhook the element clip and remove the air filter from the housing **(see illustrations)**.

3   Separate the air filter element from the element guide **(see illustration)**.

4   Check the anti-backfire screen in the filter housing for clogging or damage **(see illustration)**. Clean or replace it as necessary.
5   Clean the element and guide in a high flash point solvent, squeeze the solvent out of the foam and let the guide and element dry completely.
6   Soak the foam element in the clean engine oil, then squeeze it firmly to remove the excess oil. Don't wring it out or the foam may be damaged. The element should be thoroughly oil-soaked, but not dripping.
7   Reassemble the element and guide.
8   Installation is the reverse of removal.

Drain tube cleaning

9   Check the air cleaner housing drain tube for accumulated water and oil. If oil or water has built up in the tube, squeeze its clamp, remove the tube from the air cleaner housing and clean it out. Install the drain tube on the housing and secure it with the clamp. **Note:** *A drain tube that's full indicates the need to clean the filter element and the inside of the case.*

15 Fuel system - inspection

⚠️ *Warning: Gasoline is extremely flammable, so take extra precautions when you work on any part of the fuel system. Don't smoke or allow open flames or bare light bulbs near the work area, and don't work in a garage where a gas-type appliance (such as a water heater or clothes dryer) is present. Since gasoline is carcinogenic, wear latex gloves when there's a possibility of being exposed to fuel, and if you spill any fuel on your skin, rinse it off immediately with soap and water. Mop up any fuel spills immediately*

14.4 Check the anti-backfire screen for clogging or damage

15.1 Inspect the fuel tap, fuel line and float chamber seam for leaks

and do not store fuel-soaked rags where they could ignite. When you perform any kind of work on the fuel system, wear safety glasses and have a fire extinguisher suitable for class B type fires (flammable liquids) on hand.

1   Check the fuel tank, the fuel tap, the fuel line and the carburetor for leaks and evidence of damage **(see illustration)**.
2   If carburetor gaskets are leaking, the carburetor should be disassembled and rebuilt (see Chapter 4).
3   If the fuel tap is leaking, tightening the screws may help. If leakage persists, the tap should be disassembled and repaired or replaced with a new one.
4   If the fuel line is cracked or otherwise deteriorated, replace it with a new one.
5   Place the fuel tap lever in the Off position. Remove the fuel tank (see Chapter 4) and drain it. Remove the screws and detach the tap from the tank **(see illustration)**.
6   Clean the strainer with solvent and let it dry.
7   Installation is the reverse of removal. Be sure to use a new O-ring. Hand-tighten the

screws firmly, but don't overtighten them. If you do, the O-ring will be distorted, which will result in fuel leaks.
8   After installation, run the engine and check for fuel leaks.
9   Any time the vehicle is going to be stored for a month or more, remove and drain the fuel tank. Also remove the float chamber drain plug (in the bottom of the carburetor on the left-hand side) and drain the fuel from the carburetor.
10   Inspect the condition of the crankcase breather hose. Replace it if it's cracked, torn or deteriorated.

16 Spark plug - inspection, cleaning and gapping

1   Remove the fuel tank (see Chapter 4).
2   Twist the spark plug cap to break the seal, then pull it off the spark plug **(see illustrations)**.
3   If available, use compressed air to blow

15.5 Remove the fuel tap screws and separate the tap and strainer from the tank

16.2a Twist and pull the spark plug boot by hand to free it from the cylinder head

16.2b Pull the boot out of the spark plug well in the valve cover and cylinder head

16.3a Unscrew the spark plug with a short extension and a 5/8-inch spark plug socket . . .

16.3b . . . the plug socket should have a rubber insert that grips the plug so you can lift it out

any accumulated debris from around the spark plug. Remove the plug with a spark plug socket (see illustrations).

4   Inspect the electrodes for wear. Both the center and side electrodes should have square edges and the side electrode should be of uniform thickness. Look for excessive deposits and evidence of a cracked or chipped insulator around the center electrode. Compare your spark plugs to the color spark plug reading chart on the inside back cover. Check the threads, the washer and the ceramic insulator body for cracks and other damage.

5   If the electrodes are not excessively worn, and if the deposits can be easily removed with a wire brush, the plug can be regapped and reused (if no cracks or chips are visible in the insulator). If in doubt concerning the condition of the plug, replace it with a new one, as the expense is minimal.

6   Cleaning the spark plug by sandblast-ing is permitted, provided you clean the plug with a high flash-point solvent afterwards.

7   Before installing a new plug, make sure it is the correct type and heat range. Check the gap between the electrodes, as it is not preset. For best results, use a wire-type gauge rather than a flat gauge to check the gap (see illustration). If the gap must be adjusted, bend the side electrode only and be very careful not to chip or crack the insulator nose (see illustration). Make sure the washer is in place before installing the plug.

8   Since the cylinder head is made of aluminum, which is soft and easily damaged, thread the plug into the head by hand. Slip a short length of hose over the end of the plug to use as a tool to thread it into place. The hose will grip the plug well enough to turn it, but will start to slip if the plug begins to cross-thread in the hole - this will prevent damaged threads and the accompanying repair costs.

9   Once the plug is finger tight, the job can be finished with a socket. If a torque wrench is available, tighten the spark plug to the torque listed in this Chapter's Specifications. If you do not have a torque wrench, tighten the plug finger tight (until the washer bottoms on the cylinder head) then use a spark plug socket to tighten it an additional 1/4 turn. Regardless of the method used, do not over-tighten it.

10   Take a look at the drain hole for the spark plug well, located in the side of the cylinder head (see illustration). If oil has been running out of the hole, the valve cover gasket is probably leaking oil into the spark plug well. Try tightening the valve cover bolts to the torque listed in the Chapter 2 Specifications. If the bolts aren't loose, refer to Chapter 2 and replace the valve cover gasket with a new one.

16.7a Spark plug manufacturers recommend using a wire type gauge when checking the gap - if the wire doesn't slide between the electrodes with a slight drag, adjustment is required

16.7b To change the gap, bend the side electrode only, as indicated by the arrows, and be very careful not to crack or chip the ceramic insulator surrounding the center electrode

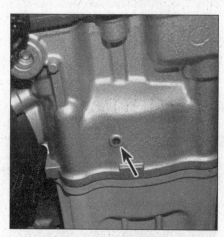

16.10 If oil has been running out of the drain hole for the spark plug well, the valve cover gasket is leaking oil and should be checked

17.1 Location of the oil level check bolt

17.3a Location of the engine drain plug

17.3b Location of the oil tank drain plug at the bottom of the frame oil tank

17 Engine oil and filter - change

1   Consistent routine oil and filter changes are the single most important maintenance procedure you can perform on a motorcycle. The oil not only lubricates the internal parts of the engine, transmission and clutch, but it also acts as a coolant, a cleaner, a sealant and a protectant. Because of these demands, the oil takes a terrific amount of abuse and should be replaced often with new oil of the recommended grade and type.

 Oil will drain from the frame tank into the crankcase if the engine is not run for several days. This may cause a very low oil level to show on the dipstick if you check it before running the engine. To be sure this is what happened, rather than a major loss of oil from the engine, remove the oil check plug from the crankcase, just below the brake pedal (see illustration). The engine should not

be running at this point. Oil should run from the hole. If it does, reinstall and tighten the check bolt and continue with the procedure. If oil doesn't run from the hole, engine oil level is very low. Reinstall the check plug and add 1.5 liters (1.6 qt) of oil through the dipstick tube, then continue the procedure. Be sure to identify the cause of the oil loss, since running the engine without oil can very quickly cause severe damage. Pay special attention to the oil hoses, checking them for cracks or loose connections.

2   Before changing the oil and filter, warm up the engine by running it for several minutes so the oil will drain easily. Be careful when draining the oil, as the exhaust pipe, the engine and the oil itself can cause severe burns.

3   Place a clean drain pan under the vehicle, positioned underneath the engine and oil tank drain plugs (see illustrations). The oil tank is built into the motorcycle's frame.

4   Remove the dipstick from the frame oil tank to vent the crankcase and act as a reminder that there is no oil in the engine (see illustration).

5   Remove the drain plugs from the engine

17.4 Remove the dipstick from the oil tank

and frame oil tank (see illustrations 17.3a and 17.3b) and allow the oil to drain into the pan.

6   Remove the oil filter cover bolts (see illustration). Take the cover off, being sure not to lose the spring inside it (see illustration).

17.6a Remove the oil filter cover bolts - the arrowhead mark (A) faces up when the cover is installed

17.6b Remove the cover, together with its O-ring - be careful not to lose the spring inside the cover

17.7a Remove the filter element, noting that the closed side goes outward . . .

17.7b . . . and the open side goes inward . . .

17.7c . . . then remove the inner O-ring

7   Remove the filter element and the inner O-ring **(see illustrations)**. If additional maintenance is planned for this time period, check or service another component while the oil is allowed to drain completely.

8   Wipe any remaining oil out of the filter housing area of the crankcase and make sure the oil passage is clear.

9   Check the condition of the drain plug threads. Replace the O-rings with new ones whenever the filter is removed.

10   Coat a new inner O-ring with clean engine oil and install it in the filter housing **(see illustration 17.7c)**. Install the filter element with its closed end facing out **(see illustration 17.7a)**.

Caution: The filter must be installed facing the correct direction or oil starvation may cause severe engine damage.

11   Coat a new cover O-ring with clean engine oil. Install the cover and O-ring with the and tighten the bolts to the torque listed in this Chapter's Specifications.

12   Install the engine and frame drain plugs, using new sealing washers if the old ones are worn or damaged. The tapered sides of the washers face downward (toward the heads of the drain plugs). Tighten the plugs to the torques listed in this Chapter's Specifications. Avoid overtightening, as damage to the engine case or frame will result.

13   Before refilling the engine, check the old oil carefully. If the oil was drained into a clean pan, small pieces of metal or other material can be easily detected. If the oil is very metallic colored, then the engine is experiencing wear from break-in (new engine) or from insufficient lubrication. If there are flakes or chips of metal in the oil, then something is drastically wrong internally and the engine will have to be disassembled for inspection and repair.

14   If there are pieces of fiber-like material in the oil, the clutch is experiencing excessive wear and should be checked.

15   If the inspection of the oil turns up nothing unusual, refill the oil tank to the proper

level with the recommended oil and install the dipstick/filler cap.

16   Start the engine and let it run for two or three minutes. Shut it off, wait a few minutes, then check the oil level with the bike held upright. If necessary, add more oil to bring the level up to the upper level mark on the dipstick. Check around the drain plugs and filter cover for leaks.

17   The old oil drained from the engine cannot be reused in its present state and should be disposed of. Check with your local refuse disposal company, disposal facility or environmental agency to see if they will accept the oil for recycling. Don't pour used oil into drains or onto the ground. After the oil has cooled, it can be drained into a suitable container (capped plastic jugs, topped bottles, milk cartons, etc.) for transport to one of these disposal sites.

18 Cooling system - inspection and coolant change

Inspection

1   The cooling system should be carefully inspected at the recommended intervals. Look for evidence of leaks, check the condition of the coolant, check the radiator for clogged fins and damage and make sure the fan operates when required.

2   Examine each of the rubber coolant hoses along its entire length. Look for swelling, cracks, abrasions and other damage. Squeeze each hose at various points. They should feel firm, yet pliable, and return to their original shape when released. If they are dried out or hard, replace them.

3   Look for leaks at each cooling system joint. Tighten the hose clamps carefully to halt minor leaks. If a hose is seriously cracked or torn at a hose clamp, tightening the clamp won't stop the leak; it might even accelerate it. If a hose leaks after tighten-

18.4 If coolant has been leaking from the water pump weep hole, there will be residue on the frame or skid plate below the water pump

ing the hose clamp, drain the coolant (see Steps 13 through 16), loosen the clamp, pull off the hose and inspect it closely. If the damage is close to the end of the hose, cut off the damaged end and reattach the hose. If the damage is too far from the end of the hose, cutting off the end of the hose is not an option; replace the hose.

4   Check for leaks at the water pump **(see illustration)**. The weep hole, which is designed to let coolant drip if the water pump seals are worn, isn't directly visible while the water pump is mounted on the engine. However, a leak will cause coolant residue to accumulate on the frame or in the skid plate below the water pump. Also check for leaks at the coolant drain plug. Replace water pump or drain plug gaskets if they've been leaking. If coolant has been leaking from the weep hole, it's time for a new water pump seal (see Chapter 3).

5   Inspect the radiator for evidence of leaks and other damage. Radiator leaks usually produce tell-tale deposits or stains on the surface

18.7 Locate the radiator cap before you remove the drain bolt

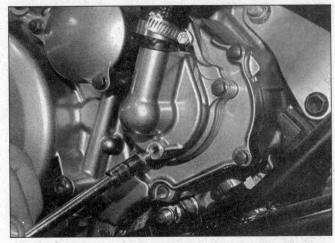

18.15a Remove the drain bolt and sealing washer to drain the coolant

of the core below the leak. If the radiator is leaking, remove it (see Chapter 3) and have it repaired by a radiator shop or replace it.

Caution: Do NOT use a liquid leak-stopping compound to try to repair leaks.

6   Inspect the radiator cooling fins for mud, dirt and insects. Debris stuck in the fins can impede the flow of air through the radiator. If the fins are dirty, force water or low-pressure compressed air through the fins from the backside of the radiator. If any of the fins are bent or distorted, straighten them carefully with a screwdriver.

7   If you're working on a DR-Z400S or SM model, remove the right side cover (see Chapter 8). On all models, locate the radiator cap on the right-hand radiator **(see illustration)**.

8   Remove the radiator cap as follows: Loosen the retaining screw in the edge of the cap and turn the cap counterclockwise until it reaches the first detent. If you hear a hissing sound (indicating there is still pressure in the system), wait until it stops. Then press down on the cap and continue turning it counterclockwise until it's free.

9   Inspect the condition of the coolant in the radiator. If it's rust-colored, or if accumulations of scale are visible in the radiator, drain, flush and refill the system with new coolant. Inspect the cap gaskets for cracks and other damage. Have the cap tested by a dealer service department or replace it with a new one. Install the cap by turning it clockwise until it reaches the first detent, then push down on the cap and continue turning it until it stops.

10   Analyze the condition of the antifreeze in the coolant with an antifreeze hydrometer. Sometimes coolant may look like it's in good condition, but might be too weak to offer adequate protection. If the hydrometer indicates a weak mixture, flush and refill the cooling system (see following).

11   Start the engine and let it reach normal operating temperature, then check for leaks again. As the coolant temperature increases,

the fan (if equipped) should come on automatically and the temperature should begin to drop. If it doesn't, check the fan and fan circuit (see Chapter 3).

12   If the coolant level is constantly low, but there is no evidence of leaks, have the system pressure checked by a dealer service department, motorcycle repair shop or service station.

Coolant change

⚠ *Warning: Don't allow antifreeze to come into contact with your skin or with painted surfaces of the vehicle. Rinse off spills immediately with plenty of water. Antifreeze is highly toxic if ingested. Never leave antifreeze in an open container or in puddles on the floor; children and pets are attracted by its sweet odor and may drink it. Check with local authorities regarding the proper disposal of used antifreeze. Many communities have collection centers that can dispose of antifreeze safely. Finally, antifreeze is combustible, so don't store it or put it near open flames.*

⚠ *Warning: Let the engine cool completely before performing this Step. Opening the radiator cap while the engine is hot will allow scalding coolant to spray out.*

Draining

13   Locate the radiator cap if you haven't already done so **(see illustration 18.7)**.

14   Put a shop rag over the radiator cap. Slowly rotate the cap counterclockwise to the first detent and allow any residual pressure to escape. When the hissing sound ceases, push down on the cap, turn it counterclockwise again and remove it.

15   Place a large, clean drain pan under the water pump, remove the drain plug **(see illustrations)** and drain the coolant into the container.

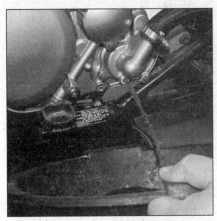

18.15b Coolant will spurt out once the radiator cap is removed, so have a container ready

HAYNES HiNT *The coolant will rush out with considerable force, so be prepared to quickly readjust the position of the drain pan.*

16   Remove the overflow tank (see Chapter 3) and drain it. Wash out the reservoir with clean water. Install the reservoir.

Flushing

17   Flush the system with clean tap water by inserting a garden hose into the radiator filler neck. Allow the water to run through the system until it is clear when it exits the drain bolt hole. If the radiator is extremely corroded, remove it (see Chapter 3) and have it cleaned by a radiator shop.

18   Using a new gasket, install the drain bolt and tighten it to the torque listed in this Chapter's Specifications.

19   Fill the cooling system with clean water mixed with a flushing compound. Make sure the flushing compound is compatible with aluminum, and follow the manufacturer's instructions carefully.

18.24 The cooling system air bleed bolt is located in the top of the left-hand radiator

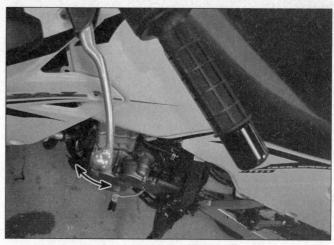

19.2 Measure clutch lever freeplay at the lever tip

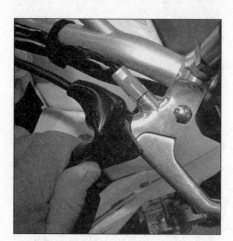

19.3a Pull the rubber boot back from the adjuster

20   Start the engine and allow it to reach normal operating temperature. Let it run for about ten minutes.

21   Stop the engine. Let the machine cool

for awhile, then cover the radiator cap with a heavy rag and turn it counterclockwise to the first stop, releasing any pressure that may be present in the system. Once the hissing stops, push down on the cap and remove it completely.

22   Drain the system.

23   Fill the system with clean water, then repeat Steps 17 and 18.

Refilling and air bleeding

24   Fill the system with the correct coolant mixture (listed in this Chapter's Specifications). To do this, unscrew the air bleed bolt from the top of the left-hand radiator **(see illustration)**. Slowly fill the system to the base of the radiator filler neck, letting air flow from the bleeder bolt hole.

25   Once the radiator is full, install the bleeder bolt and tighten it to the torque listed in this Chapter's Specifications.

26   Start the engine, warm it to normal operating temperature, then shut the engine off.

27   Let the engine cool down completely,

then recheck the coolant level (see *Daily (pre-ride) checks* at the front of this manual). Top up the coolant to the base of the filler neck, then reinstall the radiator cap.

19 Clutch lever freeplay - check and adjustment

1   The clutch cable is adjusted at the clutch lever.

2   Operate the clutch lever and check freeplay at the lever tip **(see illustration)**.

3   If freeplay isn't within the range listed in this Chapter's Specifications, pull back the adjuster cover and loosen the locknut **(see illustrations)**. Turn the adjuster to set freeplay and tighten the locknut. Slide the cover back over the adjuster.

4   Clutch freeplay can also be adjusted at the mid-line adjuster in the clutch cable if adjustment at the handlebar doesn't bring freeplay within the specified range **(see illustration)**. Loosen the locknut, turn the adjuster

19.3b Loosen the locknut (right arrow) and turn the adjuster (left arrow) to adjust the cable

19.4 Make major cable adjustments at the inline adjuster - loosen the locknut (left arrow) and turn the adjuster (right arrow)

20.3 Adjust the idle speed with the throttle stop screw

21.3 Check throttle lever freeplay at the lever tip

to change freeplay, then tighten the locknut.
5   If the previous steps don't bring cable freeplay within the specified range, the cable is stretched and should be replaced with a new one.

20 Idle speed - check and adjustment

1   Before adjusting the idle speed, make sure the spark plug gap is correct (see Section 16). Also, turn the handlebars back-and-forth and note whether the idle speed changes. If it does, the throttle cable may be incorrectly routed. Be sure to correct this problem before proceeding.
2   Start the engine and warm it up to its normal operating temperature. Make sure the transmission is in Neutral, then hook up an inductive-type tachometer.
3   Turn the throttle stop screw to bring the idle speed within the range listed in this Chapter's Specifications **(see illustration)**. Turning the screw in increases the idle speed; backing it out decreases the idle speed.
4   Snap the throttle open and shut a few times, then recheck the idle speed. If necessary, repeat the adjustment procedure.
5   If a smooth, steady idle can't be achieved, the fuel/air mixture may be incorrect. Refer to Chapter 4 for additional carburetor or fuel injection system information.

21 Throttle cables - check and adjustment

1   Before proceeding, check and, if necessary, adjust the idle speed (see Section 20).
2   Make sure the throttle lever moves easily from fully closed to fully open with the front wheel turned at various angles. The lever should return automatically from fully open

to fully closed when released. If the throttle sticks, check the throttle cables for cracks or kinks in the housing. Also, make sure the inner cables are clean and well-lubricated.
3   Measure freeplay at the throttle grip **(see illustration)**. If it's within the range listed in this Chapter's Specifications, and the throttle performs as described in Step 2, no adjustment is necessary. If not, adjust it as follows.
4   Loosen the locknut on the return cable **(see illustration)**. Turn the adjusting nut to give an exposed thread length (above the bracket) of 3 mm (0.12 inch), then tighten the locknut.
5   Pull back the rubber boot to expose the throttle cable adjuster at the handlebar **(see illustration)**. Loosen the adjuster locknut. Turn the adjuster to set freeplay, then tighten the locknut.
6   If the handlebar adjuster won't produce the specified result, loosen the throttle cable locknut at the carburetor bracket **(see illustration 21.4)**. Turn the adjusting nut to obtain the specified freeplay, then tighten the locknut.
7   Reposition the rubber boot over the adjuster.

21.4 Cable adjustment points (Mikuni carburetor shown; Keihin carburetor similar)

A   Push cable locknut
B   Push cable adjuster
C   Pull cable adjuster
D   Pull cable locknut

21.5 Slide the rubber boot off the adjuster, loosen the locknut and turn the adjuster

22.1 Check the choke knob for smooth operation

24.4 Disconnect the hoses from the valve cover

22 Choke - operation check
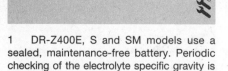

1   Operate the choke knob **(see illustration)** and note whether it operates smoothly.
2   If the choke knob doesn't operate smoothly, inspect the choke system (see Chapter 4).

23 Battery - check

1   DR-Z400E, S and SM models use a sealed, maintenance-free battery. Periodic checking of the electrolyte specific gravity is not possible. Inspect the battery as described in Chapter 5.
2   If the vehicle will be stored for an extended time, fully charge the battery, then remove it. Disconnect the negative cable and remove the battery retainer strap. Disconnect the positive cable and lift the battery out.

 Warning: Always disconnect the negative cable first and reconnect it last to avoid sparks which could cause a battery explosion.

3   Store the battery in a cool dark place. Check open circuit voltage (see Chapter 5) at least once a month and recharge the battery if it's low.

24 Valve clearance - check and adjustment

Check

1   The engine must be cool to the touch for this maintenance procedure; if possible, let the machine sit overnight before beginning.

2   Remove the seat (see Chapter 8). If you're working on a DR-Z400S or SM model, loosen the horn bracket.
3   Remove the fuel tank (see Chapter 4).
4   Disconnect the crankcase breather hoses **(see illustration)**.
5   Remove the spark plug (see Section 16). This will make it easier to turn the crankshaft.
6   Remove the valve cover (see Chapter 2).
7   Unscrew the crankshaft end plug and timing hole access plug **(see illustration)**.
8   Make sure the transmission is in Neutral. Using a socket on the crankshaft rotation bolt, turn the engine to position the piston at Top Dead Center on the compression stroke. **Note:** *Rotate the crankshaft counter-clockwise.* When this occurs, the timing mark on the rotor will align with the notch in the crankcase cover **(see illustration)**. To make sure the piston is on the compression stroke, not the exhaust stroke, check the camshaft position. The camshaft lobes should point away from each other **(see illustration)**. If the camshaft lobes are out of position, rotate the crankshaft one full turn, so the crankshaft timing mark again aligns with the notch.

9   With the engine in this position, all four valve clearances can be checked.
10   Insert a feeler gauge of the same thickness as the valve clearance listed in this Chapter's Specifications between each of the cam lobes and the lifter beneath it **(see illustration)**.
11   Pull the feeler gauge out slowly - you should feel a light drag. If there's no drag, the clearance is too loose. If there's a heavy drag, the clearance is too tight.
12   Record the locations of any valves with incorrect clearances. Recheck the clearances of these valves, trying different feeler gauges until you find the thickness that fits correctly (a light drag). Once you do, record this thickness - you'll need this information later to select a new valve adjusting shim.
13   If any of the clearances need to be adjusted, go to Step 14. If all of the clearances are within Specifications, go to Step 20.

Adjustment

14   Remove the camshaft (see Chapter 2). Remove the lifter and shim for each of the valves that need to be adjusted.
15   Determine the thickness of the shim

24.7 Unscrew the crankshaft bolt cover and the timing hole cover directly above it

24.8a Align the timing mark next to the T mark (upper arrows) with the pointer cast in the cover (lower arrow)

24.8b If the piston is on the compression stroke, the cam lobes will point away from each other like this (if they don't, rotate the crankshaft another full turn)

that was removed. It should be marked on the top of the shim (see illustration), but the ideal way is to measure it with a micrometer or vernier caliper (refer to *Tools and Workshop Tips* at the end of this manual). **Note:** *If the number on the shim does not end with zero or 5, round it off to the nearest zero or 5. For example, if the number on the shim is 238, round it off to 240. If it's 244, round it off to 245.*

16   If the clearance (measured in Steps 10 and 11 and recorded in Step 12) was too large, you need a thicker shim. If it was too small, you need a thinner shim.

17   If the valve clearance measured in Steps 10 and 11 was too great, subtract the mid-range specified clearance from the measured clearance. Record this number, then add it to the thickness of the adjusting shim you removed. This will give you the thickness of the needed new shim. For example:

Measured clearance: 0.20 mm
Specified clearance: 0.10 to 0.15 mm
Mid-range (desired) clearance: 0.12 mm

Measured clearance minus desired clearance: 0.08 mm

So if the existing shim is numbered 230 (2.30 mm thick), the new shim should be 2.38 mm thick. The closest to this is a 240 (2.40 mm thick). This is the thickness of the new shim that you will need for that valve.

18   Select new shims for any remaining valves that are not within the Specifications.

19   Install the new shims and their lifters (see Chapter 2).

20   The remainder of installation is the reverse of removal. After the camshafts are reinstalled, recheck the valve clearances to make sure they're within the Specifications.

25 Exhaust system - inspection

1   Periodically, inspect the exhaust system for leaks and loose fasteners.

2   The exhaust pipe flange nuts at the cyl-inder head are especially prone to loosening, which could cause damage to the head (see Chapter 4). Check them frequently and keep them tight. If tightening the flange nuts fails to stop the leak, replace the gasket (see Chapter 4).

3   The spark arrester should be removed and cleaned at the specified intervals.

⚠ *Warning: To avoid burns, be sure the exhaust system has cooled down before you start this procedure.*

4   Unbolt the spark arrester. Remove three bolts from the rear end of the tailpipe (see illustration).

5   Pull the spark arrester out of the muffler. Tap it lightly with a soft-faced mallet to loosen any deposits, then clean the deposits off with a wire brush. Also clean any deposits from the inside of the muffler, again using a wire brush.

6   Reinstall the spark arrester and tighten the bolt(s) to the torque listed in this Chapter's Specifications.

24.10 Slip the feeler gauge between the cam lobe and lifter to measure the clearance

24.15 The shim thickness is marked on the shim, but it should also be checked with a vernier caliper or micrometer

25.4 The spark arrester is secured by three bolts

26.1a Check the oil hoses and metal lines for cracks, damage or loose connections

26.1b Frame oil tank-to-crankcase hose location

26 Engine oil hoses - inspection

1   Locate the oil hoses that run from the oil tank to the engine **(see illustrations)**.
2   Check the hoses for cracks or deterioration. If any problems are found, replace the hoses. It's a good idea to replace the clamps with new ones whenever you replace a hose or line.

26.1c Oil return tank-to-engine hose locations

Chapter 2
Engine, clutch and transmission

Contents

Degrees of difficulty

Easy, suitable for novice with little experience	**Fairly easy,** suitable for beginner with some experience	**Fairly difficult,** suitable for competent DIY mechanic	**Difficult,** suitable for experienced DIY mechanic	**Very difficult,** suitable for expert DIY or professional

Specifications

General

Bore	90 mm (3.543 inches)
Stroke	62.6 mm (2.465 inches)
Displacement	398 cc
Compression ratio	
DR-Z400, DR-Z400E	12.2 to 1
DR-Z400S, DR-Z400SM	11.3 to 1
Cylinder compression	
DR-Z400	Not specified
DR-Z400E (automatic compression release actuated)	142 psi (1000 kPa)
DR-Z400S, DR-Z400SM (automatic compression	
release actuated)	135 psi (950 kPa)
Oil pressure at 3000 rpm, 140-degrees F (60-degrees C)	2.8 to 8.5 psi (20 to 60 kPa)

Camshaft

Lobe height (intake)
DR-Z400, DR-Z400E
    Standard .... 36.910 to 36.960 mm (1.4531 to 1.4551 inches)
    Limit .... 36.610 mm (1.4413 inches)
DR-Z400S, DR-Z400SM
    Standard .... 36.490 to 36.540 mm (1.4366 to 1.4386 inches)
    Limit .... 36.190 mm (1.4248 inches)
Lobe height (exhaust)
DR-Z400, DR-Z400E
    Standard .... 36.880 to 36.930 mm (1.4520 to 1.4539 inches)
    Limit .... 36.580 mm (1.4402 inches)
DR-Z400S, DR-Z400SM
    Standard .... 35.790 to 35.840 mm (1.4091 to 1.4110 inches)
    Limit .... 35.490 mm (1.3972 inches)
Camshaft runout limit .... 0.10 mm (0.004 inch)
Bearing oil clearance
    Standard .... 0.19 to 0.053 mm (0.0007 to 0.0021 inch)
    Limit .... 0.150 mm (0.006 inch)

Cylinder head, valves and valve springs

Cylinder head warpage limit .... 0.05 mm (0.002 inch)
Valve cover warpage limit .... 0.05 mm (0.002 inch)
Valve stem runout .... 0.05 mm (0.002 inch)
Valve stem diameter
Intake
    Standard .... 4.975 to 4.990 mm (0.1959 to 0.1965 inch)
    Limit .... Not specified
Exhaust
    Standard .... 4.955 to 4.970 mm (0.1951 to 0.1957 inch)
    Limit .... Not specified
Valve guide inside diameter (intake and exhaust)
    Standard .... 5.000 to 5.012 mm (0.1969 to 0.1973 inch)
    Limit .... Not specified
Stem-to-guide clearance
Intake
    Standard .... 0.010 to 0.037 mm (0.0004 to 0.0015 inch)
    Limit .... Not specified
Exhaust
    Standard .... 0.030 to 0.057 mm (0.0012 to 0.0022 inch)
    Limit .... Not specified
Valve seat width (intake and exhaust)
    Standard .... 0.9 to 1.1 mm (0.0354 to 0.0433 inch)
    Limit .... Not specified
Valve margin thickness limit (intake and exhaust) .... Not specified
Valve spring free length limit
Intake .... 32.6 mm (1.28 inches)
Exhaust .... 36.3 mm (1.43 inches)
Valve spring bend limit .... Not specified

Cylinder

Bore diameter
    Standard .... 90.000 to 90.015 mm (3.5433 to 3.5439 inches)
    Limit .... Not specified
Top surface warpage limit .... 0.05 mm (0.002 inch)
Out-of-round limit .... Not specified
Taper limit .... Not specified
Measuring point .... Top, center and bottom of bore, parallel
and crosswise to crankshaft centerline

Piston

Diameter .... 89.965 to 89.980 mm (3.5419 to 3.5425 inches)
Measuring point .... 15.0 mm (0.6 inch) from bottom of skirt
Piston-to-cylinder clearance
    Standard .... 0.030 to 0.040 mm (0.0012 to 0.0016 inch)
    Limit .... 0.120 mm (0.0047 inch)
Piston pin bore
    Standard .... 20.002 to 20.008 mm (0.7875 to 0.7877 inch)
    Limit .... 20.030 mm (0.7886 inch)

Piston pin outer diameter
    Standard .... 19.995 to 20.000 mm (0.7872 to 0.7874 inch)
    Limit .... 19.980 mm (0.7886 inch)
Piston pin-to-piston clearance .... Not specified
Piston ring groove width
    Top ring .... 0.78 to 0.80 mm (0.0307 to 0.0315 inch) or
                                   1.30 to 1.32 mm (0.0512 to 0.0520 inch)
    Second ring.. 0.81 to 0.83 mm (0.0319 to 0.0327 inch)
    Oil ring.. 2.01 to 2.03 mm (0.0791 to 0.0799 inch)
Ring thickness
    Top ring .... 0.71 to 0.76 mm (0.028 to 0.030 inch) or
                                   1.08 to 1.10 mm (0.0425 to 0.0433 inch)
    Second ring.. 0.77 to 0.79 mm (0.0303 to 0.0311 inch)
    Oil ring.. Not specified
Ring side clearance limit
    Top ring .... 0.180 mm (0.007 inch)
    Second ring.. 0.150 mm (0.006 inch)
    Oil ring.. Not specified
Ring end gap (not installed in engine)
    Top ring
        Standard (approximate)... 6.9 mm (0.27 inch)
        Limit .... 5.5 mm (0.22 inch)
    Second ring (approximate)
        Standard .... 11.5 mm (0.45 inch)
        Limit .... 9.2 mm (0.36 inch)
    Oil ring.. Not specified
Ring end gap (installed in engine)
    Top and second rings
        Standard .... 0.08 to 0.20 mm (0.003 to 0.008 inch)
        Limit .... 0.5 mm (0.02 inch)
    Oil ring.. Not specified

Clutch

Spring free length limit .... 49.9 mm (1.96 inches)
Metal plate thickness .... Not specified
Friction plate thickness
    Standard .... 2.92 to 3.08 mm (0.115 to 0.121 inch)
    Limit .... 2.62 mm (0.103 inch)
Metal plate warpage limit .... 0.1 mm (0.004 inch)

Transmission

Shift fork clearance in grooves
    Standard .... 0.1 to 0.3 mm (0.004 to 0.012 inch)
    Limit .... 0.05 mm (0.002 inch)
Shift fork thickness... 4.6 to 4.7 mm (0.181 to 0.185 inch)
Shift fork groove width .... 4.8 to 4.9 mm (0.189 to 0.193 inch)

Crankshaft, connecting rod and balancer

Runout limit .... 0.08 mm (0.003 inch)
Assembly width .... 62 +/- 1.0 mm (2.441 +/- 0.004 inches)
Connecting rod big-end side clearance
    Standard .... 0.30 to 0.65 mm (0.012 to 0.026 inch)
    Limit .... 1.0 mm (0.040 inch)
Connecting rod small end inside diameter
    Standard .... 20.010 to 20.018 mm (0.7878 to 0.7881 inch)
    Limit .... 20.040 mm (0.7890 inch)

Torque specifications

Valve cover bolts.. 14 Nm (120 inch-lbs)
Cylinder head small bolts... 10 Nm (86 inch-lbs)
Cylinder head main bolts (1)
    Step 1 .... 25 Nm (18 ft-lbs)
    Step 2 .... 46 Nm (33.5 ft-lbs)
Oil hose union bolt (to crankcase)................................... 23 Nm (16.5 ft-lbs)
Oil hose mounting bolts (to oil tank and engine)................ Not specified
Oil strainer to frame oil tank .... 23 Nm (16.5 ft-lbs)
Oil tube bracket bolt (outside of right crankcase) .... Not specified
Camshaft bearing cap bolts (2) .... 10 Nm (86 inch-lbs)

Torque specifications

Cam chain guide bolt	10 Nm (86 inch-lbs)
Cam chain tensioner body bolts	10 Nm (86 inch-lbs)
Cam chain tensioner cap bolt	8 Nm (72 inch-lbs)
Cylinder base bolts	14 Nm (120 inch-lbs)
Crankcase bolts	11 Nm (96 inch-lbs)
Crankcase cover bolts	Not specified
Oil pump mounting screws (3)	Not specified
Oil pump assembly screw	Do not remove
Clutch boss nut (4)	70 Nm (50.5 ft-lbs)
Clutch spring bolts	Not specified
Gearshift cam driven gear bolt	24 Nm (17.5 ft-lbs)
External shift linkage stopper (3)	19 Nm (13.5 ft-lbs)
External shift linkage pawl lifter screws (3)	Not specified
Shift pedal pinch bolt	Not specified
Primary drive gear nut	
2004 and earlier (4)	110 Nm (79.5 ft-lbs)
2005 and later (5)	150 Nm (101.5 ft-lbs)
Balancer driven gear nut (4)	50 Nm (36 ft-lbs)
Engine mounting bolts/nuts	66 Nm (47.5 ft-lbs)

1   Apply clean engine oil to the threads, bolt seating surfaces and upper and lower sides of the washers. Install the washers with the rounded sides upward.
2   Make sure the piston is at Top Dead Center on the compression stroke before tightening these bolts.
3   Apply non-permanent thread locking agent to the threads.
4   Use a new lockwasher.
5   Lubricate the threads and seating surface of the nut with clean engine oil.

1 General information

The engine/transmission unit is of the liquid-cooled, single-cylinder four-stroke design.

All models have four valves (two intake and two exhaust). The valves are operated by dual overhead camshafts, which are chain driven off the crankshaft.

The engine/transmission assembly is constructed from aluminum alloy. The crankcase is divided vertically.

The crankcase incorporates a dry sump, pressure-fed lubrication system which uses a gear-driven rotor-type oil pump and an oil filter. All models have an external oil tank, mounted in the vehicle's frame.

On all models, a wet, multi-plate clutch connects the crankshaft to the transmission. Engagement and disengagement of the clutch is controlled through a cable by a lever on the left handlebar. The transmission has five forward gears.

2 Operations possible with the engine in the frame

The components and assemblies listed below can be removed without having to remove the engine from the frame. If, however, a number of areas require attention at the same time, removal of the engine is recommended.

Starter motor (if equipped)
Starter reduction gears
Starter clutch
Alternator rotor and stator
Clutch
External shift mechanism
Cam chain tensioner and chain
Camshafts and lifters
Cylinder head
Cylinder and piston
Oil pump
Balancer gears

3 Operations requiring engine removal

It is necessary to remove the engine/transmission assembly from the frame and separate the crankcase halves to gain access to the following components:

Crankshaft and connecting rod
Transmission shafts
Shift drum and forks

4 Major engine repair - general note

1   It is not always easy to determine when or if an engine should be completely overhauled, as a number of factors must be considered.

2   High mileage is not necessarily an indication that an overhaul is needed, while low mileage, on the other hand, does not preclude the need for an overhaul. Frequency of servicing is probably the single most important consideration. An engine that has regular and frequent oil and filter changes, as well as other required maintenance, will most likely give many miles of reliable service. Conversely, a neglected engine, or one which has not been broken in properly, may require an overhaul very early in its life.

3   Exhaust smoke and excessive oil consumption are both indications that piston rings and/or valve guides are in need of attention. Make sure oil leaks are not responsible before deciding that the rings and guides are bad. Perform a cylinder compression check to determine for certain the nature and extent of the work required (see Section 5).

4   If the engine is making obvious knocking or rumbling noises, the connecting rod and/or main bearings are probably at fault.

5   Loss of power, rough running, excessive valve train noise and high fuel consumption rates may also point to the need for an overhaul, especially if they are all present at the same time. If a complete tune-up does not remedy the situation, major mechanical work is the only solution.

6   An engine overhaul generally involves restoring the internal parts to the specifications of a new engine. During an overhaul the piston rings are replaced and the cylinder walls are bored and/or honed. If a rebore is done, then a new piston is also required. Generally the valves are serviced as well, since they are usually in less than perfect condition at this point. While the engine is being overhauled, other components such as the carburetor and the starter motor (if equipped) can be rebuilt also. The end result should be a like-new engine that will give as many trouble-free miles as the original.

7   Before beginning the engine overhaul, read through all of the related procedures to familiarize yourself with the scope and requirements of the job. Overhauling an engine is not all that difficult, but it is time consuming. Plan on the vehicle being tied up for a minimum of two weeks. Check on the availability of parts and make sure that any necessary special tools, equipment and supplies are obtained in advance.

8   Most work can be done with typical shop hand tools, although a number of precision measuring tools are required for inspecting parts to determine if they must be replaced. Often a dealer service department or repair shop will handle the inspection of

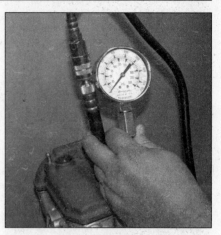

5.5 A compression gauge that screws into the spark plug hole is preferable to the type that's pressed against the opening

parts and offer advice concerning reconditioning and replacement. As a general rule, time is the primary cost of an overhaul so it doesn't pay to install worn or substandard parts.

9   As a final note, to ensure maximum life and minimum trouble from a rebuilt engine, everything must be assembled with care in a spotlessly clean environment.

5 Cylinder compression - check

1   Among other things, poor engine performance may be caused by leaking valves, incorrect valve clearances, a leaking head gasket, or worn piston, rings and/or cylinder wall. A cylinder compression check will help pinpoint these conditions and can also indicate the presence of excessive carbon deposits in the cylinder head.

2   The only tools required are a compression gauge and a spark plug wrench. Depending on the outcome of the initial test, a squirt-type oil can may also be needed.

3   Check valve clearances and adjust if necessary (see Chapter 1). Start the engine and allow it to reach normal operating temperature, then remove the spark plug (see Chapter 1). Work carefully - don't strip the spark plug hole threads and don't burn your hands.

4   Disable the ignition by disconnecting the primary (low tension) wires from the coil (see Chapter 5). Be sure to mark the locations of the wires before detaching them.

5   Install the compression gauge in the spark plug hole **(see illustration)**. Hold or block the throttle wide open.

6   Crank the engine over a minimum of four or five revolutions (or until the gauge reading stops increasing) and observe the initial movement of the compression gauge needle as well as the final total gauge read-

6.3 Location the main oil gallery plug

7.9 Disconnect the oil hose and breather hose from the valve cover

ing. Compare the results to the value listed in this Chapter's Specifications.

7 If the compression built up quickly and evenly to the specified amount, you can assume the engine upper end is in reasonably good mechanical condition. Worn or sticking piston rings and a worn cylinder will produce very little initial movement of the gauge needle, but compression will tend to build up gradually as the engine spins over. Valve and valve seat leakage, or head gasket leakage, is indicated by low initial compression which does not tend to build up.

8 To further confirm your findings, add a small amount of engine oil to the cylinder by inserting the nozzle of a squirt-type oil can through the spark plug hole. The oil will tend to seal the piston rings if they are leaking.

9 If the compression increases significantly after the addition of the oil, the piston rings and/or cylinder are definitely worn. If the compression does not increase, the pressure is leaking past the valves or the head gasket. Leakage past the valves may be due to insufficient valve clearances, burned, warped or cracked valves or valve seats or valves that are hanging up in the guides.

10 If compression readings are considerably higher than specified, the combustion chamber is probably coated with excessive carbon deposits. It is possible (but not very likely) for carbon deposits to raise the compression enough to compensate for the effects of leakage past rings or valves. Refer to Section 12, remove the cylinder head and carefully decarbonize the combustion chamber.

6 Engine oil pressure - check

1 You'll need a tune-up tachometer and a mechanical oil pressure gauge for this procedure.

2 Connect a tachometer to the engine, following manufacture's instructions.

3 Unscrew the main oil gallery plug **(see illustration)** and thread an oil pressure gauge into the hole.

4 If the engine is cold, run it at 2000 rpm to warm it up. In warm weather, run the engine for 10 minutes; in cold weather, run it for 20 minutes.

5 Raise engine speed to 3000 rpm and note the reading on the oil pressure gauge. If it's too low, the problem may be a dirty oil filter, defective O-ring or worn oil pump. If it's too high, the oil may be too high a viscosity (refer to Chapter 1 for oil viscosity specifications). If the viscosity is correct and oil pressure is too high, an obstructed oil passage may be the cause.

7 Engine - removal and installation

⚠️ **Warning: Engine removal and installation should be done with the aid of an assistant to avoid damage or injury that could occur if the engine is dropped.**

Removal

1 Remove the seat and engine skid plate (see Chapter 8).

2 Disconnect the negative cable from the battery (see Chapter 5).

3 Remove the fuel tank and exhaust system (see Chapter 4).

4 Drain the engine oil and coolant (see Chapter 1).

5 Disconnect the radiator hoses from the engine and remove the coolant overflow tank (see Chapter 3).

6 Remove the carburetor (see Chapter 4).

7 Unbolt the clutch cable bracket from the valve cover and disconnect the clutch cable

from the engine (see Section 20).

8 Disconnect the spark plug wire (see Chapter 1).

9 Disconnect the breather hose and oil hose from the valve cover **(see illustration)**.

10 Disconnect the remaining oil hoses. Remove the oil return tank (see Section 18).

11 Remove the drive sprocket from the engine, together with the chain (see Chapter 6).

12 Label and disconnect the following wires (see Chapter 5 for component locations if necessary):
   Alternator
   Starter motor (except DR-Z400)
   Neutral switch
   Engine ground wire

13 If you're working on a DR-Z400, disconnect the decompression cable from the left front corner of the engine.

14 Support the engine securely from below.

15 Remove the lower engine mounting through-bolt **(see illustration)**. Remove the engine mounting bolts, nuts and brackets at the lower front and upper rear **(see illustrations)**.

16 Remove the swingarm pivot bolt partway (see Chapter 6).

HAYNES HINT *The swingarm pivot bolt acts as an engine mounting bolt. Pull out the bolt just far enough to free the engine, but leave it in far enough to support one side of the swingarm.*

17 Have an assistant help you support the engine. Remove it from the left side.

18 Slowly lower the engine to a suitable work surface.

Installation

19 Check the engine supports for wear or damage and replace them if necessary before installing the engine.

20 Make sure the motorcycle is securely supported so it can't be knocked over during

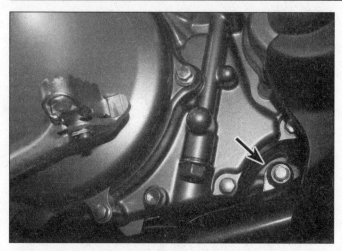

7.15a With the engine supported from below, remove the lower engine mount through-bolt

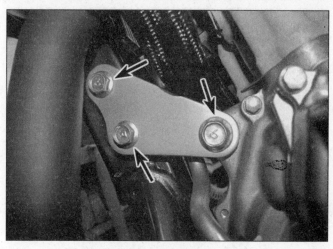

7.15b Detach the lower front mount . . .

the remainder of this procedure.

21   With the help of an assistant, lift the engine up into the frame. Install the mounting nuts and bolts at the rear, front and top. Be sure the mount brackets are installed on the correct sides of the bike (refer to their L and R marks). Finger-tighten the mounting bolts, but don't tighten them to the specified torque yet.

22   Tighten the engine mounting bolts and nuts evenly to the torques listed in this Chapter's Specifications.

23   The remainder of installation is the reverse of removal, with the following additions:

a) Use new gaskets at all exhaust pipe connections.
b) Adjust the throttle cables and clutch cable (see Chapter 1).
c) Fill the engine with oil and coolant (see Chapter 1). Run the engine and check for oil, coolant and exhaust leaks.
d) Check engine idle speed and adjust it if necessary (see Chapter 1).

8   Engine disassembly and reassembly - general information

1   Before disassembling the engine, clean the exterior with a degreaser and rinse it with water. A clean engine will make the job easier and prevent the possibility of getting dirt into the internal areas of the engine.

2   In addition to the precision measuring tools mentioned earlier, you will need a torque wrench, a valve spring compressor, oil gallery brushes (see illustration), a piston ring removal and installation tool, and a piston ring compressor. Some new, clean engine oil of the correct grade and type, some engine assembly lube (or moly-based grease) and a tube of RTV (silicone) sealant will also be required.

3   An engine support stand made from short lengths of 2 x 4s bolted together will facilitate the disassembly and reassembly procedures (see illustration). If you have an automotive-type engine stand, an adapter plate can be made from a piece of plate, some angle iron and some nuts and bolts.

4   When disassembling the engine, keep mated parts together (including gears, rocker arms and shafts, etc.) that have been in con-

7.15c . . . and the upper rear mount

tact with each other during engine operation. These mated parts must be reused or replaced as an assembly.

5   Engine/transmission disassembly should be done in the following general order with reference to the appropriate Sections.

Remove the cam chain tensioner
Remove the camshafts and lifters
Remove the cylinder head
Remove the cylinder

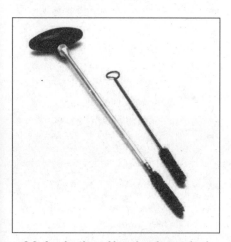

8.2 A selection of brushes is required for cleaning holes and passages in the engine components

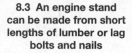

8.3 An engine stand can be made from short lengths of lumber or lag bolts and nails

9.4a Remove the valve cover bolts

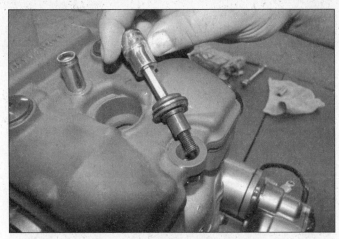

9.4b Front bolt collar and sealing washer

*Remove the piston
Remove the clutch
Remove the balancer gears
Remove the oil pump
Remove the external shift mechanism
Remove the alternator rotor
Remove the starter reduction gears
Separate the crankcase halves
Remove the shift drum and forks
Remove the transmission gears
    and shafts
Remove the crankshaft and
    connecting rod*

6   Reassembly is the reverse of disassembly.

9 Valve cover - removal and installation

1   Remove the seat, fuel tank and both side covers (see Chapters 4 and 8).
2   Remove the spark plug (see Chapter 1).

3   Disconnect the cylinder head breather hose and oil hose from the valve cover **(see illustration 7.9)**.
4   Loosen the valve cover bolts in several stages, in a criss-cross pattern, then remove them **(see illustrations)**.
5   Lift the valve cover off the cylinder head **(see illustration 9.8)**. If it's stuck, don't attempt to pry it off - tap around the sides of it with a plastic hammer to dislodge it. Remove the sealing washers if they didn't come off with the bolts.
6   Work the gasket free of the cylinder head and remove it **(see illustration 9.8)**.
7   Check the valve cover gasket for damage or deterioration and replace it as needed. It's a good idea to replace the bolt sealing washers whenever they're removed.
8   Installation is the reverse of removal, with the following additions:

a) *Coat the area of the valve cover gasket that fits into the cylinder head cutouts with non-hardening sealer* **(see illustration)**.

b) *Install new sealing washers and tighten the valve cover bolts evenly to the torque listed in this Chapter's Specifications.*

10 Cam chain tensioner - removal and installation

Removal

Caution: Once you start to remove the tensioner bolts, you must remove the tensioner all the way and reset it before tightening the bolts. The tensioner extends and locks in place, so if you loosen the bolts partway and then tighten them, the tensioner or cam chain will be damaged.

1   Loosen the tensioner cap bolt **(see illustration)**.
2   Remove the tensioner mounting bolts and detach the tensioner from the cylin-

9.4c Rear valve cover bolt

9.8 Apply non-hardening sealant to the semicircular portions of the gasket

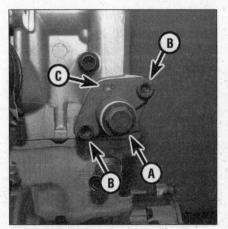

10.1 Cam chain tensioner details

A   Cap bolt and washer
B   Mounting bolts
C   UP mark

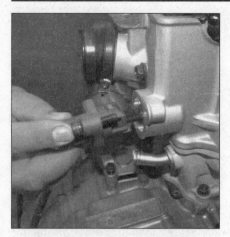

10.2a Remove the tensioner from the engine

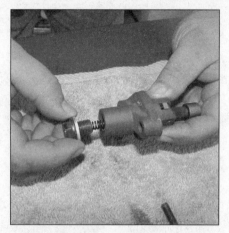

10.2b Remove the cap bolt and washer from the tensioner

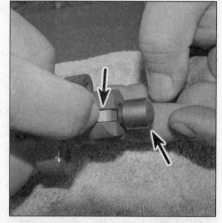

10.5 Before installing the tensioner, lift the latch (left arrow), push the tensioner piston (right arrow) all the way in, then release the latch to hold the piston in

der (see illustration). Remove the cap bolt, the sealing washer and spring (see illustration).

Installation

3   Clean all old gasket material from the tensioner body and engine.
4   Place a new gasket on the tensioner body.
5   Pull back the tensioner pushrod latch with a finger and press the pushrod all the way in, then release to latch to lock the pushrod in the retracted position (see illustration 10.2b and the accompanying illustration).
6   Position the tensioner body on the cylinder, making sure the UP mark is upward (see illustration 10.1). Install the bolts, tightening them to the torque listed in this Chapter's Specifications.
7   Install the spring and cap bolt, using a new sealing washer (see illustration 10.1). Tighten the cap bolt to the torque listed in this Chapter's Specifications.

11 Camshafts and lifters - removal, inspection and installation

Removal

Camshafts

1   Remove the valve cover (see Section 9).
2   Refer to Valve clearance - check and adjustment in Chapter 1 and place the engine at Top Dead Center on the compression stroke.
3   Remove the cam chain tensioner (see Section 10).
4   Secure the cam chain with wire so it can't fall into the chain cavity.
5   Loosen the camshaft cap bolts in several stages, in a criss-cross pattern (see illustration). Unbolt the upper cam chain guide and lift it out (see illustration). Lift the caps off the camshafts and locate the dowels (see illustrations). Put the dowels in a safe

11.5a Loosen the camshaft cap bolts in a criss-cross pattern . . .

place so they won't drop into the engine. Note: The caps are marked IN (intake) and EX (exhaust). If the marks aren't visible, make your own marks.

11.5b . . . two of the bolts secure the upper chain guide

11.5c Lift the caps and locate the dowels on the intake side . . .

11.5d . . . and on the exhaust side

11.6a Roll the camshafts out of their saddles and disengage them from the chain

11.6b Remove the face bolt and sealing washer from the side of the cylinder head

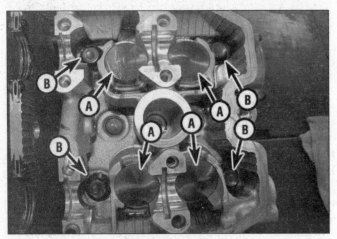

11.10a Camshaft lifters (A) and main head bolts (B)

11.10b Pull the lifters out of their bores with a magnet

6   Lift the intake camshaft out of its saddles and disengage the sprocket from the chain **(see illustration)**. Remove the exhaust camshaft in the same way. Unscrew the face bolt from the side of the cylinder head and remove it, together with its sealing washer **(see illustration)**.

> **HAYNES HiNT** *If you're removing the camshafts to adjust the valves, don't remove them all the way - just roll them out of their saddles (one at a time), leaving them attached to the chain. That way, you won't need to realign the timing marks when installing the camshafts.*

Lifters

7   Stuff a clean shop rag into the timing chain cavity so the valve adjusting shims can't fell into it when they're removed.
8   Remove the camshafts following the procedure given above. Be sure to keep tension on the cam chain.
9   Make a holder for each lifter and its adjusting shim (an egg carton or box will work). Label the sections according to

whether the lifter belongs with the intake or exhaust camshaft, and left or right valve. The lifters form a wear pattern with their bores and must be returned to their original locations if reused.
10   Label each lifter and pull each lifter out

of the bore, using a magnet or suction cup **(see illustrations)**. The shims may stay with their lifters or remain on the valve stems **(see illustrations)**. The shims are inside the lifters, so be careful not to let them fall if they come out with the lifters.

11.10c The valve adjusting shims may stay on top of the valves, as shown here . . .

11.10d . . . or come off with the lifters

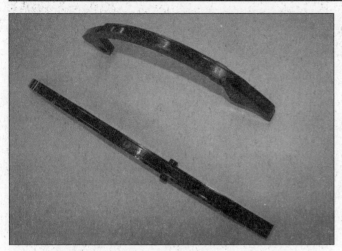

11.16 Check the chain guides for wear or damage

11.21 On DR-Z400E, S and SM models, check the contact surface of the compression release for wear or damage

Timing chain and guides

11   The rear (intake side) chain guide is bolted at the bottom, so the right crankcase cover and clutch will have to be removed (see Sections 19 and 20) for access if the guide or the cam chain need to be removed.

12   Stuff clean rags into the cam chain opening so dirt, small parts or tools can't fall into it.

Inspection

Camshaft, chain and guides

Note: *Before replacing camshafts or the cylinder head because of damage, check with local machine shops specializing in motorcycle engine work. In the case of the camshaft, it may be possible for cam lobes to be welded, reground and hardened, at a cost far lower than that of a new camshaft. If the bearing surfaces in the cylinder head are damaged, it may be possible for them to be bored out to accept bearing inserts. Due to the cost of a new cylinder head it is recommended that all options be explored before condemning it as trash!*

13   Check the camshaft lobes for heat discoloration (blue appearance), score marks, chipped areas, flat spots and spalling. Measure the height of each lobe with a micrometer and compare the results to the minimum lobe height listed in this Chapter's Specifications (micrometer use is described in *Tools and Workshop Tips* at the end of this manual). If damage is noted or wear is excessive, the camshaft must be replaced. Check the bearing surfaces for scoring or wear. Also, be sure to check the condition of the lifters (see Step 22).

14   Except in cases of oil starvation, the camshaft chain wears very little. If the chain has stretched excessively, which makes it difficult to maintain proper tension, replace it with a new one. To remove the chain from the crankshaft sprocket, remove the clutch (see Section 21).

15   Check the sprockets for wear, cracks and other damage, replacing it if necessary.

If a sprocket is worn, the chain is also worn, and possibly the sprocket on the crankshaft. If wear this severe is apparent, the entire engine should be disassembled for inspection. The sprockets are permanently attached to the camshafts, so if the sprockets must be replaced, the camshafts must be replaced as well. The crankshaft sprocket can be removed if necessary (see Section 22).

16   Check the chain guides for wear or damage, especially along the friction surfaces **(see illustration)**. Use a flashlight to look down the cam chain tunnel at the intake side chain guide. If they are worn or damaged, replace them (see Section 20).

17   Check the camshaft bearing oil clearances with Plastigage (see *Tools and Workshop Tips* at the end of this manual).

18   Compare the results to this Chapter's Specifications.

19   If oil clearance is greater than specified, measure the diameter of the cam bearing journal with a micrometer. If the journal diameter is less than the specified limit, replace the camshaft with a new one and recheck the clearance.

20   If the clearance is still too great, replace the cylinder head and bearing caps with new parts (see the **Note** that precedes Step 13).

21   On all except DR-Z400 models, check the automatic compression release in the left camshaft **(see illustration)**. Operate the lever on the sprocket end of the camshaft by hand. It should move smoothly, causing the plunger in the camshaft to extend. When released, it should return by itself. Also check the contact surface for wear. If the compression release doesn't work properly, replace the camshaft.

Lifters

22   Check the lifters and their bores for wear, scuff marks, scratches and other damage. Check the camshaft contact surface, as well as the outer surface that rides in the bore. Replace the lifters if they're visibly worn or damaged.

Installation

23   Make sure the piston is still at Top Dead Center on the compression stroke (refer to Chapter 1, Section 24 if necessary).

24   Coat the lifters and their bores with clean engine oil. Apply a small amount of moly-based grease to the shims and stick them to their respective valve stems with the thickness number upward.

25   Slide the lifters into their bores, taking care not to knock the valve shims out of position. When the lifters are correctly installed, it should be possible to rotate them with a finger.

26   Coat the camshaft contact surfaces of the lifters and the bearing surfaces of the camshafts with moly-based grease.

27   Install the exhaust camshaft, then the intake camshaft in the cylinder head, engaging the sprocket with the chain as you do so, and make sure the sprockets are in the correct positions (see Chapter 1). Install the cap dowels in their holes (if they were removed).

28   Install the camshaft bearing caps **(see illustrations 11.5a through 11.5d)**. Tighten the cap bolts in stages, in a criss-cross pattern, to the torque listed in this Chapter's Specifications.

Caution: The caps must be tightened in the proper sequence with an accurate torque wrench, or the camshafts may seize.

29   Install the cam chain tensioner (see Section 10). Release the tensioner so its piston presses against the chain.

30   Recheck the crankshaft timing mark in the timing hole cover and the match marks on both camshafts. If they are not still aligned, stop and find out why before continuing.

Caution: Don't run the engine with the marks misaligned or the valves may strike the pistons, bending the valves.

31   Rotate the crankshaft two full turns and make sure the timing marks still line up correctly.

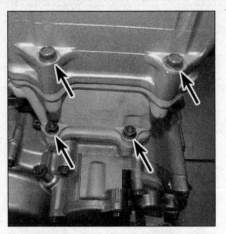

12.5 Cylinder head small bolt (upper arrows) and base nut (lower arrows) locations

12.6 Remove the head bolts and their washers

12.8 Cylinder head locating dowels

32   Check the valve clearances (see Chapter 1). This is necessary to make sure none of the shims has slipped out of position.
33   Change the engine oil (see Chapter 1).
34   The remainder of installation is the reverse of removal.

12 Cylinder head - removal, inspection and installation

Removal

1   Drain the cooling system (see Chapter 1).
2   Remove the seat, side covers and fuel tank cover (see Chapter 8).
3   Remove the fuel tank, carburetor and exhaust system (see Chapter 4).
4   Remove the valve cover and camshafts (see Sections 9 and 11).
5   Remove the two bolts that secure the left-hand side of the cylinder head **(see illustration)**.
6   Loosen the four main head bolts in several stages, in a criss-cross pattern, until they're completely loose **(see illustration 11.10a)**. Lift out the bolts and their washers **(see illustration)**.
7   Lift the cylinder head off the cylinder **(see illustration 12.8)**. If it's stuck, don't attempt to pry it off - tap around the sides of it with a plastic hammer to dislodge it.
8   Locate the dowels **(see illustration)**. There are two of them, one in each of the head bolt holes nearest the timing chain. The dowels may be in the cylinder or they may have come off with the head.
9   Remove the old head gasket from the cylinder or head.

Inspection

10   Check the cylinder head gasket and the mating surfaces on the cylinder head and

cylinder for leakage, which could indicate warpage.
11   Check the flatness of the cylinder head (refer to *Tools and workshop tips* at the end of this manual).
12   Clean all traces of old gasket material from the cylinder head and cylinder. Be careful not to let any of the gasket material fall into the crankcase, the cylinder bore or the bolt holes.

Installation

13   Install the two dowel pins, then place the new head gasket on the cylinder **(see illustration 12.8)**. Never reuse the old gasket and don't use any type of gasket sealant.

 HAYNES HiNT *The head gasket will line up almost exactly with the coolant passages and bolt holes if it's installed upside down. Make sure the coolant passages and bolt holes line up exactly.*

14   Install the exhaust side cam chain guide, fitting the lower end and the middle guide into their notches **(see illustrations 21.2 and 21.5)**.

 HAYNES HiNT *Don't forget to install the chain guide at this point. It won't be possible to install it once the cylinder head is installed.*

15   Carefully lower the cylinder head over the dowels, guiding the cam chain through the slot in the cylinder head. It's helpful to have an assistant support the cam chain with a piece of wire so it doesn't fall and become kinked or detached from the crankshaft. When the head is resting on the cylinder, wire the cam chain to another component to keep tension on it.
16   Lubricate the threads and seating surfaces of the four main cylinder head bolts with clean engine oil. Lubricate the upper and lower sides of the head bolt washers with the same oil.

17   Install the washers on the four main head bolts and install the bolts finger-tight. Tighten the four bolts in a criss-cross pattern, in several stages, to the initial torque listed in this Chapter's Specifications.
18   Loosen the bolts all the way, again in a criss-cross pattern. Retighten them to the second-step torque setting listed in this Chapter's Specifications, then tighten them exactly 1/2 turn further.
19   After the main nuts or bolts are tightened, tighten the two Allen bolts to the torque listed in this Chapter's Specifications.
20   The remainder of installation is the reverse of removal.

13 Valves/valve seats/valve guides - servicing

1   Because of the complex nature of this job and the special tools and equipment required, servicing of the valves, the valve seats and the valve guides (commonly known as a valve job) is best left to a professional.
2   The home mechanic can, however, remove and disassemble the head, do the initial cleaning and inspection, then reassemble and deliver the head to a dealer service department or properly equipped vehicle repair shop for the actual valve servicing. Refer to Section 14 for those procedures.
3   The dealer service department will remove the valves and springs, recondition or replace the valves and valve seats, replace the valve guides, check and replace the valve springs, spring retainers and keepers (as necessary), replace the valve seals with new ones and reassemble the valve components.
4   After the valve job has been performed, the head will be in like-new condition. When the head is returned, be sure to clean it again very thoroughly before installation on the engine to remove any metal particles or abrasive grit that may still be present from the

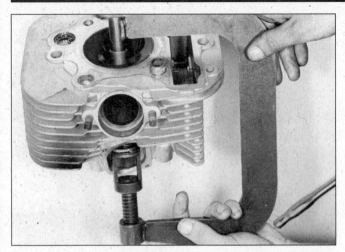

14.6 Compress the valve springs with a valve spring compressor

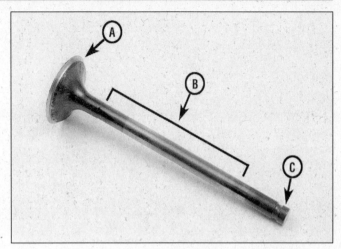

14.16 Check the valve face (A), stem (B) and keeper groove (C) for wear and damage

valve service operations. Use compressed air, if available, to blow out all the holes and passages.

14 Cylinder head and valves - disassembly, inspection and reassembly

1   As mentioned in Section 13, valve servicing and valve guide replacement should be left to a dealer service department or other repair shop. However, disassembly, cleaning and inspection of the valves and related components can be done (if the necessary special tools are available) by the home mechanic. This way no expense is incurred if the inspection reveals that service work is not required at this time.
2   To properly disassemble the valve components without the risk of damaging them, a valve spring compressor is absolutely necessary. If the special tool is not available, have a dealer service department or vehicle repair shop handle the entire process of disassembly, inspection, service or repair (if required) and reassembly of the valves.

Disassembly

3   Before the valves are removed, scrape away any traces of gasket material from the head gasket sealing surface. Work slowly and do not nick or gouge the soft aluminum of the head. Gasket removing solvents, which work very well, are available at most motorcycle shops and auto parts stores.
4   Carefully scrape all carbon deposits out of the combustion chamber area. A hand held wire brush or a piece of fine emery cloth can be used once most of the deposits have been scraped away. Do not use a wire brush mounted in a drill motor, or one with extremely stiff bristles, as the head material is soft and may be eroded away or scratched by the wire brush.

5   Before proceeding, arrange to label and store the valves along with their related components so they can be kept separate and reinstalled in the same valve guides they are removed from (plastic bags work well for this).
6   Compress the valve spring(s) on the first valve with a spring compressor **(see illustration)**, then remove the keepers and the retainer from the valve assembly. Do not compress the spring(s) any more than is absolutely necessary. Carefully release the valve spring compressor and remove the spring(s), spring seat and valve from the head. If the valve binds in the guide (won't pull through), push it back into the head and deburr the area around the keeper groove with a very fine file or whetstone.
7   Repeat the procedure for the remaining valve. Remember to keep the parts for each valve together so they can be reinstalled in the same location.
8   Once the valves have been removed and labeled, pull off the valve stem seals with pliers and discard them (the old seals should never be reused).
9   Next, clean the cylinder head with solvent and dry it thoroughly. Compressed air will speed the drying process and ensure that all holes and recessed areas are clean.
10   Clean all of the valve springs, keepers, retainers and spring seats with solvent and dry them thoroughly. Do the parts from one valve at a time so that no mixing of parts between valves occurs.
11   Scrape off any deposits that may have formed on the valve, then use a motorized wire brush to remove deposits from the valve heads and stems. Again, make sure the valves do not get mixed up.

Inspection

12   Inspect the head very carefully for cracks and other damage. If cracks are found, a new head will be required. Check the cam bearing surfaces for wear and evi-

dence of seizure. Check the camshaft for wear as well (see Section 11).
13   Using a precision straightedge and a feeler gauge, check the head gasket mating surface for warpage (see *Tools and Workshop Tips* at the end of this manual). If the head is warped it must either be machined or, if warpage is excessive, replaced with a new one.
14   Examine the valve seats in each of the combustion chambers. If they are pitted, cracked or burned, the head will require valve service that is beyond the scope of the home mechanic. Measure the valve seat width and compare it to this Chapter's Specifications. If it is not within the specified range, or if it varies around its circumference, valve service work is required.
15   Clean the valve guides to remove any carbon buildup, then measure the inside diameters of the guides (at both ends and the center of the guide) (see *Tools and Workshop Tips* at the end of this manual). Record the measurements for future reference. The guides are measured at the ends and at the center to determine if they are worn in a bell-mouth pattern (more wear at the ends). If they are, guide replacement is an absolute must.
16   Carefully inspect each valve face for cracks, pits and burned spots, and check the valve stem and the keeper groove area for cracks **(see illustration)**. Rotate the valve and check for any obvious indication that it is bent. Check the end of the stem for pitting and excessive wear and make sure the bevel is the specified width. The presence of any of the above conditions indicates the need for valve servicing.
17   Measure the valve stem diameter with a micrometer. If the diameter is less than listed in this Chapter's Specifications, the valves will have to be replaced with new ones. Also check the valve stem for bending. Set the valve in a V-block with a dial indicator touching the middle of the stem. Rotate the valve and look for a reading on the gauge (which

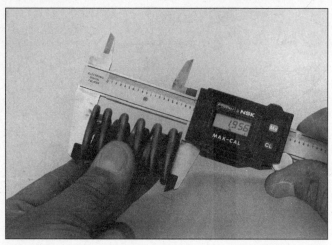

14.18a Measure the free length of the valve springs

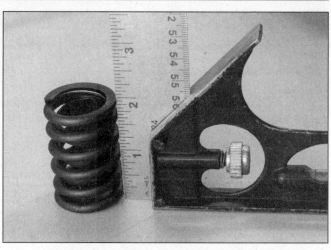

14.18b Check the valve springs for squareness

indicates a bent stem). If the stem is bent, replace the valve.

18   Check the end of each valve spring for wear and pitting. Measure the free length **(see illustration)** and compare it to this Chapter's Specifications. Any springs that are shorter than specified have sagged and should not be reused. Stand the spring on a flat surface and check it for squareness **(see illustration)**.

19   Check the spring retainers and keepers for obvious wear and cracks. Any questionable parts should not be reused, as extensive damage will occur in the event of failure during engine operation.

20   If the inspection indicates that no service work is required, the valve components can be reinstalled in the head.

Reassembly

21   If the valve seats have been ground, the valves and seats should be lapped before installing the valves in the head to ensure a positive seal between the valves and seats. This procedure requires coarse and fine valve lapping compound (available at auto parts stores) and a valve lapping tool. If a lapping tool is not available, a piece of rubber or plastic hose can be slipped over the valve stem (after the valve has been installed in the guide) and used to turn the valve.

22   Apply a small amount of coarse lapping compound to the valve face **(see illustration)**, then slip the valve into the guide. **Note:** *Make sure the valve is installed in the correct guide and be careful not to get any lapping compound on the valve stem.*

23   Attach the lapping tool (or hose) to the valve and rotate the tool between the palms of your hands. Use a back-and-forth motion rather than a circular motion. Lift the valve off the seat and turn it at regular intervals to distribute the lapping compound properly. Continue the lapping procedure until the valve face and seat contact area is of uniform width and unbroken around the entire circumference of the valve face and seat **(see illustration)**. Once this is accomplished, lap the valves again with fine lapping compound.

24   Carefully remove the valve from the guide and wipe off all traces of lapping compound. Use solvent to clean the valve and wipe the seat area thoroughly with a solvent soaked cloth. Repeat the procedure for the remaining valves.

25   Lay the spring seat in place in the cylinder head, then install new valve stem seals on the guides. Use an appropriate size deep socket to push the seals into place until they are properly seated. Don't twist or cock them, or they will not seal properly against the valve stems. Also, don't remove them again or they will be damaged.

26   Coat the valve stems with assembly lube or moly-based grease, then install one of them into its guide. Next, install the spring seat, springs and retainers, compress the springs and install the keepers. **Note:** *Install the springs with the tightly wound coils at the bottom (next to the spring seat).* When compressing the springs with the valve spring compressor, depress them only as far as is absolutely necessary to slip the keepers into place. Apply a small amount of grease to the keepers **(see illustration)** to help hold them in place as the pressure is released from the springs. Make certain that the keepers are securely locked in their retaining grooves.

14.22 Apply the lapping compound very sparingly, in small dabs, to the valve face

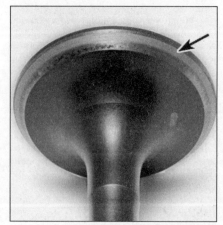

14.23 After lapping, the valve face should have a uniform, unbroken contact pattern

14.26 A small dab of grease will help hold the keepers in place on the valve while the spring compressor is released

15.4 Lift the cylinder off the piston

15.5a Locate the dowels

27 Support the cylinder head on blocks so the valves can't contact the workbench top, then very gently tap each of the valve stems with a soft-faced hammer. This will help seat the keepers in their grooves.

28 Once all of the valves have been installed in the head, check for proper valve sealing by pouring a small amount of solvent into each of the valve ports. If the solvent leaks past the valve(s) into the combustion chamber area, disassemble the valve(s) and repeat the lapping procedure, then reinstall the valve(s) and repeat the check. Repeat the procedure until a satisfactory seal is obtained.

15 Cylinder - removal, inspection and installation

Removal

1 Remove the cylinder head (see Section 12). Make sure the crankshaft is positioned at Top Dead Center (TDC).

2 Lift out the cam chain front guide **(see illustration 21.2)**.

3 Remove the nuts securing the base of the cylinder to the crankcase **(see illustration 12.5)**.

4 Lift the cylinder straight up to remove it **(see illustration)**. If it's stuck, tap around its perimeter with a soft-faced hammer. Don't attempt to pry between the cylinder and the crankcase, as you'll ruin the sealing surfaces.

5 Locate the dowel pins (they may have come off with the cylinder or still be in the crankcase) **(see illustration)**. There are two dowels, located opposite the timing chain cavity. Be careful not to let these drop into the engine. Stuff rags around the piston and remove the gasket and all traces of old gasket material from the surfaces of the cylinder and the crankcase. Be sure not to let anything block the cylinder oil jet in the crankcase **(see illustration)**.

Inspection

6 Don't attempt to separate the liner from the cylinder.

7 Check the cylinder walls carefully for scratches and score marks. The manufacturers don't specify a maximum bore limit, but if scratches and score marks are so deep they can't be removed without honing the cylinder beyond the upper diameter listed in this Chapter's Specifications, the cylinder should be replaced with a new one.

8 Using the appropriate precision measuring tools, check the cylinder's diameter. Measure parallel to the crankshaft axis and across the crankshaft axis, at the depth from the top of the cylinder listed in this Chapter's Specifications. Average the two measurements and compare the results to this Chapter's Specifications. If the cylinder walls are tapered, out-of-round, worn beyond the specified limits, or badly scuffed or scored, have the cylinder rebored and honed by a dealer service department or a motorcycle repair shop. If a rebore is done, an oversize piston and rings will be required as well. Check with your dealer service department about available oversizes.

9 As an alternative, if the precision measuring tools are not available, a dealer service department or repair shop will make the measurements and offer advice concerning servicing of the cylinder.

10 If it's in reasonably good condition and not worn to the outside of the limits, and if the piston-to-cylinder clearance can be maintained properly, then the cylinder does not have to be rebored; honing is all that is necessary.

11 To perform the honing operation you will need the proper size flexible hone with fine stones as shown in *Tools and Workshop Tips* at the end of this manual, or a bottle brush type hone, plenty of light oil or honing oil, some shop towels and an electric drill motor. Hold the cylinder block in a vise (cushioned with soft jaws or wood blocks) when performing the honing operation. Mount the hone in

15.5b Check the oil jet for clogging - it's a good idea to remove and clean it

the drill motor, compress the stones and slip the hone into the cylinder. Lubricate the cylinder thoroughly, turn on the drill and move the hone up and down in the cylinder at a pace which will produce a fine crosshatch pattern on the cylinder wall with the crosshatch lines intersecting at approximately a 60-degree angle. Be sure to use plenty of lubricant and do not take off any more material than is absolutely necessary to produce the desired effect. Do not withdraw the hone from the cylinder while it is running. Instead, shut off the drill and continue moving the hone up and down in the cylinder until it comes to a complete stop, then compress the stones and withdraw the hone. Wipe the oil out of the cylinder and repeat the procedure on the remaining cylinder. Remember, do not remove too much material from the cylinder wall. If you do not have the tools, or do not desire to perform the honing operation, a dealer service department or vehicle repair shop will generally do it for a reasonable fee.

12 Next, the cylinder must be thoroughly washed with warm soapy water to remove all traces of the abrasive grit produced dur-

16.3a There should be a punch mark to indicate the exhaust side of the piston - if not, make your own mark

16.3b Wear eye protection and remove the snap-ring from its groove with snap-ring pliers

16.4 The piston pin should come out with hand pressure - if it doesn't, a drawbolt-type removal tool can be fabricated from readily available parts

16.6 Remove the piston rings with a ring removal and installation tool

ing the honing operation. Be sure to run a brush through the bolt holes and flush them with running water. After rinsing, dry the cylinder thoroughly and apply a coat of light, rust-preventative oil to all machined surfaces.

Installation

13   Lubricate the cylinder bore with plenty of clean engine oil. Apply a thin film of moly-based grease to the piston skirt.
14   Install the dowel pins (and O-ring on the large dowel), then slip a new cylinder base gasket over them **(see illustration 15.5a)**.
15   Attach a piston ring compressor to the piston and compress the piston rings. A large hose clamp can be used instead - just make sure it doesn't scratch the piston, and don't tighten it too much.
16   Install the cylinder and carefully lower it down until the piston crown fits into the cylinder liner **(see illustration 15.4)**. While doing this, pull the camshaft chain up, using

a hooked tool or a piece of stiff wire. Push down on the cylinder, making sure the piston doesn't get cocked sideways, until the bottom of the cylinder liner slides down past the piston rings. A wood or plastic hammer handle can be used to gently tap the cylinder down, but don't use too much force or the piston will be damaged.
17   Remove the piston ring compressor or hose clamp, being careful not to scratch the piston.
18   The remainder of installation is the reverse of removal.

16 Piston - removal, inspection and installation

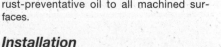

1   The piston is attached to the connecting rod with a piston pin that's a slip fit in the piston and rod.
2   Before removing the piston from the rod, stuff a clean shop towel into the crankcase hole, around the connecting rod. This will

prevent the snap-rings from falling into the crankcase if they are inadvertently dropped.

Removal

3   The piston should have a punch mark on its crown toward the exhaust (front) side of the engine **(see illustration)**. If this mark is not visible due to carbon buildup, make your own mark with a felt pen or sharp punch. Support the piston and remove the snap-ring with snap-ring pliers **(see illustration)**.
4   Push the piston pin out from the opposite end to free the piston from the rod **(see illustration)**. You may have to deburr the area around the groove to enable the pin to slide out (use a triangular file for this procedure). If the pin won't come out, you can fabricate a drawbolt piston pin removal tool from a long bolt, a nut, a piece of tubing and (see *Tools and Workshop Tips* at the end of this manual).

Inspection

5   Before inspection can be carried out, the piston must be cleaned and the old piston rings removed.
6   Using a piston ring removal and installation tool, carefully remove the rings from the piston **(see illustration)**. Do not nick or gouge the piston in the process.
7   Scrape all traces of carbon from the top of the piston. A hand-held wire brush or a piece of fine emery cloth can be used once the majority of the deposits have been scraped away. Do not, under any circumstances, use a wire brush mounted in a drill motor to remove deposits from the piston; the piston material is soft and will be eroded away by the wire brush.
8   Use a piston ring groove cleaning tool to remove any carbon deposits from the ring grooves. If a tool is not available, a piece broken off the old ring will do the job. Be very careful to remove only the carbon deposits. Do not remove any metal and do not nick or gouge the sides of the ring grooves.

16.14 Measure the piston diameter with a micrometer

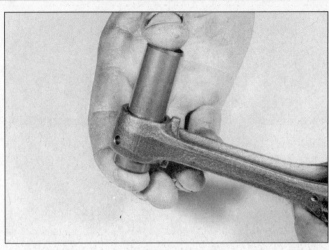

16.16 Slip the piston pin into the connecting rod and check for looseness

9   Once the deposits have been removed, clean the piston with solvent and dry them thoroughly. Make sure the oil return holes below the oil ring grooves are clear.

10   If the piston is not damaged or worn excessively and if the cylinder is not rebored, a new piston will not be necessary. Normal piston wear appears as even, vertical wear on the thrust surfaces of the piston and slight looseness of the top ring in its groove. New piston rings, on the other hand, should always be used when an engine is rebuilt.

11   Carefully inspect each piston for cracks around the skirt, at the pin bosses and at the ring lands.

12   Look for scoring and scuffing on the thrust faces of the skirt, holes in the piston crown and burned areas at the edge of the crown. If the skirt is scored or scuffed, the engine may have been suffering from over-heating and/or abnormal combustion, which caused excessively high operating temperatures. The oil pump should be checked thoroughly. A hole in the piston crown, an extreme to be sure, is an indication that abnormal combustion (pre-ignition) was

occurring. Burned areas at the edge of the piston crown are usually evidence of spark knock (detonation). If any of the above problems exist, the causes must be corrected or the damage will occur again.

13   Measure the piston ring-to-groove clearance (side clearance) by laying a new piston ring in the ring groove and slipping a feeler gauge in beside it. Check the clearance at three or four locations around the groove. Be sure to use the correct ring for each groove; they are different. If the clearance is greater than specified, a new piston will have to be used when the engine is reassembled.

14   Check the piston-to-bore clearance by measuring the bore (see Section 15) and the piston diameter **(see illustration)**. Measure the piston across the skirt on the thrust faces at a 90-degree angle to the piston pin, at the specified distance up from the bottom of the skirt. Subtract the piston diameter from the bore diameter to obtain the clearance. If it is greater than specified, the cylinder will have to be rebored and a new oversized piston and rings installed. If the appropriate precision measuring tools are not available, the piston-to-cylinder clearance can be obtained, though not quite as accurately, using feeler gauge stock. Feeler gauge stock comes in 12-inch lengths and various thicknesses and is generally available at auto parts stores. To check the clearance, slip a piece of feeler gauge stock of the same thickness as the specified piston clearance into the cylinder along with appropriate piston. The cylinder should be upside down and the piston must be positioned exactly as it normally would be. Place the feeler gauge between the piston and cylinder on one of the thrust faces (90-degrees to the piston pin bore). The piston should slip through the cylinder (with the feeler gauge in place) with moderate pressure. If it falls through, or slides through easily, the clearance is excessive and a new piston will be required. If the piston binds at the lower end of the cylinder and is loose toward the top, the cylinder is tapered, and if tight spots are encountered as the pis-

ton/feeler gauge is rotated in the cylinder, the cylinder is out-of-round. Be sure to have the cylinder and piston checked by a dealer service department or a repair shop to confirm your findings before purchasing new parts.

15   Apply clean engine oil to the pin, insert it into the piston and check for freeplay by rocking the pin back-and-forth. If the pin is loose, a new piston and possibly new pin must be installed.

16   Repeat Step 15, this time inserting the piston pin into the connecting rod **(see illustration)**. If the pin is loose, measure the pin diameter and the pin bore in the rod (or have this done by a dealer or repair shop). A worn pin can be replaced separately; if the rod bore is worn, the rod and crankshaft must be replaced as an assembly.

17   Refer to Section 17 and install the rings on the piston.

Installation

18   Install the piston with its punch mark toward the exhaust side (front) of the engine. Lubricate the pin and the rod bore with moly-based grease. Install a new snap-rings in the groove in one side of the piston (don't reuse the old snap-rings). Push the pin into position from the opposite side and install another new snap-ring. Compress the snap-rings only enough for them to fit in the piston. Make sure the snap-rings are properly seated in the grooves **(see illustration)**.

---

17 Piston rings - installation

1   Before installing the new piston rings, the ring end gaps must be checked.

2   Insert the top (No. 1) ring into the bottom of the first cylinder and square it up with the cylinder walls by pushing it in with the top of the piston. The ring should be about one-half inch above the bottom edge of the cylinder. To measure the end gap, slip a feeler gauge

16.18 Make sure both piston pin snap-rings are securely seated in the piston grooves

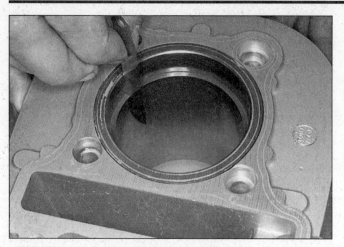

17.2 Check the piston ring end gap with a feeler gauge at the bottom of the ring travel area

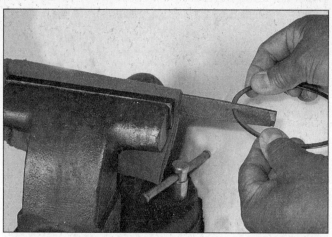

17.4 If the end gap is too small, clamp a file in a vise and file the ring ends (from the outside in only) to enlarge the gap slightly

between the ends of the ring **(see illustration)** and compare the measurement to the Specifications.

3　If the gap is larger or smaller than specified, double check to make sure that you have the correct rings before proceeding.

17.7a Installing the oil ring expander - make sure the ends don't overlap

4　If the gap is too small, it must be enlarged or the ring ends may come in contact with each other during engine operation, which can cause serious damage. The end gap can be increased by filing the ring ends very carefully with a fine file **(see illustration)**. When performing this operation, file only from the outside in.

5　Repeat the procedure for the second compression ring (ring gap is not specified for the oil ring rails or spacer).

6　Once the ring end gaps have been checked/corrected, the rings can be installed on the piston.

7　The oil control ring (lowest on the piston) is installed first. It is composed of three separate components. Slip the spacer into the groove, then install the upper side rail **(see illustrations)**. Do not use a piston ring installation tool on the oil ring side rails as they may be damaged. Instead, place one end of the side rail into the groove between the spacer expander and the ring land. Hold it firmly in place and slide a finger around the piston while pushing the rail into the groove (taking care not to cut your fingers on the

sharp edges). Next, install the lower side rail in the same manner.

Caution: Be sure the ends of the oil ring spacer butt against each other and don't overlap.

8　After the three oil ring components have been installed, check to make sure that both the upper and lower side rails can be turned smoothly in the ring groove.

9　Install the no. 2 (middle) ring next with its identification mark facing up **(see illustration)**. Do not mix the top and middle rings; their profiles are slightly different, but the difference can be hard to see. The most important indicator is the ring thickness. The top ring is thicker than the second ring. On a new piston, the top ring will not fit into the second ring's groove. If you're not sure which ring is which, measure their thicknesses with a micrometer.

10　To avoid breaking the ring, use a piston ring installation tool and make sure that the identification mark is facing up. Fit the ring into the middle groove on the piston. Do not expand the ring any more than is necessary to slide it into place.

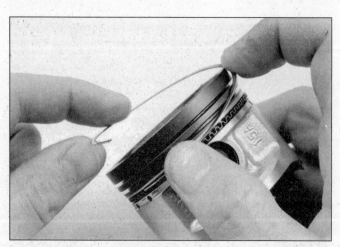

17.7b Installing an oil ring side rail - don't use a ring installation tool to do this

17.9 Install the middle ring with its identification mark up

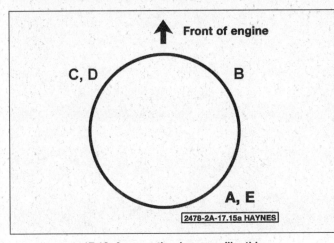

17.12 Arrange the ring gaps like this

A   Oil ring spacer
B   Oil ring upper rail
C   Oil ring lower rail
D   Second compression ring
E   Top compression ring

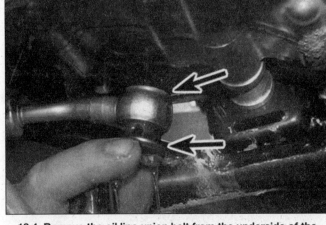

18.4 Remove the oil line union bolt from the underside of the engine and disconnect the oil line - there's a sealing washer on each side of the fitting

11   Finally, install the no. 1 (top) ring in the same manner. Make sure the identifying mark is facing up. Be very careful not to confuse the top and second rings.

12   Once the rings have been properly installed, stagger the end gaps, including those of the oil ring side rails (see illustration).

18 Oil return tank and lines - removal and installation

1   All models have an oil tank built into the frame forward of the engine, an oil return tank behind the engine on the right side of the bike, and a pair of combined oil pipes/hoses, one that connects to the left side of the engine and one that connects to the bottom of the crankcase.

2   The lower hose runs from an oil strainer at the bottom of the frame oil tank near the drain plug, to a union bolt on the underside

of the crankcase. The upper hose runs along the left side of the engine to a bolted fitting.

3   For access to either hose, remove the skid plate (see Chapter 8).

4   To remove the lower hose, loosen its clamp and disconnect it from the strainer, then remove the union bolt and sealing washers (see illustration). If necessary, unscrew the strainer from the frame oil tank and remove the gasket.

5   To remove the upper hose, remove the bolt that secures it to the oil tank. Detach the hose fitting from the oil tank and remove the dowel and O-ring. Remove the retaining clip that secures the hose (see illustration 26.1a in Chapter 1), then unbolt the fitting from the crankcase and remove the dowel and O-ring (see illustrations).

6   To disconnect the oil return tank hoses, remove the right side cover (see Chapter 8). Loosen the hose clamps and carefully pry them off the fittings (see illustration). To remove the tank, unscrew its mounting bolt and take it out.

18.5a Remove the retaining bolt, and pull the hose out of the engine

7   Installation is the reverse of removal. Replace the O-rings whenever they are removed.

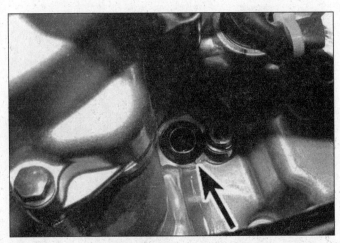

18.5b Remove the dowel and O-ring

18.6 Remove the bolt and disconnect the hoses to remove the oil return tank

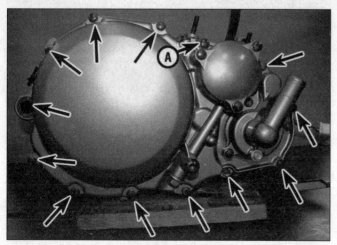

19.2 Right crankcase cover bolt locations - bolt (A) has a washer

19.3a Remove the cover - the dowels may come off with the cover . . .

19.3b . . . or stay in the engine

19.4 Remove the oil check valve, spring and ball - reinstall it with the rubber side of the check valve outward (toward the center of the engine)

19 Crankcase covers - removal and installation

Right crankcase cover

Removal

1   Drain the engine oil (see Chapter 1).
2   Remove the water pump bolts (see illustration 4.1 in Chapter 3) and the crankcase cover mounting bolts (see illustration).
3   Tap the cover gently with a soft-faced mallet to free it and remove it from the engine. Locate the dowels and remove the old gasket (see illustrations).
4   Check the condition of the oil check valve (see illustration). If its condition is in doubt, pull the bushing out of the cover, then remove the ball and spring.

Installation

5   If you removed the oil check valve, install it so the rubber part of the bushing faces out of the bore.
6   Installation is the reverse of removal.

Use a new gasket, coated on both sides with gasket sealer. Be sure the dowels and O-rings are installed.
7   Tighten the cover bolts evenly to the torque listed in this Chapter's Specifications.

Left crankcase cover

Removal

8   Drain the engine oil (see Chapter 1).
9   Remove the starter drive gear (see Chapter 5).
10   Follow the alternator wiring harness to the electrical connector and disconnect it (see Chapter 5).
11   Remove the cover bolts (see illustration). Loosen the bolts evenly in a criss-cross pattern, then remove them.
12   Pull off the cover (see illustration). Tap it with a rubber mallet if it won't come easily. Don't pry the cover off or the gasket surfaces will be damaged.
13   Locate the cover dowels (see illustration 19.12 and the accompanying illustration). They may have stayed in the crankcase or come off with the cover.
14   Remove all traces of the old gasket from the cover and crankcase.

Installation

15   Installation is the reverse of removal. Use a new gasket, coated on both sides with gasket sealer. Be sure the dowels are

19.11 Remove the left crankcase cover bolts

19.12 Pull off the cover - the dowels may stay in the engine . . .

19.13 . . . or they may come off with the cover

installed. Don't forget to refill the engine oil (see Chapter 1).

16 Tighten the cover bolts evenly to the torque listed in this Chapter's Specifications.

20 Clutch and release mechanism - removal, inspection and installation

Cable and lever

Removal

1   Loosen the handlebar cable adjuster all the way to create slack (see Chapter 1). Rotate the adjuster and locknut so their slots align with the slots in the lever and bracket **(see illustration)**. Turn the cable out of the slots so it aligns with the notch in the lever, then lower the end plug out of the lever **(see illustration)**.

2   Either unbolt the lever bracket from the top of the crankcase, or disengage the cable

20.1a Align the slots in the adjuster and locknut (left and center) with the slot in the bracket (right)

housing from the bracket **(see illustration)**.

3   Rotate the exposed end of the cable so it aligns with the slot in the lever, then lift the

20.1b Rotate the cable to align it with the lever notch, then lower the cable end plug out of the lever

cable end upward out of the lever **(see illustration)**.

4   Remove the cable bracket from the

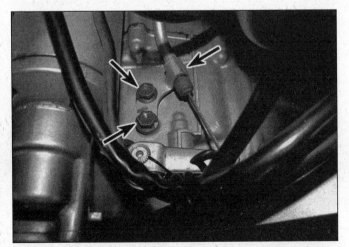

20.2 Either remove the bracket bolts (left arrows) or pull the cable back and slide it out of the slot in the underside of the bracket (right arrow)

20.3 Rotate the cable out of the release lever groove, then lift it up out of the slot

20.5 Unscrew the locknut from the pivot bolt, then unscrew the pivot bolt from the bracket

20.6 Remove the pinch bolt (right arrow) all the way, lift the lever off the shaft, then remove the retaining screw (left arrow)

20.7a Remove the washer

20.7b Pry the seal out of its bore

vehicle, together with the cable **(see illustration 20.2)**. If you haven't already done so, separate the cable from the bracket.

5   To remove the lever from the handlebar bracket, unscrew the nut from the pivot bolt, then unscrew the pivot bolt from the bracket **(see illustration)**. Pull the pivot bolt out and slip the lever out of the bracket.

6   At the crankcase, disconnect the cable as described previously. Remove the lever pinch bolt all the way, then slide the lever off the release shaft **(see illustration)**.

7   Remove the screw that secures the retaining washer and remove the washer to expose the seal **(see illustration)**. Pry out the seal, taking care not to damage the bore **(see illustration)**. Lift the pivot shaft and bearings out of the crankcase.

Inspection

8   Slide the inner cable back and forth in the housing and make sure it moves freely. If it doesn't, try lubricating it as described in Chapter 1. If that doesn't help, replace the cable.

Installation

9   Installation is the reverse of removal. Install the pivot shaft so the notch on its lower end faces toward the right side of the engine.

Refer to Chapter 1 and adjust clutch free-play.

Clutch

Removal

10   Remove the right crankcase cover (see Section 19).

11   Hold the clutch from turning with a holding tool. You can make your own holding tool from steel strap if you don't have one. **Note:** *If you've removed the right crankcase cover, you can wedge a copper washer or penny between the primary drive gear and clutch housing driven gear to keep the clutch housing from turning while you loosen the clutch spring bolts and clutch housing nut.*

12   Follow the photo sequence to remove the clutch **(see illustrations)**.

Inspection

13   Check the bolt posts and the friction surface on the pressure plate for damaged threads, scoring or wear. Replace the pressure plate if any defects are found.

14   Check the edges of the slots in the

20.12a Loosen the clutch cover bolts in a criss-cross pattern . . .

20.12b . . . then remove the bolts and springs

20.12c Remove the clutch cover, together with the release bearing

20.12d Remove the push piece from the clutch center . . .

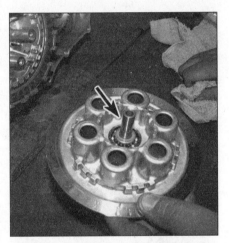

20.12e . . . and place it in the release bearing for storage - on installation, the long end goes into the clutch center

20.12f The pushrod is located in the transmission countershaft . . .

20.12g . . . pull it out with a magnet . . .

20.12h . . . and place it in the push piece for storage

20.12i Bend back the lockwasher with a hammer and chisel

20.12j Remove the metal plates and friction plates (except for the innermost friction plate), then hook the damper spring with a pick or similar tool

20.12k Pull out the damper spring - the concave side faces away from the engine

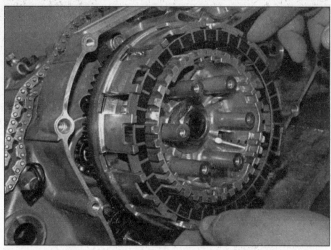

20.12l Remove the innermost friction plate - it's narrower than the others

20.12m Use a clutch holding tool or wedge the primary gears with a copper washer, then unscrew the clutch nut

20.12n Remove the splined washer

20.12o Pull off the clutch center . . .

20.12p . . . the washer may come off with the clutch center or stay in the engine

20.12q Pull off the clutch center and pull out the collar

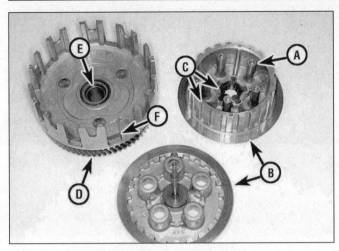

20.14a Clutch inspection points

20.14b Grip the clutch housing and try to rotate the primary gear;
if there's any play, replace the housing

A   Spring posts
B   Friction surfaces
C   Splines
D   Primary driven gear
E   Clutch housing bushing
F   Clutch housing slots

clutch housing for indentations made by the friction plate tabs **(see illustration)**. If the indentations are deep they can prevent clutch release, so the housing should be replaced with a new one. If the indentations can be removed easily with a file, the life of the housing can be prolonged to an extent. Check the bushing surface in the center of the clutch housing for score marks, scratches and excessive wear. Also, check the driven gear teeth for cracks, chips and excessive wear. If the bushing or gear is worn or damaged, the clutch housing must be replaced with a new one. Check the primary driven gear for play **(see illustration)**. If there is any, replace the clutch housing.

15   Check the splines of the clutch boss for indentations made by the tabs on the metal plates. Check the clutch boss friction surface for wear or scoring. Replace the clutch boss if problems are found.

16   Measure the free length of the clutch springs **(see illustration)** and compare the results to this Chapter's Specifications. If the springs have sagged, or if cracks are noted, replace them with new ones as a set.

17   If the lining material of the friction plates smells burnt or if it is glazed, new parts are required. If the metal clutch plates are scored or discolored, they must be replaced with new ones. Measure the thickness of the friction plates **(see illustration)**. Compare the measurements to the values listed in this Chapter's Specifications and replace with new parts any friction plates that are worn.

18   Lay the metal plates, one at a time, on a perfectly flat surface (such as a piece of plate glass) and check for warpage by trying to slip a feeler gauge between the flat surface and the plate **(see illustration)**. The feeler gauge should be the same thickness as the maximum warp listed in this Chapter's Specifications. Do this at several places around the plate's circumference. If the feeler gauge can be slipped under the plate, it is warped and should be replaced with a new one.

19   Check the tabs on the friction plates for excessive wear and mushroomed edges. They can be cleaned up with a file if the

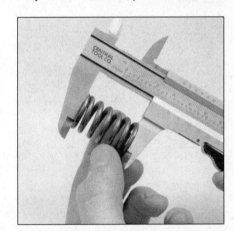

20.16 Measure the clutch spring
free length

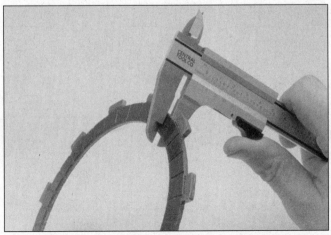

20.17 Measure the thickness of the friction plates

20.18 Check the metal plates for warpage

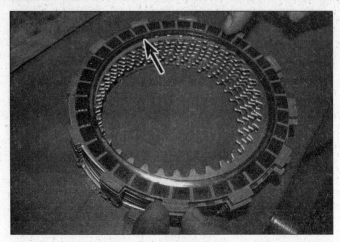

20.21a The damper spring fits inside the innermost friction plate

20.21b The tabs of the outermost friction plate (lower arrow) are offset from the other friction plate tabs (upper arrow) by one notch

deformation is not severe, but the width must be at least the minimum listed in this Chapter's Specifications. Check the friction plates for warpage as described in Step 18.

20 Check the thrust washer for score marks, heat discoloration and evidence of excessive wear.

21.2 Lift the exhaust side chain guide out of its notch

Installation

21 Installation is the reverse of removal, with the following additions:

a) Install a new lockwasher and position its tabs between the ribs of the clutch center. Tighten the clutch nut to the torque listed in this Chapter's Specifications, then bend the lockwasher tabs against one of the flats on the nut.

b) Coat the friction plates with clean engine oil before installing them.

c) Install the narrower friction plate first, then a metal plate, then alternate the remaining metal and friction plates until they're all installed. Friction plates go on first and last, so the friction material contacts the metal surfaces of the clutch center and the pressure plate. Be sure the narrower friction plate goes on first (see illustration). The last friction plate should be installed with its tab one notch offset from the tabs of the other friction plates (see illustration).

d) Apply grease to the ends of the clutch pushrod, the steel ball and the end of the adjuster rod.

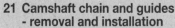

21 Camshaft chain and guides - removal and installation

1 If initial inspection reveals problems with the chain or guides, remove them for further inspection.

2 To remove the exhaust side chain guide, remove the cylinder head (see Section 12). Lift the guide out of its pocket (see illustration).

3 To remove the intake side guide or the chain, remove the left crankcase cover and the clutch (see Sections 19 and 20). Unbolt the guide and slip the chain off the crankshaft sprocket (see illustrations).

4 If you need to remove the crankshaft sprocket, remove the primary drive gear, then slide the sprocket off the crankshaft (see Section 22).

5 Installation is the reverse of removal. Be sure the screw holding the metal tab that forms the outer side pocket for the intake chain guide is tightened securely (see illustration). If you removed the

21.3a Unscrew the Allen bolt that secures the intake side chain guide . . .

21.3b . . . pull it out . . .

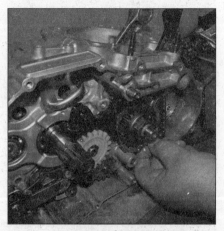

21.3c . . . disengage the chain guide from the sprocket . . .

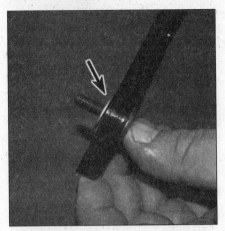

21.3d . . . and remove the washer that goes on the inner side of the chain guide

21.5 Be sure the screw that holds the chain guide pocket tab is tight

22.2 The punch marks on the balancer drive and driven gears must be in alignment with each other like this when the gears are installed

22.5a The primary drive gear nut has left-hand threads (turn clockwise to loosen) - there's a lockwasher behind it

22.5b Remove the gear and pull the Woodruff key out of its slot

22.5c Remove the cam chain sprocket from the crankshaft

crankshaft sprocket, install the Woodruff key, then slip the sprocket onto the crank-shaft.

22 Primary drive gear, crankshaft sprocket and balancer gears - removal, inspection and installation

Removal

1   If you're just planning to remove the gears, remove the right crankcase cover and the clutch (see Sections 19 and 20). If you're planning to remove the balancer weight or shaft, disassemble the crankcase halves (see Section 25).
2   Turn the crankshaft so the match marks on the balancer drive and driven gears align **(see illustration)**.
3   Bend back the tab on the balancer drive gear lockwasher.
4   Wedge a copper washer or penny

between the teeth of the balancer drive and driven gears to prevent them from turning. Loosen the driven gear nut. If you plan to remove the primary drive gear or balancer drive gear, wedge the gears from the other

side and loosen the primary drive gear nut.
5   Unscrew the nuts and remove the lock-washers **(see illustrations)**. **Note:** *The primary drive gear nut has left-hand threads (unscrews clockwise).*

22.5d Unscrew the driven gear nut . . .

22.5e . . . and take off the washer

22.6a Take the driven gear off the balancer shaft - the shouldered side of the gear (shown) faces the engine on installation

22.6b Pull the driven gear pin out of the shaft with a magnet

6   Slide off the primary drive gear, the crankshaft cam chain sprocket, then the balancer drive gear **(see illustrations 22.5a, 22.5b and the accompanying illustrations)**.

22.6c Slide the drive gear off the crankshaft . . .

Remove the Woodruff key from the crankshaft and remove the drive pins from the crankshaft and balancer shaft.

Inspection

7   Check the gears for worn or damaged teeth and replace them as a set if problems are found. The driven gear can be separated into its components - gear, hub, springs and pins - if necessary for inspection. Before you disassemble it, make sure the alignment marks on gear and hub are visible. If not, make your own marks.
8   Check the ball bearings for wear, looseness or rough movement. If any problems are found, replace the bearings as described in Section 26.
9   Check the remaining components for wear and damage and replace any worn or damaged parts. Replace the lockwasher with a new one whenever it's removed.
10   Inspect the balancer and crankshaft ball bearings. If wear, looseness or roughness can be detected, the crankcase will have to be disassembled to replace the bearings.

Installation

11   If you disassembled the balancer driven gear, reassemble it. Note that two of the springs have pins inside them and two don't. The pins go opposite each other when the gear is assembled **(see illustration)**.
12   Install the drive pins in the balancer shaft and crankshaft **(see illustrations 22.6b and 22.6d)**. Install the balancer drive and driven gears over the pins so their match marks align with each other **(see illustration 22.2)**.
13   Install the Woodruff key in the crankshaft, then install the cam chain sprocket and primary drive gear.
14   Install the lockwashers and nuts on the balancer shaft and crankshaft.
15   Wedge the gears as described in Step 4 and tighten the nuts to the torque listed in this Chapter's Specifications. **Note:** *The primary drive gear nut has left-hand threads (tightens counterclockwise).* Bend the lockwasher tab to secure the nuts.
16   The remainder of installation is the reverse of removal.

22.6d . . . and remove the drive pin with a magnet

22.11 There are small pins inside two of the springs

23.2 Oil pipe bolt location

23.7a Remove the snap-ring and remove the oil pump idler gear from its shaft - the shouldered side faces the engine on installation

23 Oil pump and pipe - removal, inspection and installation

Oil pipe

1   Remove the clutch (see Section 20).
2   Remove the oil pipe bolt and pull the oil pipe out of the crankcase **(see illustration)**.
3   Take the O-rings off the oil pipe.
4   Apply clean engine oil to new O-rings and install them on the pipe.
5   Push the pipe into the engine and secure it with the bolt.

Oil pump

Removal

6   Remove the right crankcase cover and clutch (see Sections 19 and 20).
7   Remove the snap-ring that secures the oil pump idler gear, and remove the gear from the shaft **(see illustration)**.

Caution: Don't remove the snap-ring that remains on the idler gear shaft after removing the gear (see illustration). The shaft might fall into the crankcase. If this happens, the crankcase will have to be disassembled to reinstall the shaft.

8   Remove the snap-ring from the oil pump drive gear **(see illustration)**, pull the gear off and remove its drive pin **(see illustration)**.
9   Remove the oil pump mounting screws and remove it from the engine **(see illustrations 23.8a and 23.8b)**.
10   Locate the pump dowel(s) **(see illustration 23.8b)**. They may have come off with the pump or stayed in the engine.

Inspection

11   Remove the outer rotor, inner rotor and drive pin **(see illustration 23.8b)**.

23.7b DO NOT remove the snap-ring - if the idler shaft slides into the crankcase, you'll have to separate the case halves to get it out

23.8a Remove the snap-ring (A) and remove the screws (B)

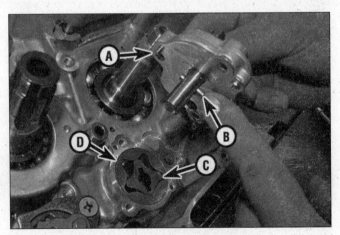

23.8b Oil pump body details

A	Dowel (two dowels on some models)	C Inner rotor
B	Drive pin	D Outer rotor

23.12 This screw can't be removed without damaging it

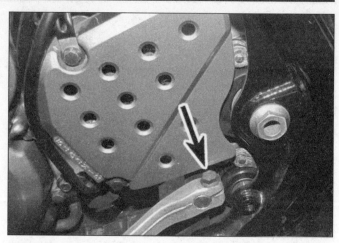

24.1 Remove the pinch bolt all the way, then slide the shift pedal off the shaft

12   The assembly screw that secures the cover to the oil pump body is secured with permanent-type thread locking agent, so it can't be removed without damaging it **(see illustration)**. The screw, cover and pump body are not available separately. If inspection shows any problems, replace the oil pump body as a unit.

13   Wash all the components in solvent, then dry them off. Check the pump body, the rotors and the cover for scoring and wear. If any damage or uneven or excessive wear is evident, replace the pump. The inner and outer rotors are available separately. If you are rebuilding the engine, it's a good idea to install a new oil pump.

14   Reassembly is the reverse of disassembly, with the following additions:

a)   *Before installing the oil pump, pack the cavities between the rotors with petroleum jelly - this will ensure the pump develops suction quickly and begins oil circulation as soon as the engine is started.*

b)   *Make sure the drive pins are in position.*

c)   *Install the outer rotor in the crankcase with its punch mark facing away from the pump body.*

Installation

15   Installation is the reverse of removal, with the following additions:

a)   *Make sure the pump dowel(s) are in position.*

b)   *Tighten the oil pump mounting screws to the torque listed in this Chapter's Specifications.*

24 External shift mechanism - removal, inspection and installation

Shift pedal

1   Look for alignment marks on the end of the shift pedal and shift shaft. If they aren't visible, make your own marks with a felt pen or sharp punch. Remove the shift pedal

pinch bolt completely (it fits in a groove) and slide the pedal off the shaft **(see illustration)**.

2   Check the shift pedal for wear or damage such as bending. Check the splines on the shift pedal and shaft for stripping or step wear. Replace the pedal or shaft if these problems are found.

3   Check the shift shaft seal in the alternator cover for signs of leakage. If the seal has been leaking, remove the left crankcase cover (see Section 19). Pry the seal out of the cover, then tap in a new one with a seal driver or socket the same diameter as the seal.

4   Install the shift pedal or shift arm. Line up its punch marks and tighten the pinch bolt to the torque listed in this Chapter's Specifications.

External shift linkage

5   Remove the shift pedal (see Step 1).

6   Remove the right crankcase cover and the clutch (see Sections 19 and 20).

7   Remove the linkage **(see illustrations)**.

24.7a On the right-hand side of the engine, remove the snap-ring and washer from the shift shaft

24.7b On the left-hand side of the engine, pull out the shift shaft . . .

24.7c . . . and remove the bushing from the post on the pawl assembly

24.7d Remove the screws and remove the pawl assembly

24.7e Note how the pawls fit in the unit . . .

8   Check the shift shaft for bends and damage to the splines. If the shaft is bent, you can attempt to straighten it, but if the splines are damaged it will have to be replaced. Check the condition of the return spring, shift arm and the pawl spring. Replace the shift shaft if they're worn, cracked or distorted.

9   Installation is the reverse of removal, with the following additions:

a) *Apply non-permanent thread locking agent to the return spring pin and tighten it securely.*

b) *Apply non-permanent thread locking agent to the gearshift cam driven gear bolt and tighten it to the torque listed in this Chapter's Specifications.*

c) *Check the engine oil level and add some, if necessary (see Chapter 1).*

24.7f . . . then disassemble it for inspection

24.7g Remove the bolt, then remove the stopper arm and spring

25 Crankcase - disassembly and reassembly

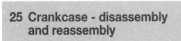

1   To examine and repair or replace the balancer shaft, crankshaft, connecting rod, bearings and transmission components, the crankcase must be split into two parts.

Disassembly

2   Remove the engine from the vehicle (see Section 7).

3   Remove the alternator and starter clutch (see Chapter 5).

4   Remove the right crankcase cover and the clutch (see Sections 19 and 20).

5   Remove the external shift mechanism (see Section 24).

6   Remove the valve cover, cam chain tensioner, camshafts, cylinder head, cylinder, piston and crankcase oil pipe (see Sections 9, 10, 11, 12, 15, 16 and 23).

7   Remove the cam chain and intake side

24.7h Remove the center bolt from the shift drum driven gear

24.7i Remove the gear - its notch engages the pin on installation

25.11a Left side crankcase bolts (upper left bolt hidden)

25.11b Right side crankcase bolts (four lower right bolts hidden)

guide (see Section 21).

8   Remove the oil pump (see Section 23).

9   Remove the balancer gears (see Section 22).

10   Check carefully to make sure there

25.12a Set up a puller like this to separate the crankcase halves

aren't any remaining components that attach the upper and lower halves of the crankcase together.

11   Loosen the crankcase bolts in two or three stages, in a criss-cross pattern (see illustrations).

12   Place the engine on blocks so the transmission shafts and crankshaft can extend downward. Set up a three-legged puller against the end of the crankshaft so it can pull the upper case half off the crankshaft (see illustration). Tap gently on the ends of the transmission shafts, balancer shaft and crankshaft as the case halves are being separated. Make sure the case halves separate evenly (see illustration). Carefully pry the crankcase apart at the pry points. Don't pry against the mating surfaces or they'll develop leaks.

13   Lift the right crankcase half off the left half.

14   Locate the crankcase dowels (see illustrations). !f they aren't secure in their holes, remove them and set them aside for safekeeping.

15   Refer to Sections 26 through 29 for

information on the internal components of the crankcase.

Reassembly

16   Remove all traces of old gasket and sealant from the crankcase mating surfaces with a sharpening stone or similar tool. Be careful not to let any fall into the case as this is done and be careful not to damage the mating surfaces.

17   Check to make sure the dowel pins are in place in their holes in the mating surface of the crankcase (see illustrations 25.14a and 25.14b).

18   Coat both crankcase mating surfaces with Three Bond sealant 0636-070 (or equivalent).

19   Pour some engine oil over the transmission gears, balancer shaft and crankshaft bearing surfaces and the shift drum. Don't get any oil on the crankcase mating surfaces.

20   Carefully place the removed crankcase half onto the other crankcase half. While doing this, make sure the transmission shafts, shift drum, crankshaft and bal-

25.12b The halves will separate like this - if they don't separate evenly as shown, make sure you've removed all the bolts, reposition the puller and try again

25.14a This case dowel stayed in the left side of the crankcase . . .

25.14b . . . and this one stayed in the right side

26.3 Check the bearings inside the case for wear and for rough or noisy movement

26.4a Oil strainer bolt locations

ancer shaft fit into their bearings in the upper crankcase half.

21   Install the crankcase half bolts or screws in the correct holes and tighten them so they are just snug. Then tighten them in two or three stages, in a criss-cross pattern, to the torque listed in this Chapter's Specifications.

22   Turn the transmission shafts to make sure they turn freely. Also make sure the crankshaft and balancer shaft turn freely.

23   The remainder of installation is the reverse of removal.

26 Crankcase components - inspection and servicing

1   Separate the crankcase and remove the following:

a) Transmission shafts and gears
b) Crankshaft and main bearings
c) Shift drums and forks
d) Balancer shaft

2   Clean the crankcase halves thoroughly with new solvent and dry them with compressed air. All oil passages should be blown out with compressed air and all traces of old gasket sealant should be removed from the mating surfaces.

Caution: Be very careful not to nick or gouge the crankcase mating surfaces or leaks will result. Check both crankcase sections very carefully for cracks and other damage.

3   Check the bearings in the case halves (see illustration 25.14a and the accompanying illustration). If they don't turn smoothly, replace them (see Tools and Workshop Tips at the end of this manual).

4   Check the oil strainer screen for clogging or damage. If problems are found, remove the screen for cleaning or replacement. It's a good idea to remove the screen and check its oil passage in the crankcase whenever the crankcase is disassembled (see illustrations). When you reinstall the screen, make sure the oil passages in the screen and crankcase line up exactly.

5   Pull out the oil jet and remove its O-ring (see illustration 15.5b). Make sure the jet is clear by blowing through it with compressed air or aerosol carburetor cleaner. Coat a new O-ring with engine oil, install it on the jet, and push the jet back into its passage in the crankcase.

6   If any damage is found that can't be repaired, replace the crankcase halves as a set.

7   Assemble the case halves (see Section 25) and check to make sure the crankshaft and the transmission shafts turn freely.

27 Balancer shaft - removal and installation

1   Separate the crankcase halves (see Section 25).

2   Lift the balancer shaft out of its bearing in the left case half (see illustration).

3   Installation is the reverse of removal.

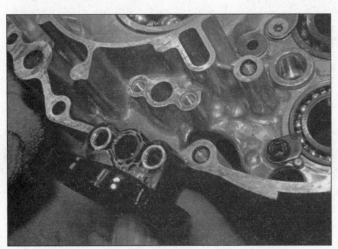

26.4b Check the screen and passages for clogging

27.2 Rotate the balancer weight out of the crankshaft slot, then pull the balancer shaft out of the crankcase

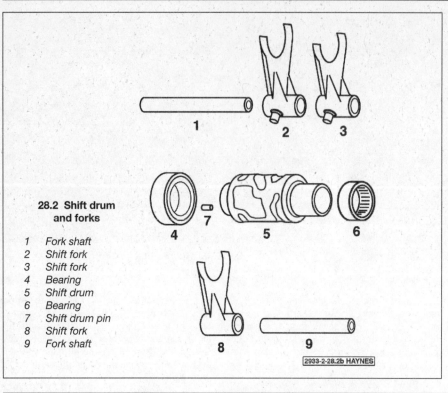

28.2 Shift drum and forks

1 Fork shaft
2 Shift fork
3 Shift fork
4 Bearing
5 Shift drum
6 Bearing
7 Shift drum pin
8 Shift fork
9 Fork shaft

2933-2-28.2b HAYNES

28 Transmission shafts and shift drum - removal, inspection and installation

Note: When disassembling the transmission shafts, place the parts on a long rod or thread a wire through them to keep them in order and facing the proper direction.

Removal

1 Separate the crankcase halves (see Section 25). The transmission components remain in one case half when the case is separated.

2 Remove the shift drum, shift forks **(see illustrations)** and transmission shafts from the crankcase.

3 Using snap-ring pliers, remove the snap-rings and take the gears off the shafts **(see illustration)**.

4 Place the gears in order on a coat hanger or dowel so they won't be mixed up.

Inspection

5 Wash all of the components in clean solvent and dry them off.

6 Inspect the shift fork grooves in the gears. If a groove is worn or scored, replace

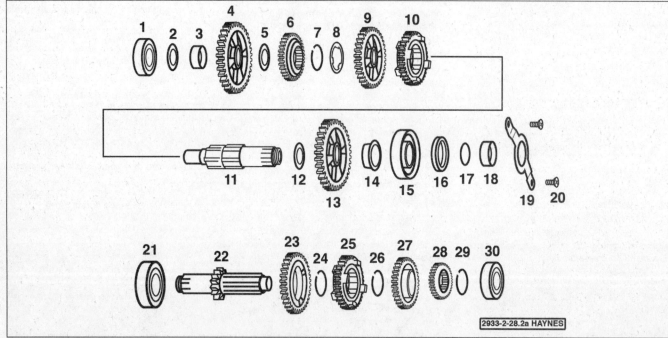

2933-2-28.2a HAYNES

28.3 Transmission shafts and gears

1	Bearing	11	Mainshaft	21	Bearing
2	Thrust washer	12	Thrust washer	22	Mainshaft/integral first gear
3	Bushing	13	Mainshaft fourth gear	23	Mainshaft fifth gear
4	Mainshaft first gear	14	Bushing/washer	24	Snap-ring
5	Thrust washer	15	Bearing	25	Mainshaft third gear
6	Mainshaft fifth gear	16	Oil seal	26	Snap-ring
7	Snap-ring	17	O-ring	27	Mainshaft fourth gear
8	Spline washer	18	Sprocket spacer	28	Mainshaft second gear
9	Mainshaft third gear	19	Retainer	29	Snap-ring
10	Mainshaft fourth gear	20	Screw	30	Bearing

29.2 Use a puller like this to push the crankshaft out of the case half

29.3 Measure the gap between the connecting rod and the crankshaft with a feeler gauge

29.5 Check the cam chain sprocket and the ball bearing on the end of the crankshaft

the affected part and inspect its corresponding shift fork.

7 Check the shift forks for distortion and wear, especially at the fork ears. If they are discolored or severely worn they are probably bent. Inspect the guide pins for excessive wear and distortion and replace any defective parts with new ones.

8 Check the shift fork guide bars evidence of wear, galling and other damage. Make sure the shift forks move smoothly on the guide bars. If the shafts are worn or bent, replace them with new ones.

9 Check the edges of the grooves in the shift drums for signs of excessive wear.

10 Hold the inner race of the shift drum bearing with fingers and spin the outer race. Replace the bearing if it's rough, loose or noisy. Replace the shift drum driven gear if it's worn or damaged (see Section 24).

11 Check the gear teeth for cracking and other obvious damage. Check the bushing surface in the inner diameter of the freewheeling gears for scoring or heat discoloration. Replace damaged parts.

12 Inspect the engagement dogs and dog holes on gears so equipped for excessive wear or rounding off. Replace the paired gears as a set if necessary.

13 Check the transmission shaft bearings in the crankcase for wear or heat discoloration and replace them if necessary (see Section 26).

Installation

14 Installation is the reverse of removal, noting the following points:

a) Use new snap-rings. Install the snap-rings with their rounded edges facing the direction of thrust (toward the component they're securing). Refer to "Tools and Workshop Tips" at the end of this manual if necessary.

b) Lubricate the components with engine oil before assembling them.

c) Install the shift forks, making sure they face in the proper direction (see illustration 28.2).

d) After assembly, check the gears to make sure they're installed correctly (see illustration 28.3). Move the shift drum through the gear positions and rotate the gears to make sure they mesh and shift correctly. If they don't, stop and find out why before completing assembly of the crankcase.

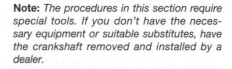

29 Crankshaft and connecting rod - removal, inspection and installation

Note: *The procedures in this section require special tools. If you don't have the necessary equipment or suitable substitutes, have the crankshaft removed and installed by a dealer.*

Removal

1 Separate the crankcase halves (see Section 25). The transmission shafts need not be removed.

2 The crankshaft may be loose enough in its bearing that you can lift it out of the left crankcase half. If not, push it out with a crankshaft puller (see illustration).

Inspection

3 Measure the side clearance between connecting rod and crankshaft with a feeler gauge (see illustration). If it's more than the limit listed in this Chapter's Specifications, it may be possible to have the crankshaft rebuilt. However, this is a specialized job that should be done by a dealer service department or qualified machine shop.

4 Set up the crankshaft in V-blocks with a dial indicator contacting the big end of the connecting rod. Move the connecting rod side-to-side against the indicator pointer and compare the reading to the value listed in this Chapter's Specifications. If it's beyond the limit, the crankshaft can be disassembled and the needle roller bearing replaced. However, this is a specialized job that should

be done by a dealer service department or qualified machine shop.

5 Check the crankshaft splines, the ball bearing at the sprocket end of the crankshaft and the bearing journals for visible wear or damage (see illustration). Suzuki lists the ball bearing end of the crankshaft as a separately available part, but check with your dealer first; it may be more practical to replace the entire crankshaft if the ball bearing or cam sprocket is worn or damaged. Replace the crankshaft if any of the other conditions are found.

6 Set the crankshaft in a lathe or a pair of V-blocks, with a dial indicator contacting each end (see illustration). Rotate the crankshaft and note the runout. If the runout at either end is beyond the limit listed in this Chapter's Specifications, replace the crankshaft and connecting rod as an assembly.

7 Measure the assembly width of the crankshaft (from the outside of one crank throw to the outside of the other crank throw). If it exceeds the limit listed in this Chapter's Specifications, replace the crankshaft.

29.6 Measure runout on each side of the crankshaft (A); if the assembly width (B) is greater than specified, replace the crankshaft

29.8 These tools are used to pull the crankshaft into the crankcase

Installation

8   Start the crankshaft into the case half. If it doesn't go in easily, pull it in the rest of the way with a crankshaft puller such as manufacturer tools 09919-32812, 09910-32820 and 09911-11310 **(see illustration)**.

Caution: Do not tap the crankshaft in with a mallet, even a soft-faced one. This can cause misalignment of the crankshaft and subsequent engine damage.

9   The remainder of installation is the reverse of removal.

30 Kickstarter (DR-Z400) - removal, inspection and installation

Removal

1   Remove the bolt that secures the kickstarter lever to the right side of the crankcase and remove the lever.
2   Remove the clutch (see Section 20).
3   Remove two screws that secure the driven gear retainer to the crankcase. Remove the retainer, spacer and kickstarter driven gear.

4   Pull the kickstarter out of the crankcase, then remove the guide (it's on the crankcase behind the driven gear).

Inspection

5   Check all parts for visible wear or damage before you take the assembly apart. Check the drive and driven gears for chipped or broken teeth.
6   Look for a punch mark on the kickstarter cog that aligns with a scribed line on the inner end of the shaft, between two of the splines. The marks are necessary for correct reassembly of the kickstarter. If you don't see them, make your own.
7   Remove the washer, spring and kickstarter ratchet from the inner end of the shaft, then remove the snap-ring, washer and drive gear **(see illustration)**.
8   Remove the oil seal, guide and spring from the outer end of the shaft **(see illustration 30.7)**.
9   Check the disassembled parts and replace any that are worn or damaged. Replace the snap-ring with a new one.
10   Reassembly is the reverse of disassembly.

Installation

11   Installation is the reverse of removal, with the following additions:

a)   *Align the punch mark on the ratchet with the line on the shaft.*
b)   *Hook the inner end of the spring into the slot in the guide. Hook the outer end of the spring into the hole in the crankcase below the kickstarter.*

31 Initial start-up after overhaul

1   Make sure the engine oil level is correct, then remove the spark plug from the engine. Place the engine kill switch in the Off position and unplug the primary (low tension) wires from the coil.
2   Crank the engine over with the starter

several times to build up oil pressure. Reinstall the spark plug, connect the wires and turn the switch to On.
3   Make sure there is fuel in the tank, then operate the choke.
4   Once you've made sure that there is oil pressure, allow the engine to run at a moderately fast idle until it reaches operating temperature.
5   Check carefully for oil leaks and make sure the transmission and controls, especially the brakes, function properly before road testing the machine. Refer to Section 31 for the recommended break-in procedure.
6   Upon completion of the road test, and after the engine has cooled down completely, recheck the valve clearances (see Chapter 1).

32 Recommended break-in procedure

1   Any rebuilt engine needs time to break in, even if parts have been installed in their original locations. For this reason, treat the machine gently for the first few miles to make sure oil has circulated throughout the engine and any new parts installed have started to seat.
2   Even greater care is necessary if the cylinder has been rebored or a new crankshaft has been installed. In the case of a rebore, the engine will have to be broken in as if the machine were new. This means greater use of the transmission and a restraining hand on the throttle for the first few operating days. There's no point in keeping to any set speed limit - the main idea is to vary the engine speed, keep from lugging (laboring) the engine and to avoid full-throttle operation. These recommendations can be lessened to an extent when only a new crankshaft is installed. Experience is the best guide, since it's easy to tell when an engine is running freely.
3   If a lubrication failure is suspected (oil doesn't seep from the check bolt, or the engine makes noise), stop the engine immediately and try to find the cause. If an engine is run without oil, even for a short period of time, irreparable damage will occur.

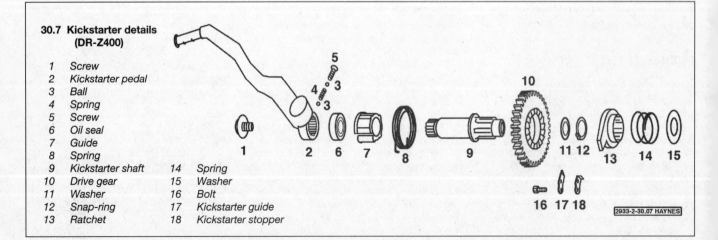

30.7 Kickstarter details (DR-Z400)

1	Screw
2	Kickstarter pedal
3	Ball
4	Spring
5	Screw
6	Oil seal
7	Guide
8	Spring
9	Kickstarter shaft
10	Drive gear
11	Washer
12	Snap-ring
13	Ratchet
14	Spring
15	Washer
16	Bolt
17	Kickstarter guide
18	Kickstarter stopper

2933-2-30.07 HAYNES

Chapter 3
Cooling system

Contents

Degrees of difficulty

Easy, suitable for novice with little experience		**Fairly easy,** suitable for beginner with some experience		**Fairly difficult,** suitable for competent DIY mechanic		**Difficult,** suitable for experienced DIY mechanic		**Very difficult,** suitable for expert DIY or professional	

Specifications

General

Radiator cap relief pressure	95 to 125 kPa (13.5 to 17.8 psi)
Thermostat opening temperature	Approximately 75-degrees C (167-degrees F)
Thermostat valve lift	6 mm (0.24 inch) or more at 90-degrees C (194-degrees F)
Fan switch operating temperature	
Off to on	Approximately 96-degrees C (205-degrees F)
On to off	Approximately 91-degrees C (196-degrees F)

Torque specifications

Cooling fan switch to radiator	13 Nm (114 inch-lbs)
Water pump cover bolts	10 Nm (84 inch-lbs)

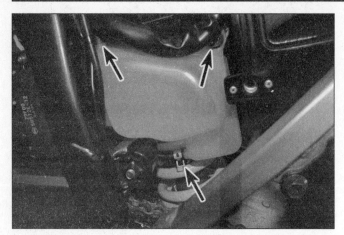

3.2 Coolant reservoir tank mounting bolt locations

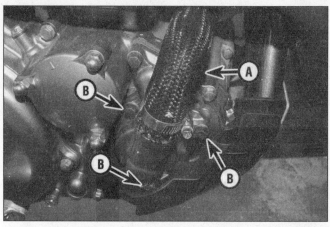

4.1a Lower radiator hose (A) and water pump cover bolt (B) locations (DR-Z400S and SM models)

1 General information

The vehicles covered by this manual are equipped with a liquid cooling system which utilizes a water/antifreeze mixture to carry away excess heat produced during combustion. The combustion chamber and cylinder are surrounded by a water jacket, through which the coolant is circulated by the water pump. The pump is mounted to the right side of the crankcase near the front and is driven by a gear. The twin radiators are mounted at the front of the frame. The coolant is pumped upward through the cylinder water jacket and cylinder head, then flows from the cylinder head to the radiators where it is cooled, then flows through the radiator bottom hose and water pump, then back into the engine. On DR-Z400S and SM models, a thermostat, mounted in the cylinder head, regulates coolant flow. When the engine is cold, the thermostat closes and coolant circulates through the water pump, thermostat bypass hose, coolant hoses and radiator. As the engine warms up, the thermostat opens, allowing coolant to be circulated through the engine coolant passages.

The cooling system on DR-Z400S and SM models includes a temperature warning light and fan. All models have a reservoir tank. As the coolant heats up, it expands and flows into the reservoir tank. As it cools, the coolant is pulled back into the cooling system.

2 Radiator cap - check

If problems such as overheating or loss of coolant occur, check the entire system as described in Chapter 1. The radiator cap opening pressure should be checked by a dealer service department or service station equipped with the special tester required to do the job. If the cap is defective, replace it with a new one.

3 Coolant reservoir - removal and installation

1 Locate the coolant reservoir.
2 Remove the tank mounting bolt (see illustration) and lift off the tank. Disconnect the siphon hose from the tank.
3 Installation is the reverse of removal.

4 Coolant hoses - removal and installation

1 The coolant hoses are all secured by screw-type clamps to fittings on the engine and radiator. On DR-Z400S and SM models, the water pump hose runs to the bottom of the left-hand radiator and another hose runs from the cylinder head to the top of the right-hand radiator, and the two radiators are joined at the top by a third hose (see illustrations).

4.1b A radiator hose runs from the front of the engine to the bottom of the left-hand radiator

4.1c The upper hose on DR-Z400S and SM models runs from the thermostat housing in the cylinder head to the bottom of the right-hand radiator

4.1d The radiators are joined at the top by a hose

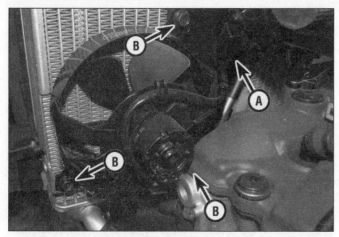

5.2 Fan connector (A) and mounting screw (B - bottom right mounting screw hidden) locations

6.4 Each radiator is secured to the frame by two bolts (right-hand radiator shown)

On DR-Z400 and DR-Z400E models, one hose runs from the water pump to the bottom of both radiators, and another hose runs from the cylinder head to the top of both radiators.

2   To remove a hose, loosen its clamp and carefully pry it off the fitting.

3   If the hose is stuck, pry the edge up slightly with a pointed tool and spray brake or electrical contact cleaner into the gap. Work the tool around the fitting, lifting the edge of the hose and spraying into the gap until the hose comes free of the fitting.

4   In extreme cases, you may have to slit the hose and cut it off the fitting with a knife. Make sure you can get a replacement hose before doing this.

5   Cooling fan and circuit (DR-Z400S and DR-Z400SM models) - check and replacement

Check

1   Check the battery to make sure it's fully charged (see Chapter 5).

2   If the engine is overheating and the cooling fan isn't coming on, disconnect the fan motor connector **(see illustration)** and connect the fan motor directly to a fully charged 12-volt battery using a pair of jumper wires. The fan motor should run. If it doesn't run, replace the fan motor with a new one.

3   Check the main fuse (see Chapter 5). If the fuse is blown, check the fan circuit for a short to ground (see the Wiring diagrams at the end of this manual).

4   If the fan motor runs when connected directly to the battery, disconnect the electrical connector from the fan thermoswitch. It's mounted in the rear side of the upper tank on the left-hand radiator.

5   Connect a short jumper wire between the terminals of the fan thermoswitch connector in the wiring harness (not between the

terminals of the switch itself). With the ignition key in the ON position, the fan should run. If it does, replace the thermoswitch with a new one.

6   As a further test of the thermoswitch, remove it from the radiator and suspend it in a pan of water with a thermometer so it doesn't touch the sides.

> **Warning: Antifreeze is poisonous. DO NOT use a cooking pan for this test.**

Connect an ohmmeter between the terminals of the switch and heat the water. The ohmmeter should indicate no continuity (infinite resistance) with the water cold. It should show continuity (little or no resistance) when the water is heated to approximately 96-degrees C (205-degrees F). Turn off the heat and let the water cool. The ohmmeter should once again show no continuity when the water cools to approximately 91-degrees C (196-degrees F).

7   If the switch doesn't perform as specified, replace it (see Steps 8 through 12).

Switch replacement

8   Drain the cooling system (see Chapter 1).

9   If you haven't already done so, disconnect the electrical connector from the thermoswitch.

10   Unscrew the thermoswitch from the radiator.

11   Lubricate the O-ring of the new switch with grease (Suzuki Supergrease A or equivalent).

12   Tighten the thermoswitch to the torque listed in this Chapter's Specifications.

Fan and motor replacement

13   If you haven't already done so, disconnect the wiring connectors for the fan and switch(es).

14   Remove the three screws that secure the fan to the radiator **(see illustration 5.2)**. Lift the fan off, together with the fan motor.

15   Installation is the reverse of removal.

6   Radiators - removal and installation

> **Warning: The engine must be completely cool before beginning this procedure.**

1   Remove the seat, side covers, radiator grilles and fuel tank (see Chapters 8 and 4). Drain the cooling system (see Chapter 1).

2   Disconnect the electrical connectors for the fan motor, fan switch and temperature warning light switch.

3   Disconnect the radiator hoses (see Section 4).

4   Remove the radiator mounting bolts **(see illustration)**.

5   Lift the radiator away from the frame, together with the cooling fan (left-hand radiator, DR-Z400S and SM models only). Inspect the mounting bolt grommets and replace them if they're worn or deteriorated.

6   Installation is the reverse of removal, with the following additions:

a) Tighten the mounting bolts securely, but don't overtighten them and distort the grommets.

b) Fill the cooling system (see Chapter 1).

c) Run the engine and check for coolant leaks.

7   Thermostat (DR-Z400S and DR-Z400SM models) - removal, check and installation

Removal

1   Drain the cooling system below the level of the thermostat (see Chapter 1).

2   Place rags beneath the thermostat housing to catch any residual coolant that drips out, then unbolt the thermostat hous-

7.3 Pull the thermostat out of the head

7.11 These flat spots align the thermostat in the correct orientation to the hole

ing from the front of the cylinder head (see illustration 4.1c).

3   Remove the thermostat from the cylinder head (see illustration).

8.7a Remove the drive gear snap-ring

Check

4   Remove any coolant deposits, then visually check the thermostat for corrosion, cracks and other damage. If it was open when it was removed, the thermostat is defective.

5   To check the thermostat operation, submerge it in a container of the specified coolant (50/50 antifreeze and water) along with a thermometer. The thermostat should be suspended so it does not touch the sides of the container.

⚠️ Warning: Antifreeze is poisonous. Do not use a cooking pan to test the thermostat.

6   Gradually heat the water in the container with a hot plate or stove and check the temperature when the thermostat just starts to open.

7   Compare the opening temperature to the values listed in this Chapter's Specifications.

8   Continue heating the water until the valve is fully open.

9   Measure how far the thermostat valve has opened and compare to the valve listed in this Chapter's Specifications.

10   It these specifications are not met, or if the thermostat doesn't open while the coolant is heated, replace it with a new one.

Installation

11   Apply clean coolant to the rubber seal on the thermostat and install the thermostat into the cylinder head. There's a flat spot on each side of the thermostat recess that only allows the thermostat to be installed in the correct orientation (see illustration).

12   Install the thermostat housing and tighten its bolts securely, but don't over-tighten them and strip the threads.

13   Fill and bleed the cooling system (see Chapter 1).

14   The remainder of installation is the reverse of removal.

8.7b Remove the drive gear and pin

8.7c Remove the washer

8.8a Water pump cover O-ring location

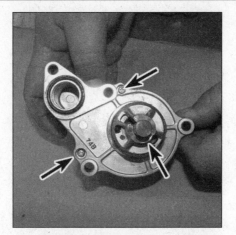

8.8b Water pump cover screws and impeller snap-ring

8.8c Remove the O-ring from the pump body and pull out the impeller, together with its shaft

8 Water pump - removal, inspection and installation

Removal and disassembly

Note: The following procedure describes removing the water pump completely. If you're only planning to remove the cover so you can inspect the impeller, ignore that steps that don't apply.

1   Drain the engine oil and cooling system (see Chapter 1).

2   Disconnect the spring from the brake pedal and unbolt the rear master cylinder (see Chapter 7). Leave the fluid line connected to the master cylinder.

3   Disconnect the spring from the brake light switch (see Chapter 5).

4   Disconnect the coolant hose from the water pump **(see illustration 4.1a)**.

5   Remove the pump cover bolts **(see illustration 4.1a)**. The bolts are different lengths, so tag them for reinstallation. Don't try to remove the pump cover yet - the reason to remove the bolts now is that they are easier to loosen while the pump is still attached to the engine.

6   Refer to Chapter 2 and remove the right crankcase cover from the engine together with the water pump. This is necessary because the pump cover is secured to the pump body from the inner side by two screws, and the only way to get at them is to remove the crankcase cover together with the water pump, then remove the drive gear and pull the pump body out of the crankcase cover.

7   The impeller and shaft are one piece. To remove them, remove the snap-ring, drive gear, pin and washer from the inner end of the shaft **(see illustrations)**. Pull the water pump body out of the crankcase cover.

8   Remove the pump cover O-ring and screws, then remove the cover from the pump body **(see illustrations)**. Remove the remaining snap-ring from the inner end of the shaft, then pull the impeller and shaft out of the pump body **(see illustration)**.

Inspection

9   Check the oil seal and mechanical seal for wear or damage. These seals separate the coolant from the engine oil. If the oil is milky or foamy, coolant may have been leaking into it past the seals. Refer to Section 9 and replace them.

10   The pump O-rings should be replaced whenever the pump is disassembled

Installation

11   Installation is the reverse of removal, with the following additions:

a) Use new O-ring.
b) Engage the impeller shaft pin with the drive gear.
c) Tighten the water pump bolts to the torque listed in this Chapter's Specifications.
d) Fill and bleed the cooling system and fill the engine oil (see Chapter 1).
e) Run the engine and check for coolant leaks.

9 Water pump seals - replacement

1   If coolant has been leaking from the weep hole, the water pump seals need to be replaced. There are four seals: a rubber seal inside the impeller, a Teflon seal next to the rubber seal, a conventional rubber seal inside the water pump body and a mechanical seal, which is spring-loaded to rub against the Teflon seal. **Note:** The mechanical seal can't be removed without destroying it. Be sure you have a new one before removing it from the pump.

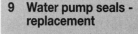

HAYNES HINT *If the Teflon seal inside the impeller is worn and is not included with a new mechanical seal, you can turn the old one over and put it back in the impeller so its other surface is exposed to the mechanical seal (see illustration).*

9.1a Remove the Teflon seal from the impeller shaft and pry the rubber seal out of the impeller

9.1b To install a new mechanical seal, you'll need a tool like this one

9.3a Pry out the rubber portion of the seal - you'll have to destroy the seal to remove it, so have a new one on hand

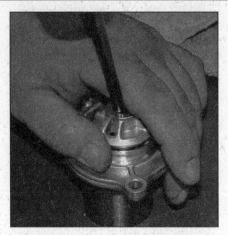

9.3b Insert a punch through the pump body to drive the metal part of the mechanical seal out of its bore

9.3c Remove the mechanical seal once it's loose - use Loctite 518 or equivalent on the sides of the metal portion

9.3d Once the mechanical seal is out, pry the rubber seal out of the pump body

 TOOL TiP *To drive the new seal in, you'll need a tool that bears on the flange of the mechanical seal, and also fits in the recess of the pump body. It should also have a center protrusion that fits inside the seal to keep it from collapsing as it's being installed (see illustration).*

2   Remove and disassemble the water pump (see Section 8).
3   Carefully start the seals from their bores with a screwdriver, being careful not to gouge the crankcase cover or impeller **(see illustration)**. Finish removal of the mechanical seal and the conventional seal behind it by inserting a punch into the access holes in the water pump body, driving the mechanical seal out, then prying out the rubber seal **(see illustrations)**.
4   Tap in new seals, using a driver tool **(see illustration 9.1b)**. If the new mechanical seal is not coated with sealant on the outer edge, coat it with Loctite 518 or equivalent.

Chapter 4
Fuel and exhaust systems

Contents

Degrees of difficulty

| Easy, suitable for novice with little experience | | Fairly easy, suitable for beginner with some experience | | Fairly difficult, suitable for competent DIY mechanic | 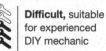 | Difficult, suitable for experienced DIY mechanic | 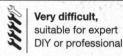 | Very difficult, suitable for expert DIY or professional | |

Specifications

Fuel*

DR-Z400, DR-Z400E
    US and Canada... Premium unleaded gasoline, 90 pump octane minimum
    All others .... Premium unleaded gasoline, 95 Research octane minimum
DR-Z400S, DR-Z400SM
    US and Canada... Unleaded gasoline, 87 pump octane minimum
    All others .... Unleaded gasoline, 91 Research octane minimum

Gasoline containing up to ten per cent ethanol may be used.

Carburetor

Mikuni

DR-Z400S, SM
    Type .... Mikuni BSR36
    ID mark
        2006 and earlier
            US and Canada... 29FB
            California 29FC
            UK, Europe, Israel 29FA
        2007 and 2008
            US and Canada... 29FB
            California 29FC
            UK, Australia 29FA
            Europe (frame number JS1B811200100001-on) 29FN
            Europe (frame number JS1B811100100001-on) 29FP

Carburetor (continued)

Mikuni (continued)

DR-Z400S, SM
    2009 and later
        DR-Z400S 29FA
        DR-Z400SM 29FN
    Main jet 142.5
    Needle jet P-0M
    Needle/clip position
        2006 and earlier
            US, California, Canada .... 5DH-37/not applicable
            UK, Europe, Israel 5DH-36/2
        2007 and later
            US, California, Canada 5DH-37/1
            UK, Europe, Australia 5DH-36/2
    Pilot jet 22.5
    Pilot air jet
        2006 and earlier
            US, California, Canada 135
            UK, Europe, Israel 165
        2007 and 2008 (jet no. 1)
            US, California, Canada 140
            UK, Europe, Australia 65
        2007 and 2008 (jet no. 2)
            US, California, Canada 135
            UK, Europe, Australia 165
        2009 and later (DR-Z400S)
            US, California, Canada 135
            UK, Europe 165
        2009 and later (DR-Z400SM, jet no. 1)
            US, California, Canada 140
            UK, Europe 65
        2009 and later (DR-Z400SM, jet no. 2)
            US, California, Canada 135
            UK, Europe 165
    Standard pilot screw setting
        2006 and earlier
            US, California, Canada .... Not specified
            UK, Europe, Israel .... 3 turns out
        2007 and later
            UK, Australia .... 3 turns out
            Europe (frame number JS1B811200100001-on) .... 3 turns out
            Europe (frame number JS1B811100100001-on) .... 2-3/4 turns out
    Float height
        2003 and earlier .... 13.0 +/- 1.0 mm (0.51 +/- 0.04 inch)
        2004 through 2008
            US (except California), Canada .... 16.3 +/- 1.0 mm (0.64 +/- 0.04 inch)
            California, UK, Europe, Israel .... 13.0 +/- 1.0 mm (0.51 +/- 0.04 inch)
        2009 and later (DR-Z400S) .... 13.0 +/- 1.0 mm (0.51 +/- 0.04 inch)
        2009 and later (DR-Z400SM)
            US, California, Canada .... 14.0 +/- 1.0 mm (0.55 +/- 0.04 inch)
            UK, Europe .... 16.3 +/- 1.0 mm (0.64 +/- 0.04 inch)
DR-Z400E
    Type .... Mikuni BSR36
    ID mark 29F2
    Main jet 140
    Needle jet P-0M
    Needle/clip position .... 5DH-56/not applicable
    Pilot jet 22.5
    Pilot air jet 155
    Standard pilot screw setting .... 2-1/2 turns out
    Float height .... 13.0 +/- 1.0 mm (0.51 +/- 0.04 inch)

Keihin

Type..	FCR39H
ID mark	
DR-Z400 (2005 and earlier)	
US, Canada	29F1
All others...	29F0
DR-Z400E (2005 and earlier)	
US, Canada	29F4
Europe (2000 only)...	29F6
All others...	29F3
DR-Z400/DR-Z400E (2006 and later)	
US, Canada	29F8
Europe	29F6
All others...	29F3
Main jet	
US, Canada...	142
All others	165
Main air jet	200
Jet needle/clip position	
2006 and later US, Canada..	OBDYP/4
All others	OBDXP/4
Needle jet	
2000	45
2001 and later	2.9 mm (0.11 inch)
Slow jet..	45
Slow air jet	60
Air jet	90
Pilot screw setting...	1-1/2 turns out
Float height..	9.0 +/- 1.0 mm (0.35 +/- 0.04 inch)

Throttle position sensor

Mikuni carburetor	
Throttle closed	3.5 to 6.5 k-ohms
Throttle wide open...	78 percent of throttle closed reading
Keihin carburetor	
Throttle closed	Approximately 5 k-ohms
Throttle wide open	3.09 to 4.63 k-ohms

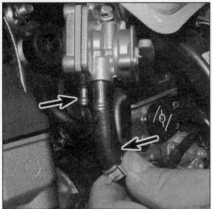

2.2 Fuel tap vacuum line (left arrow, Mikuni carburetor only) and fuel line (right arrow)

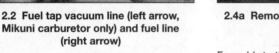

1 General information

All DR-Z400S and SM models, as well as 2004 and later DR-Z400E California models, use a constant-vacuum Mikuni BRS36 carburetor with a butterfly-type throttle valve.

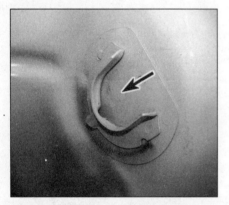

2.4c Pull the tank rearward so the mounting notches clear the mounting insulators

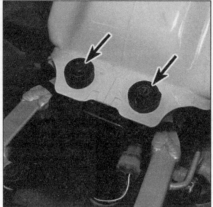

2.4a Remove the mounting bolts at the rear of the tank

For cold starting, a choke plunger is actuated by a knob. The carburetor is equipped with a throttle position sensor.

All 2004 and earlier DR-Z400 and DR-Z400E models, as well as 2005 and later non-California versions, use a Keihin flat-slide carburetor with an accelerator pump.

The exhaust system consists of a pipe and muffler. US and Canadian models have a spark arrester that can be removed for cleaning.

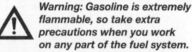

2 Fuel tank - removal and installation

⚠️ *Warning: Gasoline is extremely flammable, so take extra precautions when you work on any part of the fuel system. Don't smoke or allow open flames or bare light bulbs near the work area, and don't work in a garage where a gas-type appliance (such as a water heater or clothes dryer) is present. Since gasoline is carcinogenic, wear fuel-resistant gloves when there's a possibility of being exposed to fuel, and, if you spill any fuel on your skin, rinse it off immediately*

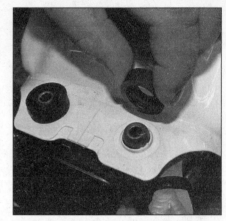

2.4b Pull off the mounting grommets

with soap and water. Mop up any spills immediately and do not store fuel-soaked rags where they could ignite. When you perform any kind of work on the fuel system, wear safety glasses and have an extinguisher suitable for a class B type fire (flammable liquids) on hand.

Removal

1   Remove the seat and side covers (see Chapter 8). If you're working on a DR-Z400 or DR-Z400E, pull the fuel tank breather hose out of the handlebar.

2   Turn the fuel tap to Off and disconnect the fuel line **(see illustration)**. If you're working on a DR-Z400S or SM, disconnect the fuel tap vacuum line as well.

3   If you're working on a DR-Z400 or DR-Z400E, unhook the rubber strap that secures the rear of the tank. Remove the mounting bolt from each side at the lower front of the tank. Lift the tank off.

4   If you're working on a DR-Z400S or SM, remove the mounting bolts and grommets at the rear of the tank **(see illustrations)**. Pull it backward to clear the mounts at the front and lift it far enough to disconnect the breather hose from the underside **(see illustrations)**. If necesary, pour the fuel from the tank into an approved gasoline container.

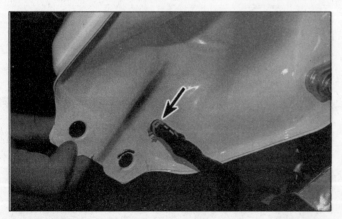

2.4d Lift the tank and disconnect the vent line, if equipped

2.5 Check the mounting insulators (left arrow), heat shield (center) and frame insulator (right) for wear or damage

4.3 Loosen the clamping bands at the front and rear of the carburetor (Mikuni shown, Keihin similar)

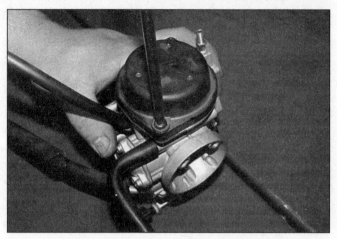

5.3a Remove the screws that secure the cap

Installation

5   Before installing the tank, check the condition of the mounting isolator and heat shield on the frame **(see illustration)**, the rubber strap or bushings at rear of the tank, and the fuel line to the carburetor (and vacuum line on S and SM models) - if they're hardened, cracked, or show any other signs of deterioration, replace them.

6   Installation is the reverse of removal. Make sure the tank does not pinch any wires. Tighten the tank mounting bolts securely, but don't overtighten them and strip the threads.

3   Carburetor overhaul - general information

1   Poor engine performance, hesitation, hard starting, stalling, flooding and backfiring are all signs that major carburetor maintenance may be required.

2   Keep in mind that many so-called carburetor problems are really not carburetor problems at all, but mechanical problems within the engine or ignition system malfunctions. Try to establish for certain that the carburetor is in need of maintenance before beginning a major overhaul.

3   Check the fuel tap and its strainer screen, the fuel lines, the intake manifold clamps, the O-ring between the intake manifold and cylinder head, the vacuum hoses, the air filter element, the cylinder compression, crankcase vacuum and compression, the spark plug and the ignition timing before assuming that a carburetor overhaul is required. If the bike has been unused for more than 24 hours, drain the float chamber and refill the tank with fresh fuel.

4   Most carburetor problems are caused by dirt particles, varnish and other deposits which build up in and block the fuel and air passages. Also, in time, gaskets and O-rings shrink or deteriorate and cause fuel and air

leaks which lead to poor performance.

5   When the carburetor is overhauled, it is generally disassembled completely and the parts are cleaned thoroughly with a carburetor cleaning solvent and dried with filtered, unlubricated compressed air. The fuel and air passages are also blown through with compressed air to force out any dirt that may have been loosened but not removed by the solvent. Once the cleaning process is complete, the carburetor is reassembled using a new top gasket, O-rings and, generally, a new inlet needle valve and seat.

6   Before disassembling the carburetor, make sure you have the necessary gasket, O-rings and other parts, some carburetor cleaner, a supply of rags, some means of blowing out the carburetor passages and a clean place to work.

4   Carburetor - removal and installation

1   Remove the left fuel tank side cover (see Chapter 8).

2   Disconnect the fuel line from the carburetor (see Section 2).

3   Loosen the clamping bands at the front and rear of the carburetor **(see illustration)**.

4   Disconnect the wiring connector for the throttle position sensor **(see illustration 4.3)**.

5   Free the carburetor from the intake tube and the air cleaner tube.

6   Remove the carburetor partway and disconnect the throttle cables (see Section 7).

7   Note how the hoses are routed and free them from the retainer. Remove the carburetor.

8   Installation is the reverse of the removal steps, with the following additions:

 a) *Adjust the throttle freeplay (see Chapter 1).*
 b) *Adjust the idle speed (see Chapter 1).*

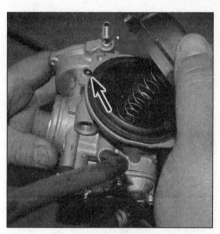

5.3b Lift off the cap, noting the position of the small O-ring on the carburetor body

5   Carburetor - disassembly, cleaning and inspection

 Warning: Gasoline is extremely flammable, so take extra precautions when you work on any part of the fuel system. See the Warning in Section 2.

Disassembly

1   Remove the carburetor (see Section 4).

2   Set the carburetor on a clean working surface. Take note of how the vent hoses are routed, including locations of hose retainers. Remove the throttle position sensor (see Section 9).

Mikuni carburetor

3   To disassemble the carburetor, refer to the **accompanying illustrations**.

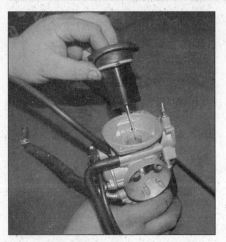

5.3c Pull out the diaphragm and piston, together with the jet needle

5.3d Remove the float chamber screws . . .

5.3e . . . and lift off the float chamber, together with its O-ring

5.3f Remove the float screw

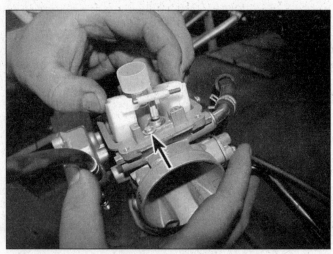

5.3g Lift out the float together with the needle valve and remove the screw that secures the needle valve seat

5.3h Remove the needle valve seat and fuel strainer

5.3i Hold the needle jet holder with a wrench on the hex and unscrew the main jet

5.3j Unscrew the needle jet holder and lift it out together with its O-ring

5.3k Unscrew the main jet

5.3l Unscrew the starter (choke) jet

5.3m Unscrew the pilot jet. On California models, drill and pry out the plug for access to the idle mixture screw. On all models, turn the screw in until it bottoms lightly, counting the number of turns, then unscrew it all the way

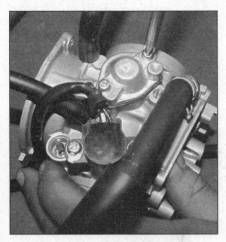

5.3n Remove the diaphragm cover screws

5.3o Remove the cover and spring

5.3p Remove the diaphragm, noting how its rod engages the hole in the carburetor body

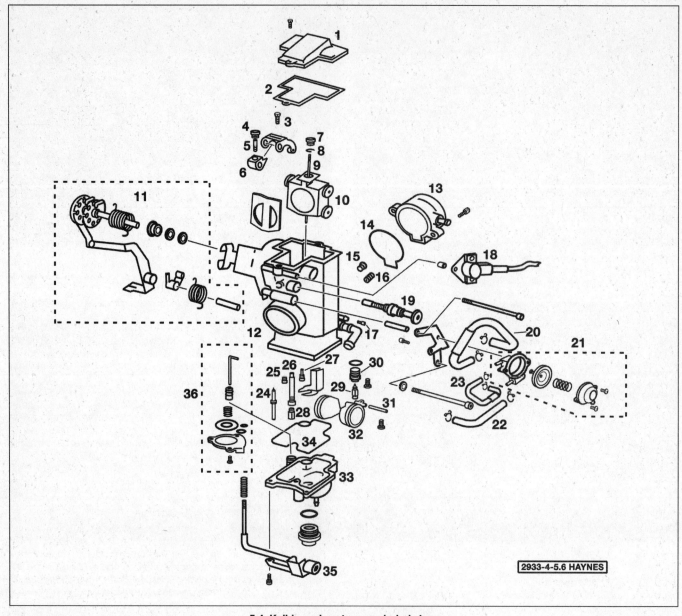

5.4 Keihin carburetor - exploded view

1	Top cap	10	Throttle valve	19	Choke plunger	28	Main jet
2	Gasket	11	Throttle lever assembly	20	Hose	29	Needle valve
3	Screw	12	Carburetor body	21	Coasting enricher	30	Needle valve seat
4	Adjusting screw locknut	13	Intake duct	22	Hose	31	Float pin
5	Adjusting screw	14	O-ring	23	Hose	32	Float
6	Throttle valve lever	15	Slow air jet	24	Pilot screw	33	Float chamber
7	Jet needle holder	16	Main air jet	25	Starter (choke) jet	34	Gasket
8	Jet needle clip	17	Air jet	26	Needle jet	35	Throttle stop screw
9	Jet needle	18	Throttle position sensor	27	Pilot jet	36	Accelerator pump

Keihin carburetor

4 Note how the hoses are installed on the carburetor, then remove them **(see illustration)**.

5 If you're working on a DR-Z400, remove the nut and bolt that secure the air valve to the left side of the carburetor and remove the air valve.

6 Place a wrench on the hex of the choke plunger and unscrew it from the carburetor **(see illustration 5.4)**.

7 Remove the screws that secure the top cover and remove the cover.

8 Loosen the throttle stop adjuster locknut and unscrew the adjuster. Count and record the number of turns required to remove the

adjuster for use on installation.

9 Rotate the throttle lever (inside the top of the carburetor) so the rollers on the throttle valve (slide) can be disengaged, then pull the throttle valve up and out of the carburetor, together with the jet needle **(see illustration 5.4)**.

10 Remove the nut that secures the jet

needle to the throttle slide, then pull the needle up and out, together with its clip.
11   Remove two screws that secure the intake joint to the carburetor body, then remove the joint and the O-ring.
12   On the bottom of the carburetor, remove the screws that secure the accelerator pump cover. Remove the cover, two O-rings, diaphragm and spring.
13   Remove the float chamber screws and remove the float chamber.
14   As you pull the float chamber off, slide the rubber boot off the accelerator pump shaft, taking care not to damage it.
15   Remove the plastic baffle plate from the main jet.
16   Remove the screw that secures the needle valve, then pull out the float pin and remove the float, together with the needle valve.
17   Remove the screw that secures the needle valve seat to the carburetor body and remove the seat.
18   Unscrew the main jet, main air jet, slow jet, needle jet and starter (choke) jet from inside the float chamber.
19   Unscrew the main air jet and slow air jet from the rear of the carburetor, above the throttle bore.
20   Unscrew the air jet from the left side of the carburetor.
21   Turn the pilot screw in until it bottoms, counting the number of turns to the nearest 1/8 turn. Record this number for use on assembly.

Caution: Don't bottom the pilot screw hard or it will be damaged.

Cleaning

Caution: Use only a carburetor cleaning solution that is safe for use with plastic parts (be sure to read the label on the container).

22   Submerge the metal components in the carburetor cleaner for approximately thirty minutes (or longer, if the directions recommend it).
23   After the carburetor has soaked long enough for the cleaner to loosen and dissolve most of the varnish and other deposits, use a brush to remove the stubborn deposits. Rinse it again, then dry it with compressed air. Blow out all of the fuel and air passages in the carburetor body.

Caution: Never clean the jets or passages with a piece of wire or a drill bit, as they will be enlarged, causing the fuel and air metering rates to be upset.

Inspection

24   Check the operation of the choke plunger. If it doesn't move smoothly, replace it. Check the plunger seat for wear or damage and replace it if problems are found.
25   Check the tapered portion of the pilot screw for wear or damage. Replace the screw if necessary.
26   Check the carburetor body, float chamber and carburetor top for cracks, distorted sealing surfaces and other damage. If any defects are found, replace the faulty component, although replacement of the entire carburetor will probably be necessary (check with your parts supplier for the availability of separate components).
27   Check the jet needle for straightness by rolling it on a flat surface (such as a piece of glass). Replace it if it's bent or if the tip is worn.
28   Check the tip of the fuel inlet valve needle. If it has grooves or scratches in it, it must be replaced. Push in on the rod in the other end of the needle, then release it - if it doesn't spring back, replace the valve needle.
29   Check the O-rings on the float chamber and the main jet access plug (in the float chamber). Replace them if they're damaged.
30   Check the floats for damage. This will usually be apparent by the presence of fuel inside one of the floats. If the floats are damaged, they must be replaced.
31   Check that the throttle valve moves up-and-down smoothly in the carburetor body. Check the surface of the throttle valve for wear. If it's worn excessively or doesn't move smoothly in the bore, replace the carburetor.

6.7 With the float needle seated (but the spring not compressed), measure the float height from the float bowl mating surface

6 Carburetor - reassembly and float height check

Reassembly

Caution: When installing the jets, be careful not to over-tighten them - they're made of soft material and can strip or shear easily.

Note: *When reassembling the carburetor, be sure to use new O-rings.*

1   Install the clip on the jet needle if it was removed. Place it in the needle groove listed in this Chapter's Specifications. Install the needle and clip in the throttle valve.
2   Install the pilot screw along with its spring, washer and O-ring, turning it in until it seats lightly. Turn the screw out the number of turns recorded during removal.
3   Reverse the disassembly steps to install the jets.
4   Invert the carburetor. Attach the fuel inlet valve needle to the float. Set the float into position in the carburetor, making sure the valve needle seats correctly. Install the float pivot pin.
5   Measure float height (see Step 7) before the float chamber is installed.
6   Install the float chamber gasket or O-ring. Place the float chamber on the carburetor and install the screws, tightening them securely. Install the main jet access plug in the bottom of the float chamber, using a new O-ring, and tighten it securely.

Float check

7   Position the carburetor so the valve needle is just seated, but the spring isn't compressed **(see illustration)**. If necessary, hold the float chamber so the float pin is at the top and the float hangs downward. Measure the distance from the float chamber gasket surface to the top of the float and compare your measurement to the float height listed in this Chapter's Specifications. Bend the float tang as necessary to change the adjustment.

7 Throttle cables - removal and installation

1   These vehicles are equipped with two throttle cables, an accelerator (pull) cable that opens the throttle plate in the carburetor and a decelerator (push) cable that closes the throttle plate.
2   Remove the fuel tank (see Section 2).
3   At the handlebar, loosen the throttle cable adjuster all the way (see Chapter 1).
4   Look for a punch mark on the handlebar next to the split in the throttle cable housing. If you don't see a mark, make one so the housing can be installed in the correct position.

7.5a Remove the throttle housing screws

7.5b Separate the housing halves for access to the cables

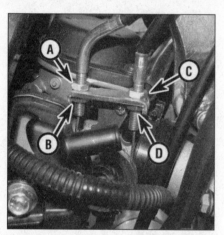

7.6a At the carburetor, loosen the cable locknuts (Mikuni shown, Keihin similar)

A   Pull cable locknut
B   Pull cable adjusting nut
C   Push cable locknut
D   Push cable adjusting nut

7.6b Slip the push cable out of the bracket notch (arrow)

5   Remove the screws that secure the halves of the throttle housing to each other and separate the halves (see illustrations).

6   At the carburetor, loosen the cable lock-nuts to create slack in the cables (see illustration). Slip each cable out of the bracket slot, then lift each cable out of the groove, turn it to align with the removal slot and slip the cable end plug out of the pulley (see illustrations).

7   Rotate the cable ends out of the pulley at the throttle grip, then slide the end plugs sideways out of the pulley (see illustration).

8   Note how the cable is routed and remove it from the vehicle.

9   Route the cable into place. Make sure it doesn't interfere with any other components and isn't kinked or bent sharply.

10   Lubricate the carburetor ends of the cable with multi-purpose grease. Reverse the disconnection steps to connect the throttle cables to the carburetor throttle pulley.

11   Reverse the disconnection steps to connect the cables to the throttle grip.

12   Operate the throttle and make sure it returns to the idle position.

7.6c Turn the cable and lift the end plug out of the slot in the throttle pulley

7.6d Remove the pull cable in the same manner as the push cable

7.7 At the throttle grip, rotate the cables out of the pulley until their end plugs align with the cable slots, then slip the end plugs sideways out of the pulley

8.2 Remove the heat shield bolts and the muffler clamp bolt

8.3a Remove the forward muffler bolt. . .

8.3b . . . and the top muffler bolt

 Warning: If the throttle doesn't return, find and solve the problem before continuing with installation. A stuck throttle can lead to loss of control of the vehicle.

13 Adjust the cables (see Chapter 1).
14 Turn the handlebars back and forth to make sure the cables do not cause the steering to bind.
15 Once you're sure the cables operate properly, install the fuel tank (see Section 2).
16 With the engine idling, turn the handlebars through their full travel (full left lock to full right lock) and note whether idle speed increases. If it does, the cable is routed incorrectly. Correct this dangerous condition before riding the motorcycle.

8 Exhaust system - removal and installation

1 Remove the right side cover (see Chapter 8).

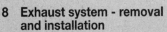

8.4 Remove the nuts or bolts, detach the pipe from the cylinder head and remove the gasket from the exhaust port

2 Unbolt the heat shield from the exhaust pipe and remove it **(see illustration)**. Loosen the muffler clamp bolt and remove the forward exhaust pipe bolt.
3 Unscrew the rearward exhaust pipe bolt and the muffler mounting bolt **(see illustrations)**. Work the muffler free of the pipe and remove the gasket.
4 Detach the front pipe from the cylinder head and remove it from the machine **(see illustration)**.
5 To replace the muffler core, refer to Chapter 1.
6 Installation is the reverse of removal. Use a new gasket in the exhaust port and at the joint between the pipe and muffler.

9 Throttle position sensor - check, removal and installation

Check

1 All models use a throttle position sensor. Before checking the throttle position

9.2 Loosen the screws to adjust the throttle position sensor - unscrew them all the way to remove the sensor (Mikuni shown; Keihin similar)

sensor, check and adjust engine idle speed and throttle cable freeplay (see Chapter 1). The check procedure is performed with the engine off.
2 Locate the sensor on the carburetor **(see illustration)**. Follow its wiring harness to the connector and disconnect it.
3 Connect an ohmmeter between the terminals of the black and blue wires (in the sensor side of the connector, not the wiring harness side). Compare the reading to the value listed in this Chapter's Specifications (throttle fully closed).
4 Connect the ohmmeter to the black and yellow wire terminals in the sensor side of the connector.
5 Open the throttle all the way and note the ohmmeter reading. If it's not within the value listed in this Chapter's Specifications, adjust the sensor (see Steps 6 and 7).

Adjustment

6 This procedure requires a Torx bit.
7 Loosen the mounting screws **(see illustration 9.2)**. Carefully rotate the sensor back and forth to get the correct ohmmeter reading, then tighten the screw.

Replacement

8 Disconnect the electrical connector. Remove the mounting screws and remove the sensor.
9 Install the sensor, making sure its slot aligns with the tab in the carburetor. Tighten the mounting screws, leaving them loose enough so the sensor can be rotated.
10 Adjust the sensor resistance (see Steps 6 and 7).
11 Once the correct reading is obtained, mark the sensor position on the carburetor with a felt pen.
12 Tighten the mounting screws, making sure that the felt pen marks stay aligned.
13 Remove the ohmmeter.
14 Refer to Chapter 1 and reset idle speed.

10.2 Disconnect the top hose (right arrow) and any additional hoses from the housing - refer to the diagram (left arrow) for hose connections

10.3 Loosen the clamp screw so the housing can be disengaged from the clamp

10.4 Remove one bolt from the top, one from the left front and one from the rear of the housing

10 Air cleaner housing - removal and installation

1   Remove the seat and fuel tank (see Chapter 8 and Section 2).
2   Disconnect the hoses from the air cleaner housing **(see illustration)**.
3   Loosen the clamping band that secures the carburetor intake duct to the front of the air cleaner housing **(see illustration)**.
4   Remove the mounting bolts, one from the top **(see illustration)**, one from the left front corner and one from the rear. Work the air cleaner housing free of the outlet tube and lift it out of the frame.
5   Installation is the reverse of removal.

11 Evaporative emission control system - check

1   This is system is used on California

S and SM models to store fuel tank vapors while the engine is not running. The vapors are drawn into the engine for burning when the engine is started.
2   Check the system hoses for deterioration, cracks and loose connections, referring to the diagram on the motorcycle **(see illustration 10.2)**. Replace any hoses that have problems.
3   Check the canister for cracks, dents or other damage. If any problems are found, remove its mounting bolt and disengage the lower side of the clamp **(see illustrations)**.
4   Check the rollover valve for damage **(see illustration)**. Replace it if problems are found.

12 Pulse air (PAIR) system - check and replacement

1   The PAIR system is used on UK, European, Israeli and Australian models to suck air into the exhaust system just downstream of the exhaust port. This allows combus-

tion to continue for a longer time, reducing unburned hydrocarbons in the exhaust.
2   Check the components (they're located at the front of the cylinder head) for visible damage. Pay special attention to the hoses, and replace them if they're cracked or deteriorated.
3   Disconnect the vacuum hose from the top of the PAIR valve. Unbolt the air supply tube from the cylinder head, then remove the valve mounting bolts and remove the assembly from the cylinder head.
4   Disconnect the hoses from the PAIR valve.
5   Check the reed valve (on the side of the PAIR valve that faces the engine) for carbon build-up. Don't try to clean it; replace the valve if carbon has built up on it.
6   Blow air into the inlet port (metal). It should flow from the outlet port (plastic). It shouldn't flow from the outlet port to the inlet port. If air flows both ways or neither way, replace the valve.

11.3a To remove the EVAP canister, remove the bolt . . .

11.3b . . . unhook the mounting clamp at the bottom, pull the canister out and disconnect its hoses

11.4 Rollover valve location

Chapter 5
Ignition and electrical systems

Contents

Degrees of difficulty

Easy, suitable for novice with little experience	**Fairly easy,** suitable for beginner with some experience	**Fairly difficult,** suitable for competent DIY mechanic	**Difficult,** suitable for experienced DIY mechanic	**Very difficult,** suitable for expert DIY or professional

Specifications

Battery

Type	Maintenance free
Capacity	
2000	12 volts, 6.5 amp-hours
2001 and later	12 volts, 6.0 amp-hours

Ignition system

Spark distance	8 mm (5/16-inch) or more
Ignition coil resistance	
Primary	0.1 to 1.0 ohms
Secondary	12 to 20 k-ohms
Ignition coil primary peak voltage	150 volts or more
Pick-up coil peak voltage	5.0 volts or more
Signal coil peak voltage	1.4 volts or more

Charging system

Alternator stator coil resistance
Charging coil .... 0.50 to 1.25 ohms (yellow to yellow)
Signal coil .... 0.05 to 0.20 ohms (white to black)
Pick-up coil .... 390 to 600 ohms (green to blue)

Alternator
No-load voltage (engine cold) .... 75 volts AC or more

Regulator/rectifier
Regulated voltage .... 13.5 to 15.0 volts at 5000 rpm

Starter motor
Relay resistance .... 3 to 5 ohms

Fuse ratings
Main fuse .... 20 amps
Spare fuse .... 20 amps

Torque specifications
Alternator rotor nut .... 120 Nm (87 ft-lbs)
Starter clutch bolts* .... Not specified
Starter mounting bolts .... 10 Nm (84 inch-lbs)
Starter clutch slip torque .... 30 to 55 Nm (22 to 40 ft-lbs)
Coolant temperature warning light switch .... 13 Nm (114 inch-lbs)

Use non-permanent thread locking agent on the bolt threads.

1 General information

The electrical system on DR-Z400E, S and SM models includes a battery and charging system, lighting system (including warning lights) and an electric starter. DR-Z400S and SM models have turn signals. The electrical system on DR-Z400 (kick start) models does not include a battery. The alternator on all models produces alternating current, which is converted to direct current to operate the lights and ignition system.

The ignition system consists of an alternator that generates the current, a capacitive discharge ignition (CDI) unit that receives and stores it, and a pulse generator that triggers the CDI unit to discharge its current into the ignition coil, where it is stepped up to a voltage high enough to jump the spark plug gap. To aid in locating a problem in the ignition circuit, wiring diagrams are included at the end of this manual.

The CDI ignition system functions on the same principle as a breaker point ignition system with the pulse generator and CDI unit performing the tasks previously associated with the breaker points and mechanical advance system. As a result, adjustment and maintenance of ignition components is eliminated (with the exception of spark plug replacement).

Note: *Keep in mind that electrical parts, once purchased, can't be returned. To avoid unnecessary expense, make very sure the faulty component has been positively identified before buying a replacement part.*

2 Electrical troubleshooting

Electrical problems often stem from simple causes, such as loose or corroded connections. Prior to any electrical troubleshooting, always visually check the condition of the wires and connections in the circuit.

If testing instruments are going to be utilized, use the diagrams to plan where you will make the necessary connections in order to accurately pinpoint the trouble spot.

The basic tools needed for electrical troubleshooting include a test light or voltmeter, an ohmmeter or a continuity tester (which includes a bulb, battery and set of test leads) and a jumper wire, preferably with a circuit breaker incorporated, which can be used to bypass electrical components.

A continuity check is performed to see if a circuit, section of circuit or individual component is capable of passing electricity through it. Connect one lead of a self-powered test light or ohmmeter to one end of the circuit being tested and the other lead to the other end of the circuit. If the bulb lights (or the ohmmeter indicates little or no resistance), there is continuity, which means the circuit is passing electricity through it properly. The kill switch can be checked in the same way.

Remember that the electrical circuit on these motorcycles is designed to conduct electricity through the wires, kill switch, etc. to the electrical component (CDI unit, etc.). From there it is directed to the frame (ground) where it is passed back to the alternator. Electrical problems are basically an interruption in the flow of electricity.

Because of their nature, the individual ignition system components can be checked but not repaired. If ignition system troubles occur, and the faulty component can be isolated, the only cure for the problem is to replace the part with a new one. Keep in mind that most electrical parts, once purchased, can't be returned. To avoid unnecessary expense, make very sure the faulty component has been positively identified before buying a replacement part.

Most battery damage is caused by heat, vibration, and/or low electrolyte levels, so keep the battery securely mounted, inspect it at regular intervals and make sure the charging system is functioning properly.

3 Battery - inspection and maintenance

1   The battery used is a maintenance free type.
2   Remove the seat (see Chapter 8). Check around the base inside of the battery for sediment, which is the result of sulfation caused by low electrolyte levels. These deposits will cause internal short circuits, which can quickly discharge the battery. Look for cracks in the case and replace the battery if either of these conditions is found.

 Warning: Always disconnect the negative cable first and reconnect it last to prevent sparks that could cause the battery to explode.

3   Check the battery terminals and cable ends for tightness and corrosion. If corrosion is evident, remove the cables from the battery and clean the terminals and cable ends with a wire brush or knife and emery paper. If you need to remove the battery, remove the retainer and lift it out of the carrier **(see illustration)**. Reconnect the cables and apply a thin coat of petroleum jelly to the connections to slow further corrosion.
4   The battery case should be kept clean to prevent current leakage, which can discharge the battery over a period of time (especially when it sits unused). Wash the outside of the case with a solution of baking soda and water. Do not get any baking soda solution in the battery cells. Rinse the battery thoroughly, then dry it.
5   If acid has been spilled on the frame

3.3 Disconnect the cables from the terminals, negative first (upper arrow). Remove the retainer bolt (lower arrow), swing it out and lift the battery out

or battery box, neutralize it with the baking soda and water solution, dry it thoroughly, then touch up any damaged paint.
6   If the motorcycle sits unused for long periods of time, disconnect the cables from the battery terminals. Charge the battery approximately once every month (see Section 4).

4 Battery - charging

1   If the machine sits idle for extended periods or if the charging system malfunctions, the battery can be charged from an external source.
2   Be sure the battery charger you use is designed for maintenance-free batteries.
3   When charging the battery, always remove it from the machine. If the battery case is translucent, check the electrolyte level by looking through the case before hooking up the charger. If the electrolyte level is low, the battery must be discarded; never remove the sealing plug to add water.
4   Disconnect the battery cables (negative cable first), then connect a digital voltmeter between the battery terminals and measure the voltage (open circuit voltage).
5   If open circuit voltage is 12.8 volts or higher, the battery is fully charged. If it's lower, recharge the battery. Charge at 0.65 amps for 5 to 10 hours.
6   A quick charge can be used in an emergency, provided the maximum charge rates and times are not exceeded (exceeding the maximum rate or time may ruin the battery). A quick charge should always be followed as soon as possible by a charge at the standard rate and time.
7   Hook up the battery charger leads (positive lead to battery positive terminal and negative lead to battery negative terminal), then, and only then, plug in the battery charger.

5.1a The fuse holder is located above the battery . . .

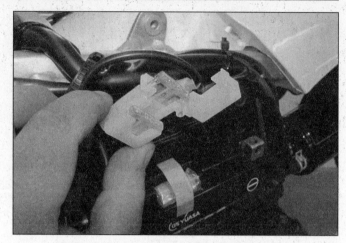

5.1b . . . it contains a main fuse and spare fuse

Warning: The gas escaping from a charging battery is explosive, so keep open flames and sparks well away from the area. Also, the electrolyte is extremely corrosive and will damage anything it comes in contact with.

8   Allow the battery to charge for the specified time listed in Step 5. If the battery overheats or gases excessively, the charging rate is too high. Either disconnect the charger or lower the charging rate to prevent damage to the battery.
9   After the specified time, unplug the charger first, then disconnect the leads from the battery.
10   Wait 30 minutes, then measure voltage between the battery terminals. If it's 12.8 volts or higher, the battery is fully charged. If it's between 12.0 and 12.7 volts, charge the battery again (refer to Step 5 for charge rate and time).

5   Fuses - check and replacement
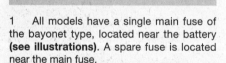

1   All models have a single main fuse of the bayonet type, located near the battery **(see illustrations)**. A spare fuse is located near the main fuse.
2   The fuse can be checked visually without removing it from its holder; just look through the plastic to see if the metal element inside is broken. If so, pull the fuse out and push a new one in.
3   If the fuse blows, be sure to check the wiring harnesses very carefully for evidence of a short circuit. Look for bare wires and chafed, melted or burned insulation. If a fuse is replaced before the cause is located, the new fuse will blow immediately.
4   Never, under any circumstances, use a higher rated fuse or bridge the fuse terminals, as damage to the electrical system - or even a fire - could result.
5   Occasionally a fuse will blow or cause

an open circuit for no obvious reason. Corrosion of the fuse ends and fuse holder terminals may occur and cause poor fuse contact. If this happens, remove the corrosion with a wire brush or emery paper, then spray the fuse end and terminals with electrical contact cleaner.

6   Ignition system - check

Warning: Because of the very high voltage generated by the ignition system, extreme care should be taken when these checks are performed.

1   If the ignition system is the suspected cause of poor engine performance or failure to start, a number of checks can be made to isolate the problem.

Engine will not start
2   Disconnect the spark plug wire (see Chapter 1). Connect the wire to a spare spark plug and lay the plug on the engine with the threads contacting the engine. If necessary, hold the spark plug with an insulated tool. Crank the engine over and make sure a

well-defined, blue spark occurs between the spark plug electrodes.

Warning: Don't remove the spark plug from the engine to perform this check - atomized fuel being pumped out of the open spark plug hole could ignite, causing severe injury!

3   If no spark occurs, the following checks should be made:
4   Check the ignition coil primary resistance, secondary resistance and peak voltage (see Section 7).
5   Check the ignition pickup coil and signal coil (see Section 9).
6   Make sure all electrical connectors are clean and tight. Check all wires for shorts, opens and correct installation.
7   If the preceding checks produce positive results but there is still no spark at the plug, check the CDI unit (see Section 8).

Engine starts but misfires
8   If the engine starts but misfires, make the following checks before deciding that the ignition system is at fault.
9   The ignition system must be able to produce a spark across an eight-millimeter (5/16-inch) gap (minimum). A simple test fixture **(see illustration)** can be constructed to make sure the minimum spark gap can be

6.9 A simple spark gap testing fixture can be made from a block of wood, two nails, a large alligator clip, a screw and a piece of wire

7.3 The ignition coil is mounted on the frame above the engine

jumped. Make sure the fixture electrodes are positioned eight millimeters apart.

10   Connect the spark plug wire to the protruding test fixture electrode, then attach the fixture's alligator clip to a good engine ground.

11   Crank the engine over with the starter and see if well-defined, blue sparks occur between the test fixture electrodes. If the minimum spark gap test is positive, the ignition coil is functioning properly. If the spark will not jump the gap, or if it is weak (orange colored), refer to Steps 4 through 10 and perform the component checks described.

7   Ignition coil - check, removal and installation

1   The primary and secondary coil resistances can be measured with an ohmmeter. If the coil is undamaged, and if the resistances are as specified, it is probably capable of proper operation. If you have a voltmeter that can measure peak voltage, you can make this additional test to confirm coil operation.

2   To inspect or remove the coil, remove the seal and fuel tank (see Chapters 8 and 4).

3   Check the coil visually for cracks and other damage **(see illustration)**.

Peak voltage check

4   Disconnect the spark plug wire from the plug (see Chapter 1 if necessary). Connect a new spark plug into the wire, then lay it on the engine so its electrode touches one of the small head bolts.

5   Connect the voltmeter to the coil primary wires (positive probe to black/white wire's terminal; negative probe to white/black wire's terminal).

6   Turn the ignition switch to the On position. Place the transmission in neutral, pull in the clutch lever and crank the engine with the starter for a few seconds. Check the peak voltage indicated by the voltmeter and compare it to the value listed in this Chapter's Specifications. If it's OK, perform the resistance checks in Steps 7 and 8. If peak voltage isn't as specified, replace the coil with a new one.

Resistance check

7   Connect an ohmmeter between the primary (small) terminals **(see illustration)**. Set the ohmmeter selector switch in the Rx1 position and compare the measured resistance to the primary resistance values listed in this Chapter's Specifications. If the resistance is

not as specified, the coil is probably defective and should be replaced with a new one.

8   Connect the ohmmeter between the coil primary positive terminal and the spark plug cap **(see illustration 7.7)**. Place the ohmmeter selector switch in the Rx100 position and compare the measured resistance to the secondary resistance values listed in this Chapter's Specifications. If the resistance is not as specified, the coil is probably defective and should be replaced with a new one.

Removal and installation

9   If you haven't already done so, perform Step 2 for access to the coil.

10   Disconnect the spark plug wire, remove the coil mounting bolts and take it out of the vehicle.

11   Installation is the reverse of removal.

8   CDI unit - check, removal and installation

Check

1   The CDI unit is tested by process of elimination (when all other possible causes of ignition problems have been checked and eliminated, the CDI unit is at fault).

2   Check the ignition coil, pulse generator, signal coil and kill switch as described elsewhere in this Chapter.

3   Carefully check the wiring harnesses for breaks or bad connections.

4   If the harness and all other system components tested good, the CDI unit may be defective. Before buying a new one, it's a good idea to substitute a known good CDI unit.

Removal and installation

5   Locate the CDI unit under the seat (it can be identified by its wire colors) **(see illustration)**. Unplug its connector and remove the mounting screws.

6   Installation is the reverse of removal.

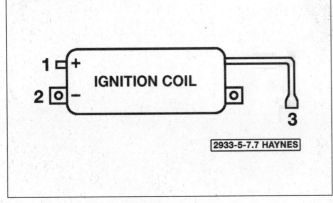

7.7 Ignition coil test

1   Measure primary winding resistance
2   Measure secondary winding resistance

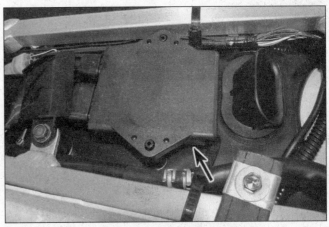

8.5 The CDI unit is located under the seat

9.1 Follow the alternator wiring harness to its connector and unplug it

9.7 Unscrew the rotor nut and remove the washer - you may need to pry it out

9 Alternator and regulator/rectifier - check and replacement

Alternator check

1   Locate the alternator wiring harnesses on the left side of the engine and follow them to their connectors **(see illustration)**.
2   To check the ignition system pickup coil, disconnect the connector for the blue and green wires. Connect an ohmmeter to the wires in the alternator side of the connector (not the wiring harness side). If the readings are much outside the value listed in this Chapter's Specifications, replace the pickup coil (see Steps 16 through 19).
3   To check the signal coil, disconnect the connector for the black and white wires. Connect an ohmmeter to the wires in the alternator side of the connector (not the wiring harness side). If the readings are much outside the value listed in this Chapter's Specifications, replace the pickup (see Steps 16 through 19).
4   To check charging coil resistance, disconnect the connector for the three brown wires. Connect an ohmmeter between two wires at a time and measure the resistance between each pair. Compare the reading to the value listed in this Chapter's Specifications. If it's not within the specified range, replace the stator coil (see Steps 16 through 19).
5   To check for a shorted charging coil, connect the ohmmeter between each brown wire, one wire at a time, and ground. The ohmmeter should indicate no continuity (infinite resistance). If it doesn't, replace the stator coil (see Steps 16 through 19).

Rotor replacement

Removal

Note: *To remove the alternator rotor, the special Suzuki puller or an aftermarket equivalent*

will be required. Don't try to remove the rotor without the proper puller, as it's almost sure to be damaged. Pullers are readily available from dealers and aftermarket tool suppliers.
6   Remove the left crankcase cover (see Chapter 2).
7   Hold the alternator rotor with a universal holder. You can also use a strap wrench. If you don't have one of these tools and the engine is in the frame, the rotor can be locked by placing the transmission in gear and holding the rear brake on. Unscrew the rotor nut and remove the washer **(see illustration)**.
8   Thread an alternator puller into the center of the rotor and use it to remove the rotor **(see illustrations)**. If the rotor doesn't come off easily, tap sharply on the end of the puller to release the rotor's grip on the tapered crankshaft end.
9   Once you've pulled the rotor off, check the Woodruff key **(see illustration 9.8c)**; if it's not secure in its slot, pull it out and set it aside for safekeeping. A convenient method

9.8a Thread the puller onto these threads on the rotor

9.8b Tighten the puller screw against the crankshaft, then hold the puller body with a wrench on the flats and tighten the puller screw to push the rotor loose

9.8c Pull off the rotor, together with the starter clutch (lower arrow) and locate the Woodruff key (upper arrow); be sure it's in its slot on installation

9.9 Be sure there aren't any small metal objects stuck to the rotor magnets; an inconspicuous item like this Woodruff key can ruin the rotor and stator if the engine is run

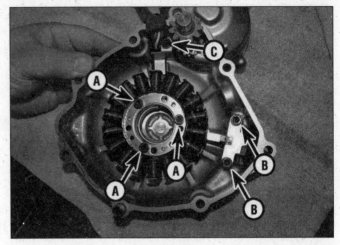

9.18 The stator coils and ignition pulse generator are secured by Allen bolts

A   Stator coil bolts
B   Pulse generator bolts

C   Wiring harness retaining bolts

is to stick the Woodruff key to the magnets inside the rotor **(see illustration)**, but be certain not to forget it's there, as serious damage to the rotor and stator coils will occur if the engine is run with anything stuck to the magnets.

Alternator installation

10   Take a look to make sure there isn't anything stuck to the inside of the rotor **(see illustration 9.9)**.
11   Degrease the center of the rotor and the end of the crankshaft.
12   Make sure the Woodruff key is positioned securely in its slot **(see illustration 9.8c)**.
13   Align the rotor slot with the Woodruff key. Place the rotor on the crankshaft.
14   Install the rotor washer and nut. Hold the rotor from turning with one of the methods described in Step 7 and tighten the nut to the torque listed in this Chapter's Specifications.
15   The remainder of installation is the reverse of removal.

Stator coil and pickup coil replacement

16   The stator coil and the pickup coil are replaced as a unit.
17   Remove the left engine cover and alternator rotor (see Steps 6 through 9).
18   Remove the Allen bolts that secure the stator coils and pickup coil **(see illustration)**. Remove them from the inside of the left crankcase cover.
19   Installation is the reverse of removal. Tighten the Allen bolts to the torque listed in this Chapter's Specifications.

Regulator/rectifier

20   The regulator/rectifier is located on the left side of the bike **(see illustration 9.24)**.

Check

21   Testing of the voltage regulator/rectifier requires a special Suzuki tester. Ordinary ohmmeters will produce a wide variety of readings which may indicate that the regulator/rectifier is defective when it is actually good.
22   Check the charging system running volt-age. To do this, connect a voltmeter between the battery terminals with the engine idling and compare the reading to the output voltage listed in this Chapter's Specifications. If the charging system running voltage is too high, the regulator/rectifier may be defective. It may also be defective if the output was too low and no other cause (alternator or wiring problems) can be found.
23   If you suspect the regulator/rectifier, take it to a dealer service department or other repair shop for further checks, or substitute a known good unit and recheck the charging system output.

Replacement

24   Disconnect the electrical connector from the regulator/rectifier. Remove its mounting bolts and lift it off **(see illustration)**.
25   Installation is the reverse of removal.

10   Handlebar switches - check, removal and installation

1   Handlebar switches include the lighting switch and headlight flasher (2002 and earlier non-US models), headlight high and low beam switch, dimmer switch, turn signal switch (if equipped), kill switch and starter button.

Check

2   Follow the wires from the switch to their connectors and unplug them.
3   Connect an ohmmeter between the wire terminals in the switch side of the connectors (not the side that leads back to the wiring harness). Check switch continuity in all positions, referring to the wiring diagrams at the end of this manual.
4   If continuity isn't as shown in the wiring diagrams, replace the switch (see Steps 5 through 7).

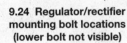

9.24 Regulator/rectifier mounting bolt locations (lower bolt not visible)

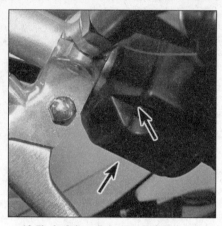

10.5a Right handlebar switch housing mounting screw locations

10.5b Left handlebar switch housing mounting screw locations

Removal and installation

5   To remove the switch housing, remove its mounting screws (see illustrations), separate the front and rear halves and remove it from the handlebar. Remove the wiring harness retainers and unplug the switch electrical connectors.

6   If the switch problem appears to be caused by corrosion, try cleaning the switch contacts. If this doesn't help, the entire switch unit must be replaced. The switches aren't available separately.

7   Installation is the reverse of removal. Be sure the post molded into the switch housing fits into the hole in the top of the handlebar.

11.2 The starter relay is mounted on the right side of the frame

11 Starter circuit - component check and replacement

1   The electric starter circuit used on these models includes a clutch switch that prevents the starter from operating unless the clutch lever is pulled in.

2   Remove the seat (see Chapter 8) and locate the starter relay (see illustration).

3   Disconnect the battery cables from the relay, negative cable first, then disconnect the wiring connector from the starter relay.

4   Connect an ohmmeter between the battery terminals on the relay (see illustration). The ohmmeter should indicate infinite resistance (no continuity).

5   Connect a fully charged battery (the vehicle's battery will work) to the relay terminals, using lengths of wire. The ohmmeter should now indicate continuity (little or no resistance).

6   If the relay doesn't perform as described, remove it from its mount and install a new one.

7   If the relay performs as it should, check the clutch switch (see Section 18).

12 Starter motor - check and replacement

Check

 Warning: This check may cause sparks. Make sure there is no leaking gasoline or anything else flammable in the vicinity.

 Warning: Make sure the transmission is in Neutral, or the vehicle will jump forward during Step 2.

Caution: The jumper cable used for this procedure must be of a gauge at least as heavy as the battery cable or it may melt.

1   Locate the starter motor and disconnect its cable (see illustration).

2   Connect a jumper cable from the battery positive terminal directly to the starter motor terminal. The starter should crank the engine.

3   If the starter doesn't crank at all, replace it. If it turns but doesn't crank the engine, remove and inspect the starter reduction gears and slipper clutch (see Section 13).

Replacement

4   If you haven't already done so, disconnect the starter cable.

5   Remove the starter mounting bolts and lift it out of the engine (see illustration).

6   Installation is the reverse of removal.

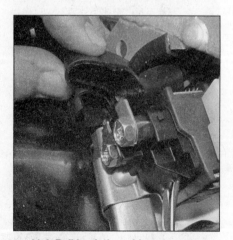

11.4 Pull back the rubber covers to expose the relay's battery terminals

12.1 Locate the starter motor and disconnect its cable

12.5 Remove the starter mounting bolts, noting that one of them secures a ground cable

13.2 Remove the slipper clutch cover bolts and remove the cover

13.3a Note how the slipper clutch fits in the recess . . .

13.3b . . . and pull it out

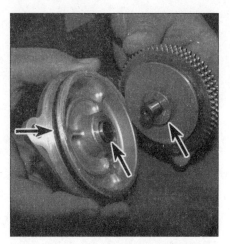

13.4a Remove the cover O-ring (left) and check the cover bushing (center) and washer (right)

13.4b Check the bushing in the crankcase cover (upper arrow) - spin the idler gear (lower arrow) to check the starter clutch

Use a new O-ring and tighten the bolts to the torque listed in this Chapter's Specifications.

13 Starter slipper clutch and reduction gears - removal and installation

1   These vehicles use two reduction gears, an idler gear and a starter clutch drive gear. The starter motor turns a slipper clutch (torque limiter). The slipper clutch turns the idler gear. The idler gear turns the starter clutch drive gear (large gear), which is mounted on the crankshaft behind the alternator rotor. The starter clutch turns the crankshaft.

Slipper clutch removal

2   Remove the slipper clutch cover from the left side of the crankcase (see illustration).

3   Pull the slipper clutch out of the engine (see illustrations).
4   If worn, remove the slipper clutch bushings from the cover and crankcase (see illustrations).

Idler gear removal

5   Remove the left crankcase cover (see Chapter 2).
6   The idler gear may come out with the cover or stay in the crankcase. Pull the shaft out of the cover or crankcase, remove the snap-ring and slip the idler gear off its shaft (see illustration). Remove the washers from the gear shaft.

Starter driven gear removal

7   Remove the left crankcase cover and alternator rotor (see Chapter 2 and Section 9). Remove the thrust washer behind the rotor.

13.6 The idler gear may come off with the crankcase cover or remain in the engine - remove its snap-ring to separate the idler gear from the shaft

13.8 Note which direction the starter clutch driven gear faces, then slip it off the crankshaft

13.11 Do not remove this snap-ring - it's not available separately, and the slipper clutch must be replaced as a unit

8   Slip the starter clutch driven gear off the crankshaft, noting which direction it faces **(see illustration)**.

Inspection

9   Check the idler and driven gears for wear or damage such as chipped teeth. Check the shaft for scoring or heat damage that might indicate lack of lubrication. Replace the gears if problems are found. The idler gear can be disassembled by removing its snap-ring **(see illustration 13.6)**.

10   Check the slipper clutch bushings for wear or damage and replace them if problems are found.

11   Check the slipper clutch for visible damage, such as broken gear teeth. Replace it as a unit if problems are found. **Note:** *Do not remove the slipper clutch snap-ring* **(see illustration)**. The slipper clutch can't be disassembled. Place the slipper clutch in a vise, with the jaws padded with wood blocks, so the triple gears are gripped by the vise jaws and the single gear is upward. Rotate the single gear with a torque wrench. Attaching the torque wrench to the single gear requires a special adapter.

12   Check the needle roller bearing on the inside of the driven gear. Since needle roller bearing wear is difficult to see, the driven gear bearing should be replaced if its condition is in doubt.

Installation

13   Installation is the reverse of removal.

14 Starter clutch - removal and installation

1   If the starter motor spins but doesn't crank the engine, you can perform a quick check to see if the starter clutch could be causing the problem.

2   Remove the slipper clutch (see Sec-

tion 13). Reach into the slipper clutch recess and spin the starter idler gear with a finger **(see illustration 13.4b)**. It should spin freely and smoothly in one direction and not at all in the other direction. If it spins both ways, the starter clutch is probably damaged. If the movement of the gear is rough or uneven, the starter clutch or one of the reduction gears may be damaged. Remove the starter clutch for further inspection.

Removal

3   Remove the alternator rotor (see Section 9). The starter clutch is mounted in the back of the rotor **(see illustration 9.8c)**.

4   Mark the starter clutch so you can reinstall it facing the correct direction. Remove the six Torx bolts that secure the starter clutch to the alternator rotor and remove the starter clutch.

Inspection

5   Check all parts for visible wear and damage and replace any parts that show problems.

6   Test the starter clutch. Place it in position on the back of the alternator rotor. Place the starter reduction gear in the starter clutch. Hold the rotor steady, with the reduction gear toward you, and try to twist the clutch. It should twist freely in a counterclockwise direction, but not at all in the clockwise direction.

7   If the gear will turn both ways or neither way, the starter clutch is bad. If the gear will turn freely clockwise, but not at all counterclockwise, the starter clutch rollers are installed upside down.

Installation

8   Installation is the reverse of removal. Tighten the starter clutch bolts to the torque listed in this Chapter's Specifications and use non-hardening Loctite on the bolt threads. Be sure to check the starter clutch function (see Step 6) before completing final installation.

15 Lighting circuit - check

1   If the headlight or taillight doesn't work, check the bulb. If it's good, check the socket for corrosion and the wiring for breaks or bad connections.

2   If neither light works, check the switch. Disconnect its wiring connector and connect an ohmmeter to the switch terminals. The ohmmeter should show little or no resistance when the switch is On, and infinite resistance when it's Off. If not, replace it.

3   If a brake light doesn't work, check it in the same manner as the headlight and taillight (see Steps 1 and 2). If none of the lights work and the switch is good, check the red wire between the starter relay and the ignition switch for breaks or bad connections.

16 Bulb replacement

⚠ Warning: If the bulb has just burned out, it will be hot enough to burn you. Allow it to cool before touching it.

Caution: Don't touch the bulb glass with your fingers or it will burn out prematurely. If you do touch it, clean the glass with rubbing alcohol or soap and water.

Headlights

1   Remove the headlight cover (see Chapter 8).

2   Remove the headlight assembly mounting bolts and pull the assembly forward for

16.2 Remove the mounting bolts from each side (right-side bolts shown) and pull the headlight assembly forward

16.3 Pull the cover off of the bulb

access to the bulb **(see illustration)**.
3   Disconnect the headlight wiring connector from the rear of the headlight. If you're working on a UK or European model, disconnect the electrical connector for the position light as well. Pull the rubber cap off the headlight assembly **(see illustration)**.
4   If the bulb is secured by a wire retaining clip, release the clip, swing it out of the way and pull the bulb out of the socket. If the bulb doesn't have a wire retaining clip, twist it to align its tabs with the notches in the socket and pull it out.
5   Installation is the reverse of removal.

Tail/brake light
6   If you're working on a DR-Z400S or SM model, remove the lens securing screws and remove the lens **(see illustration)**. Press the bulb into its socket and turn it counterclockwise to remove. Install in the reverse order. Don't over-tighten the screws or the lens may crack.
7   The taillight on DR-Z400 and DR-Z400E models is a light emitting diode (LED) type.

If it fails, the entire unit must be replaced. Remove the mounting nut(s) from inside the fender, disconnect the wiring harness and take the light off the fender. Installation is the reverse of removal.

Turn signals
8   Remove the lens securing screw and remove the lens **(see illustration)**.
9   Press the bulb into its socket and turn it counterclockwise to remove. Install in the reverse order. Don't over-tighten the screws or the lens may crack.

Warning lights
10   The warning lights are light emitting diodes (LEDs), contained in a single unit. Individual lights can't be replaced separately from the warning light unit. If a warning light fails to work, the warning light unit must be replaced as an assembly.
11   Remove the headlight cover (see Chapter 8).
12   Follow the wiring harness from the

16.6 Remove the lens securing screws and remove the lens

warning light unit to the connector and disconnect it.
13   Remove the mounting screw from the underside of the unit **(see illustration)**. Pull it up and out of the speedometer.
14   Installation is the reverse of removal.

16.8 The turn signal lenses are each secured by a single screw (right front shown; others similar)

16.13 The warning light unit is secured by a screw (right arrow) - the speedometer is secured to the bracket by three nuts (left arrows)

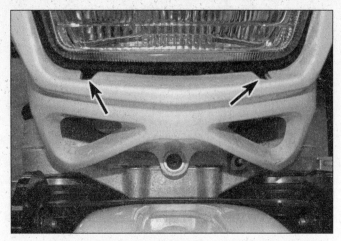

17.2a The adjusting screws are accessible through these notches

17.2b Headlight vertical (A) and horizontal (B) adjustment screw locations (headlight cover removed for clarity)

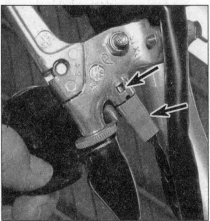

18.1 The clutch switch (lower arrow) is located in the lever bracket - compress the prong (upper arrow) and pull on the switch to remove it

19.5 Remove the mounting screws (lower arrow) and free the wiring harness from its retainers (upper arrows) to remove the gear position switch

(the switch side, not the wiring harness side). Connect the other lead to the blue wire's terminal. There should be no resistance between the switch and ground when the transmission is in Neutral. In any other gear, there should be infinite resistance.

3   Connect one lead of an ohmmeter to the black/white wire's terminal in the switch connector (the switch side, not the wiring harness side). Connect the other lead to the blue wire's terminal.

4   With the transmission in neutral, the ohmmeter should indicate continuity (little or no resistance). With the transmission in any of the gears, the switch should indicate no continuity (infinite resistance).

5   If the switch doesn't perform as described, remove its mounting screws and free the wiring harness from the retainers (see illustration). Pull the switch out of the engine and install a new one, using a new O-ring.

20 Brake light switches - check and replacement

Check

1   Locate the switch (see illustration 20.3 or 20.5). Follow the wiring harness from the switch to its connector and disconnect it.

2   Connect an ohmmeter between the terminals in the switch side of the connector. Operate the brake lever or pedal. With the lever pulled in or the pedal pressed, there should be no resistance (zero ohms). With the lever or pedal released, there should be infinite resistance.

Replacement

3   If the front brake light switch doesn't perform as described, replace it. The switch is not adjustable. To replace it, follow the wiring harness to the connector and disconnect it. Remove the switch mounting screw (see illustration), free the wiring harness from its

17 Headlight adjustment

1   The headlight can be adjusted vertically and horizontally.

2   The adjuster screws can be reached through the access holes under the headlight (see illustrations). Turn the screw on the left-hand side of the bike to make horizontal adjustments. Turn the screw on the right side of the bike to make vertical adjustments.

18 Clutch switch - check and replacement

1   The clutch switch is mounted in the clutch lever pivot (see illustration).

2   Follow the wiring harness from the switch to its connector and disconnect it.

3   Connect an ohmmeter between the terminals in the switch side of the connector. With the clutch lever pulled in, there should be no resistance (zero ohms). With the lever released, there should be infinite resistance.

4   If the switch doesn't perform as described, slide back the lever pivot cover, press the switch retainer prong and pull the switch out of the clutch lever pivot (see illustration 18.1). Push a new switch in until the retainer prong engages, then connect the wiring harness and reposition the cover.

19 Neutral switch - check and replacement

1   Remove the seat for access to the switch connector (see Chapter 8). Disconnect the electrical connector from the switch (it's located just behind the fuel tank).

2   Connect one lead of an ohmmeter to the black wire's terminal in the switch connector

20.3 Remove the screw to detach the front brake light switch from the lever pivot

20.5 The rear brake light switch is secured by a screw

retainers and remove the switch. Installation is the reverse of removal.

4   The rear brake light switch can be adjusted (see Chapter 1).

5   If adjustment of the rear brake light switch doesn't help, replace the switch with a new one. Disconnect the wiring connector and free the harness from its retainers. Remove the switch mounting screw **(see illustration)** and take it off the pedal bracket. Reverse the removal procedure to install the new switch, then adjust it (see Chapter 1).

21 Ignition switch - check and replacement

1   The ignition switch (main key switch) is located above the handlebar **(see illustration)**.

Check

2   To check the switch, follow its wiring harness to the connector and disconnect it. The following tests will be made with an

ohmmeter connected to the switch side of the connector (not the wiring harness side).

3   Place the switch in the Off position. Connect an ohmmeter between all four wires (red, orange, green and brown), two wires at a time. The ohmmeter should indicate no continuity (infinite resistance) in all cases. If it doesn't, replace the switch.

4   Place the switch in the On position. Connect an ohmmeter to the orange and red wires. The ohmmeter should indicate continuity (zero ohms). If it doesn't, replace the switch.

5   With the switch still in the On position, move the ohmmeter to the green and brown wires. The ohmmeter should again indicate continuity (zero ohms). If it doesn't, replace the switch.

6   Place the switch in the Park position. Connect an ohmmeter between red and brown wires. The ohmmeter should indicate continuity (zero ohms). If it doesn't, replace the switch.

Replacement

7   Locate and disconnect the switch wiring connector (see Step 2).

8   Remove the switch mounting bolts and lift the switch off of the handlebar bracket.

9   Installation is the reverse of removal.

22 Speedometer and drive unit - removal and installation

Note: *DR-Z400S and SM models are equipped with a cable-driven speedometer that includes an odometer and a trip meter.*

Speedometer

1   Remove the headlight cover (see Chapter 8).

2   Follow the wiring harnesses from the speedometer to their connectors and disconnect them.

3   Unscrew the cable from the speedometer **(see illustration)**.

4   Remove the speedometer mounting nuts **(see illustration 16.13 and the accompanying illustration)**. Lift the speedometer out of the bracket.

5   If necessary, remove the bolts that

21.1 The ignition switch is secured by two of the handlebar bracket bolts

22.3 Unscrew the speedometer cable nut

22.4 On installation, make sure the mounting grommets are positioned as shown

22.7 Remove the screw and pull the cable out of the drive unit

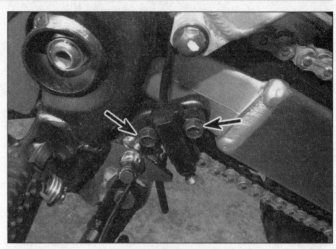

23.5 Remove the mounting bolts to remove the sidestand switch from the bracket

secure the speedometer bracket to the upper triple clamp. You may need to unbolt the headlight assembly for access to the bolts.
6 Installation is the reverse of removal **(see illustration 22.4)**.

Cable

7 Disconnect the cable from the speedometer **(see illustration 22.3)**. At the bottom of the cable, remove the screw that secures it to the drive unit **(see illustration)**.
8 Free the cable from its retainers, pull it out of the drive unit and take it off the motorcycle.
9 Installation is the reverse of removal.

Drive unit

10 Remove the screw that secures the speedometer cable to the drive unit and pull it out **(see illustration 22.7)**.
11 Remove the front wheel (see Chapter 7). Pull the drive unit off the wheel.
12 Installation is the reverse of removal. Lubricate the drive unit with Suzuki Supergrease A or equivalent and align the drive unit's two grooves with the tabs on the wheel hub.

23 Sidestand switch - check and replacement

1 The sidestand switch, used on DR-Z400S and SM models, is part of a system that prevents the starter from cranking when the transmission is in gear unless the sidestand is up and clutch is disengaged. With the transmission in neutral, the engine will crank with the sidestand down, as long as the clutch is disengaged.
2 Follow the wiring harness from the switch to its connector and disconnect it **(see illustration 23.5)**.
3 Connect an ohmmeter between the switch terminals in the connector (the switch side of the connector, not the wiring harness

side). Connect the ohmmeter positive lead to the green wire and the ohmmeter negative lead to the black/white wire.
4 With the switch plunger extended (sidestand down), the ohmmeter should indicate no current flow (infinite resistance). With the switch plunger pressed (sidestand up), the ohmmeter should indicate little or no resistance.
5 If the switch doesn't perform as described, unbolt it from the bracket and install a new one **(see illustration)**.

24 Turn signal-sidestand relay - check and replacement

1 The relay handles two systems, then turn indicators and the sidestand/clutch switch interlock. It is tested by process of elimination - when all other components in the system have been checked, and the wiring has been checked for breaks or bad connections, then the relay is replaced.
2 The relay is mounted behind the left side of the headlight cover **(see illustration)**. To replace it, remove the headlight cover (see Chapter 8), pull the relay out of the connector and install a new one. Reinstall the headlight cover.

25 Coolant temperature warning light switch - check and replacement

1 If the coolant temperature warning light comes on when the engine is not overheating, the light may be shorted to ground, either through a defective switch that stays on all the time, through worn insulation on the wire from the lamp to the switch, or through a wire that has come loose and is making contact with the bike. Check the wiring for breaks or loose connections, referring to the

wiring diagrams in Chapter 9. If the wiring is good, the switch may be defective. Test it as described in Step 3.
2 If the warning light does not come on at all, check the wiring to the light, referring to the wiring diagrams in Chapter 9. If the wiring is good, test the switch as described in Chapter 3.

⚠️ *Warning: The engine must be cool during the following procedure to prevent burns from hot coolant.*

3 Unscrew the switch from the rear side of the tank at the top of the right-hand radiator. Test the switch in the same manner as the cooling fan switch, described in Chapter 3. The switch should go from On to Off at approximately 117-degrees C (243-degrees F), and from Off to On at approximately 100-degrees C (212-degrees F).
4 If you removed the switch for testing, reinstall it, using a new O-ring lubricated with multipurpose grease. Tighten the switch to the torque listed in this Chapter's Specifications.

24.2 The turn signal/sidestand relay is mounted inside the headlight cover

Chapter 6
Steering, suspension and final drive

Contents

Degrees of difficulty

Easy, suitable for novice with little experience	**Fairly easy,** suitable for beginner with some experience	**Fairly difficult,** suitable for competent DIY mechanic	**Difficult,** suitable for experienced DIY mechanic	**Very difficult,** suitable for expert DIY or professional

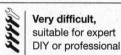

Specifications

Front suspension
Fork oil type (all models).. Suzuki fork oil SS-05 or equivalent

DR-Z400, DR-Z400E
Fork oil capacity (per fork leg) .... 720 cc (24.3 US fl oz, 25.4 Imp fl oz)
Fork oil level (fully compressed, spring removed) .... 122 mm (4.8 inches) from top
Fork spring length
    Standard .... 510.6 mm (20.1 inches)
    Limit .... 500 mm (19.7 inches)
Suspension settings (standard)
    Rebound damping .... 15 clicks out from fully in
    Compression damping.. 12 clicks out from fully in
Fork installed position .... Fork tube groove even with top of upper triple clamp

2001 and earlier DR-Z400S

Fork oil capacity (per fork leg)	709 cc (24.0 US fl oz, 25.0 Imp fl oz)
Fork oil level (fully compressed, spring removed)	165 mm (6.5 inches) from top
Fork spring length	
Standard	573.2 mm (22.57 inches)
Limit	561 mm (22.1 inches)
Suspension settings (standard)	
Spring preload	Third groove from top
Compression damping	7 clicks out from fully in
Fork installed position	5 mm (0.2 inch) above top of upper triple clamp

2002 and later DR-Z400S

Fork oil capacity (per fork leg)	710 cc (24.0 US fl oz, 25.0 Imp fl oz)
Fork oil level (fully compressed, spring removed)	129 mm (5.07 inches) from top
Fork spring length	
Standard	573.2 mm (22.57 inches)
Limit	561 mm (22.1 inches)
Suspension settings (standard)	
Rebound damping	16 clicks out from fully in
Compression damping	13 clicks out from fully in
Fork installed position	Fork tube groove even with top of upper triple clamp

DR-Z400SM

Fork oil capacity (per fork leg)	
Outer	350 cc (11.83 US fl oz, 12.32 Imp fl oz)
Inner	182 cc (6.15 US fl oz, 6.4 Imp fl oz)
Fork oil level	Not applicable
Fork spring length	
Standard	450.0 mm (17.7 inches)
Limit	441 mm (17.3 inches)
Suspension settings (standard)	
Rebound damping	17 clicks out from fully in
Compression damping	13 clicks out from fully in
Fork installed position	Fork tube groove even with top of upper triple clamp

Rear suspension and final drive

DR-Z400, DR-Z400E

Shock absorber spring length	
Standard (all models)	258.0 mm (10.2 inches)
Minimum (2002 and later)	247.5 mm (9.74 inches)
Maximum (2002 and later)	259.5 mm (10.22 inches)
Shock absorber settings	
2001 and earlier	
Rebound damping	13 clicks out from fully in
Compression damping	12 clicks out from fully in
2002	
Rebound damping	13 clicks out from fully in
High speed compression damping	1-1/4 turns out
Low speed compression damping	12 clicks out from fully in
2003 and later	
Rebound damping	13 clicks out from fully in
High speed compression damping	1-1/4 turns out
Low speed compression damping	10 clicks out from fully in
Drive chain	
Type	RK520KZO
Number of links	112
20-link length limit	319.4 mm (12.6 inches)

2001 and earlier DR-Z400S

Shock absorber spring length	258.0 mm (10.2 inches)
Shock absorber compression damping	11 clicks out from fully in
Drive chain	
Type	RK520KZO
Number of links	112
20-link length limit	319.4 mm (12.6 inches)

2002 and later DR-Z400S

Shock absorber spring length	258.0 mm (10.2 inches)
Shock absorber settings	
Rebound damping	13 clicks out from fully in
Compression damping	
High speed	1-1/4 turns out
Low speed	10 clicks out from fully in
Drive chain	
Type	RK520KZO
Number of links	112
20-link length limit	319.4 mm (12.6 inches)

DR-Z400SM

Shock absorber spring length	254.0 mm (10.0 inches)
Shock absorber settings	
Rebound damping	14 clicks out from fully in
Compression damping	
High speed	1-1/8 turns out
Low speed	10 clicks out from fully in
Drive chain	
Type	RK520KZO
Number of links	110
20-link length limit	319.4 mm (12.6 inches)

Torque specifications

DR-Z400, DR-Z400E

Handlebar clamp bolts	23 Nm (16.5 ft-lbs)
Upper triple clamp bolts	30 Nm (21.5 ft-lbs)
Lower triple clamp bolts	32 Nm (23 ft-lbs)
Fork cap bolts	23 Nm (16.5 ft-lbs)
Fork base bolts	80 Nm (58 ft-lbs)
Damper rod locknut (2002 and later)	22 Nm (16 ft-lbs)
Steering stem nut to upper triple clamp	90 Nm (65 ft-lbs)
Steering stem adjusting nut	
Initial torque	45 Nm (32.5 ft-lbs)
Final torque	Loosen 1/4 to 1/2 turn
Rear shock absorber spring adjuster locknut	90 Nm (65 ft-lbs)
Rear shock absorber mounting bolt nuts	55 Nm (40 ft-lbs)
Rear suspension linkage pivot bolt nuts	100 Nm (72.5 ft-lbs)
Swingarm pivot bolt nut	77 Nm (55.5 ft-lbs)

DR-Z400S

Handlebar clamp bolts	23 Nm (16.5 ft-lbs)
Upper triple clamp bolts	30 Nm (21.5 ft-lbs)
Lower triple clamp bolts	32 Nm (23 ft-lbs)
Fork cap bolts	23 Nm (16.5 ft-lbs)
Fork base bolts	80 Nm (58 ft-lbs)
Damper rod locknut (2002 and later)	22 Nm (16 ft-lbs)
Steering stem nut to upper triple clamp	90 Nm (65 ft-lbs)

Torque specifications (continued)

DR-Z400S (continued)

Steering stem adjusting nut	
Initial torque	45 Nm (32.5 ft-lbs)
Final torque	Loosen 1/4 to 1/2 turn
Rear shock absorber spring adjuster locknut	90 Nm (65 ft-lbs)
Rear shock absorber mounting bolt nuts	55 Nm (40 ft-lbs)
Rear suspension linkage pivot bolt nuts	100 Nm (72.5 ft-lbs)
Swingarm pivot bolt nut	77 Nm (55.5 ft-lbs)

DR-Z400SM

Handlebar clamp bolts	23 Nm (16.5 ft-lbs)
Handlebar bracket-to-post bolts and nuts	45 Nm (32.5 ft-lbs)
Triple clamp bolts	23 Nm (16.5 ft-lbs)
Compression damper to top of fork	30 Nm (21.5 ft-lbs)
Fork base bolts	70 Nm (50.5 ft-lbs)
Damper rod locknut	22 Nm (16 ft-lbs)
Fork top to outer fork tube	35 Nm (25.5 ft-lbs)
Steering stem nut to upper triple clamp	90 Nm (65 ft-lbs)
Steering stem adjusting nut	
Initial torque	45 Nm (32.5 ft-lbs)
Final torque	Loosen 1/4 to 1/2 turn
Rear shock absorber spring adjuster locknut	90 Nm (65 ft-lbs)
Rear shock absorber mounting bolt nuts	55 Nm (40 ft-lbs)
Rear suspension linkage pivot bolt nuts	100 Nm (72.5 ft-lbs)
Swingarm pivot bolt nut	77 Nm (55.5 ft-lbs)

2.2 Look for punch marks that indicate handlebar alignment and the front side of the bracket; if they aren't visible, make your own marks

2.3 Handlebar bracket bolt locations

1 General information

The front forks on these models are of the conventional coil spring, hydraulically-damped telescopic type. 2001 and earlier DR-Z400S models have damper rod forks. 2002 and later DR-Z400S models, as well as all DR-Z400 and DR-Z400E models, use cartridge forks. DR-Z400SM models use inverted cartridge forks.

The steering stem is supported by tapered roller bearings.

The rear suspension consists of a single coil spring/shock absorbers with a progressive rising rate linkage and a swingarm.

The final drive is by a chain and sprockets. Rubber dampers are installed between the rear wheel coupling and the wheel on all models.

2 Handlebars - removal and installation

1 These motorcycles use a one-piece handlebar, secured to the upper triple clamp by upper and lower brackets. On all except DR-Z400SM models, the lower brackets are integral with the upper triple clamp. The SM lower brackets are secured to the upper triple clamp by mounting posts, which are threaded on the bottom and secured to the upper triple clamp by nuts.

2 Before removing the handlebars, look for a punch mark indicating the position of the handlebar in the brackets and another one indicating which end of the bracket faces forward (see illustration). Make your own mark if you can't see one.

3 If the handlebars must be removed for access to other components, such as the forks or the steering head, remove the

bracket bolts (see illustration) and lift off the brackets and remove the handlebar. It's not necessary to disconnect the cables, wires or hoses, but it is a good idea to support the assembly with a piece of wire or rope, to avoid unnecessary strain on the cables, wires and (on the right side) the brake hose.

4 Check the handlebar for cracks and distortion and replace it if any undesirable conditions are found.

5 Installation is the reverse of removal, with the following additions:

a) *If you removed the lower brackets from a DR-Z400SM model, tighten the bracket nuts to the torque listed in this Chapter's Specifications.*

b) *Tighten all four bracket bolts evenly to one-half of the torque listed in this Chapter's Specifications. Then tighten the forward bolt on each bracket to the torque listed in this Chapter's Specifications, then tighten the rear bolts to the specified torque. This will leave a gap at the rear of the bracket (see illustration). Don't try to close the gap by tightening the bolts further or the brackets will break.*

2.5 There should be a gap at the rear of each bracket after the bolts are tightened

3 Forks - removal and installation

Removal

1 Support the bike securely upright. Jack up the front of the frame to take the weight off the front wheel.

2 Remove the brake caliper and hang it from the bike with a piece of rope or wire (see Chapter 7). It's not necessary to disconnect the caliper brake hose for fork removal.

3 Remove the wheel (see Chapter 7).

4 Remove the front fender (see Chapter 8).

5 Detach the speedometer cable retainer from the right fork leg and the brake hose retainer from the left fork leg.

⚠ *Warning: Do not remove the fork cap completely in Step 6, or the spring may fly out.*

6 If you plan to disassemble the forks, loosen the cap bolts now (this will be easier while the fork leg is still mounted in the triple clamps) (see illustration). This is a good time

3.6 Loosen the fork cap bolt while the fork is still held in the triple clamps

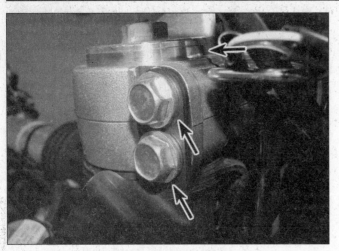

3.7a Loosen the upper triple clamp bolts

3.7b Loosen the lower triple clamp bolts to free the fork leg from the triple clamps

to loosen the damper rod bolt in the bottom end of each fork tube, as the spring pressure should keep the damper rod from spinning inside the fork tube when the bolt is turned **(see illustration 4.7)**. Note: *If the damper rod bolt just spins without loosening, refer to the disassembly procedure to remove it.*

7   Loosen the upper and lower triple clamp bolts **(see illustrations)**. Twist the fork tubes and slide them downward and out of the triple clamps.

Installation

8   Slide each fork leg into the lower triple clamp.
9   Slide the fork legs up, installing the tops of the tubes into the upper triple clamp. Position the tubes so they protrude from the upper triple clamp the amount listed in this Chapter's Specifications.
10   The remainder of installation is the reverse of removal. Tighten the triple clamp bolts to the torque listed in this Chapter's Specifications.

11   Pump the front brake lever several times to bring the pads into contact with the disc.

4   Forks (2001 and earlier DR-Z400S) - disassembly, inspection and reassembly

Disassembly

1   Remove the forks (see Section 3). Work on one fork leg at a time to avoid mixing up the parts.
2   Remove the clamps that secure the rubber boot to the fork tube. **Note:** *Once the lower clamp is removed, it must be replaced with a new one.*

⚠ Warning: Be careful of spring pressure as you remove the cap bolt. The spring is under considerable compression and will come out forcefully.

3   Remove the fork cap bolt **(see illustration)**.

4   Remove the fork spring from the top of the fork.
5   Remove the clamps that secure the boot to the fork and remove the boot.
6   Invert the fork assembly over a container and allow the oil to drain out.
7   Prevent the damper rod from turning using a holding handle (part no. 09950-54821 or equivalent). Unscrew the base bolt at the bottom of the outer tube and retrieve the O-ring **(see illustration)**. **Note:** *If you don't have access to these special tools, you can fabricate your own using a bolt with a head that fits inside the damper rod, two nuts, a socket (to fit on the nuts), a long extension and a ratchet. Thread the two nuts onto the bolt and tighten them against each other. Insert the assembly into the socket and tape it into place. Now, insert the tool into the fork tube and engage the bolt head (or the special Suzuki tool) into the round hole in the damper rod.*
8   Remove the oil lock piece from the damper rod **(see illustration)**.
9   Pull out the damper rod and its spring

4.3 Hold the fork cap with one wrench and loosen the locknut with another

4.7 Loosen the base bolt in the underside of the fork leg

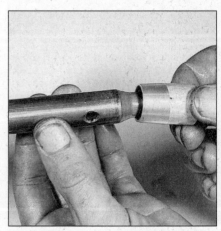

4.8 Remove the oil lock piece from the damper rod

4.9 Pull out the damper rod and remove the spring from the rod

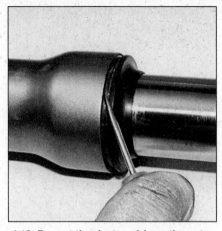

4.10 Pry out the dust seal from the outer fork leg

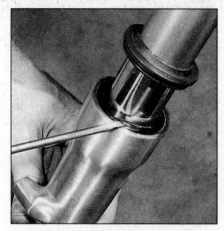

4.11 Pry out the retaining ring

(see illustration). Don't remove the Teflon ring from the damper rod unless you plan to replace it.

10   Pry the dust seal from the outer tube **(see illustration)**.

11   Pry the retaining ring from its groove in the outer tube **(see illustration)**.

12   Hold the outer tube and yank the inner tube upward, repeatedly (like a slide hammer), until the seal, washer and outer tube guide bushing pop loose **(see illustration)**.

13   Slide the seal, washer and outer tube guide bushing from the inner tube **(see illustration 4.12)**.

Inspection

14   Clean all parts in solvent and blow them dry with compressed air, if available. Check the inner and outer fork tubes, the guide bushings and the damper rod for score marks, scratches, flaking of the chrome and excessive or abnormal wear. Look for dents in the tubes and replace them if any are found. Check the fork seal seat for nicks,

gouges and scratches. If damage is evident, leaks will occur around the seal-to-outer tube junction. Replace worn or defective parts with new ones.

15   Have the fork inner tube checked for runout at a dealer service department or other repair shop.

> ⚠ *Warning: If it is bent, it should not be straightened; replace it with a new one.*

16   Measure the overall length of the spring and check it for cracks and other damage. Compare the length to the minimum length listed in this Chapter's Specifications. If it's defective or sagged, replace both fork springs with new ones. Never replace only one spring.

17   If it's necessary to replace the inner guide bushing (the one that won't come off that's on the bottom of the inner tube), pry it apart at the slit and slide it off **(see illustration)**. Make sure the new one seats properly **(see illustration)**.

18   Check the friction ring on the damper rod and replace it if it's worn.

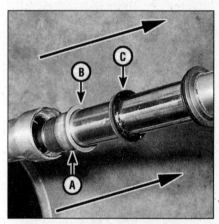

4.12 Pull the slider and fork tube in opposite directions with a few sharp jerks (like a slide hammer); the outer tube bushing (A), back-up ring (B) and oil seal (C) will pop out of the outer tube

4.17a If you need to remove the outer tube's bushing from the inner tube, spread it carefully and slip it off the end

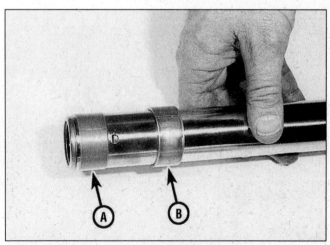

4.17b Place the outer tube bushing (A) in the groove on the inner tube and slip the inner tube bushing (B) over the inner tube

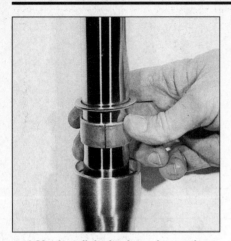

4.22a Install the back-up ring on the inner tube

4.22b Using a split-type seal driver (this is a Kent-Moore, but any suitable equivalent will work) . . .

4.22c . . . tap down gently and repeatedly to seat the bushing; make sure the bushing is fully seated against the shoulder inside the fork tube

Reassembly

19   Place the rebound spring over the damper rod and slide the rod assembly into

4.22d If you don't have a bushing driver, you can use a section of pipe instead; tape the ends of the pipe so it doesn't scratch the fork tube

the inner fork tube until it protrudes from the lower end of the tube.

20   If you haven't already done so, install the oil lock piece onto the end of the damper rod. The flange end (wide end) of the oil lock piece faces downward when the fork is installed on the bike.

21   Insert the inner tube/damper rod assembly into the outer tube until the base bolt (with a new O-ring) can be threaded into the damper rod from the lower end of the outer tube. **Note:** *Keep the two tubes fairly horizontal so the damper rod base doesn't fall off. Using the tool described in Step 7, hold the damper rod and tighten the base bolt to the torque listed in this Chapter's Specifications.*

22   Lubricate the bushings with the fork oil listed in this Chapter's Specifications. Slide the outer guide bushing down the inner tube (see illustration 4.17b and the accompanying illustration). Using a special bushing driver or equivalent and a used guide bushing placed on top of the guide bushing being installed, drive the bushing into place until it is fully seated (see illustrations). If you don't

have access to one of these tools, it is highly recommended that you take the assembly to a Suzuki dealer service department or other motorcycle repair shop to have this done. It is possible, however, to drive the bushing into place using a section of tubing and an old guide bushing (see illustration). Wrap tape around the ends of the tubing to prevent it from scratching the fork tube.

23   Slide the washer down the inner tube, into position over the guide bushing (see illustration 4.22a).

24   Lubricate the lips of the fork seal with the recommended fork oil (see illustration) and slide it down the inner tube, with the lips facing down (see illustration). Drive the seal into place with a special seal driver (Suzuki part no. 09940-52861) (see illustration) or a home-made substitute (see illustration). If you don't have access to one of these, it is recommended that you take the assembly to a Suzuki dealer service department or other motorcycle repair shop to have the seal driven in. If you are very careful, the seal can be driven in with a hammer and a drift punch.

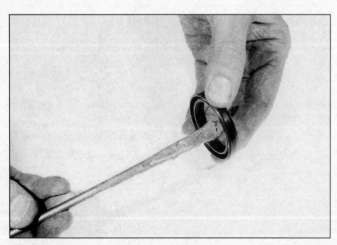

4.24a Coat the inner lip and the outer circumference of the new seal with fork oil

4.24b Install the seal on the fork tube; be careful not to damage the seal lip on the upper edge of the fork tube

4.24c Tap the seal gently and repeatedly with a seal driver until it's fully seated in the fork tube (but don't keep hitting it after it bottoms)

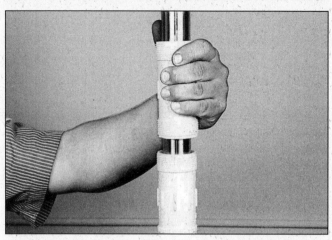

4.24d Using two PVC plumbing fittings of the correct diameter, place one fitting on the seal and strike it with the other fitting

4.25 Compress the stopper ring and fit it securely into its groove in the outer fork tube (if the ring doesn't snap into place, it might be too fatigued to re-use)

4.26 Drive the dust seal into place

4.27a Pour the specified fork oil into the tube . . .

Work around the circumference of the seal, tapping gently on the outer edge of the seal until it's seated. Be careful - if you distort the seal, you'll have to disassemble the fork again and end up taking it to a dealer anyway!

25 Install the retaining ring, making sure the ring is completely seated in its groove **(see illustration)**.

26 Install the dust seal, making sure it seats completely **(see illustration)**.

27 Compress the fork fully and add the recommended type and quantity of fork oil listed in this Chapter's Specifications **(see illustrations)**.

28 Install the fork spring with the narrow-diameter coils at the bottom. Install the cap bolt, but don't tighten it yet.

29 Install the fork (see Section 3). If you won't be installing the fork right away, store it in an upright position to prevent leakage.

30 Once the fork is securely held in the triple clamps, tighten the fork cap bolt to the torque listed in this Chapter's Specifications.

5 Forks (DR-Z400, DR-Z400E, 2002 and later DR-Z400S) - disassembly, inspection and reassembly

Disassembly

1 Remove the forks (see Section 3), loosening the fork cap if you plan to disassemble the forks **(see illustration 3.6)**. Work on one fork leg at a time to avoid mixing up the parts **(see illustration)**.

2 Loosen the clamps and remove the rubber boot from the fork leg.

3 Unscrew the cap bolt from the fork tube.

4 Hold the locknut with a wrench and unscrew the base bolt from the fork cartridge **(see illustration 4.7)**. Remove the washer and spring from the fork.

5 Invert the fork over a drain pan and pump the inner tube slowly inward and out-

ward to drain the oil. This will probably take several minutes.

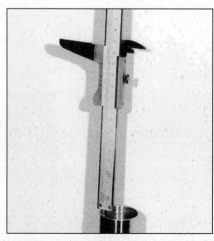

4.27b . . . until it reaches the specified level inside the tube

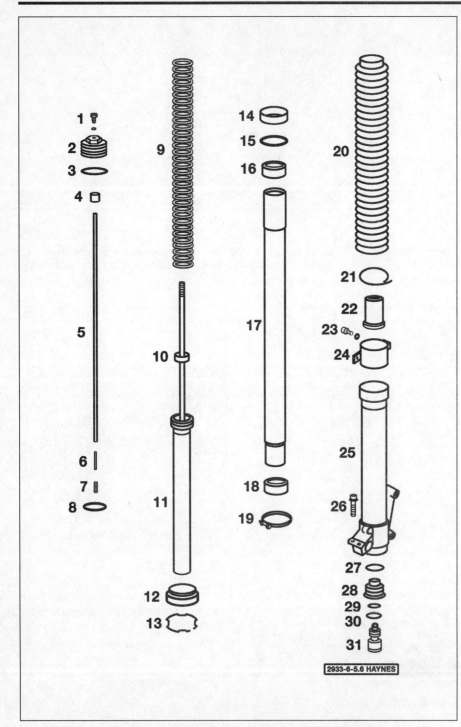

5.1 Front fork details (DR-Z400, DR-Z400E, 2002 and later DR-Z400S)

1	Air relief screw	12	Dust seal	23	Holder		
2	Fork cap bolt	13	Stopper ring	24	Holder screw		
3	O-ring	14	Oil seal	25	Outer fork tube		
4	Locknut	15	Oil seal retainer	26	Axle pinch bolt		
5	Pushrod	16	Bushing	27	O-ring		
6	Needle	17	Inner fork tube	28	End plate		
7	Spring	18	Bushing	29	O-ring		
8	Spring washer	19	Boot clamp	30	O-ring		
9	Spring	20	Boot	31	Base bolt		
10	Damper rod wear ring	21	Boot clamp				
11	Cartridge	22	Oil lock piece				

6   Pull the pushrod, needle and spring out of the cartridge.

7   Remove the dust seal and oil seal stopper ring **(see illustrations 4.10 and 4.11)**.

8   Remove the base bolt from the outer fork tube.

9   Pull the cartridge out of the outer fork tube.

10   Separate the inner and outer fork tubes (see Section 4, Steps 10 through 13).

Inspection

11   Inspect the fork as described in Section 4, Steps 14 through 18.

Reassembly

12   Assembly is the reverse of the disassembly procedure, with the following additions:

 a) *Refer to Steps 1 through 6 to assemble the inner and outer tubes, bushings and seals* **(see illustration 5.1)**.

 b) *If you removed the locknut from the cartridge, thread it on all the way.*

 c) *Install the spring on the cartridge needle, then install the needle into the cartridge rod point first and install the pushrod on top of it.*

 d) *Before installing the spring, hold the fork upright and pour the specified fork oil into the inner tube until it's full. Slowly pump the rod up and down until no more bubbles can be seen in the oil, then compress the fork all the way and measure the oil level in the fork tube* **(see illustration 4.27b)**. *Add oil, or remove it with a suction tool if necessary, to bring the level to the value listed in this Chapter's Specifications.*

 e) *Install the spring with its narrow-diameter coils at the bottom.*

 f) *Align the gaps in the rubber boot clamps with the center of the axle boss at the bottom of the fork.*

 g) *Install the cap bolt on the damper rod threads, then tighten the locknut against the cap bolt to the torque listed in this Chapter's Specifications.*

 h) *Thread the cap bolt into the fork and tighten it slightly.*

13   Install the fork (see Section 3). If you won't be installing the fork right away, store it in an upright position to prevent leakage.

14   Once the fork is securely held in the triple clamps, tighten the fork cap bolt to the torque listed in this Chapter's Specifications.

6   Forks (DR-Z400SM) - disassembly, inspection and reassembly

Disassembly

1   Remove the forks (see Section 3). Work on one fork leg at a time to avoid mixing up the parts.

2   Before beginning disassembly, obtain

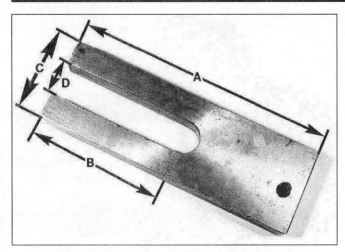

6.2 This support tool can be made from 1 to 1.5 mm (1/32 to 1/16-inch) thick steel plate

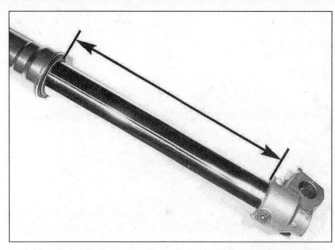

6.5 The distance from the dust seal to the axle holder should be the same when the fork is reassembled

A	55 mm (2 inches)	C	33 mm (1-5/16 inches)
B	25 mm (1 inch)	D	12.5 mm (1/2 inch)

Suzuki tool 09910-20115, or make a support tool of aluminum plate (see illustration).

3   Turn the rebound adjuster all the way in (clockwise), recording the number of clicks until it stops, then turn the adjuster all the way counterclockwise. Do the same for the compression adjuster (see Section 15).

4   Remove the plastic protectors form the fork legs if you haven't already done so. Thoroughly clean the outside of the fork, paying special attention to the surface of the inner fork tube and the cavity around the center bolt on the bottom of the fork.

5   Before disassembling the fork, measure and record the distance from the dust seal to the axle holder (see illustration).

6   Unscrew the damper from the outer fork tube, using a 50 mm hex wrench, then compress the fork until the dust seal contacts the axle holder (see illustration).

7   Turn the fork upside down over a drain pan and drain the oil from the fork tube and the small hole in the damper (see illustration).

8   Thread the damper back into the fork tube, tightening it with your fingers only.

9   Support the fork in a padded vise gripping the axle holder.

Caution: Don't tighten the vise enough to damage the axle holder.

Unscrew the center bolt until it disengages from the fork, but don't try to remove it completely yet (see illustration).

10   Push in on the fork cap so the center bolt and locknut protrude from the bottom of the fork, then slip the support tool in above the locknut (see illustration).

Caution: Do not remove the locknut from the damper during Step 11, or the damper rod will fall out of position, with no way to reinstall it.

6.6 After unscrewing the damper, compress the fork until the dust seal touches the axle holder

6.7 Drain the oil from the fork tube and the small hole in the damper

6.9 Place the fork in a vise and unscrew the center bolt

6.10 Push the center bolt out and slide the support tool over the damper, then release the center bolt

6.11 Hold the locknut and unscrew the center bolt; DO NOT unscrew the locknut or the damper rod will fall out of place and the damper will be ruined

6.12 Remove the center bolt and pull the pushrod out of the damper rod

11   Hold the locknut with one wrench and unscrew the center bolt with another **(see illustration)**.
12   Pull the pushrod out of the damper **(see illustration)**.
13   Unscrew the damper from the fork, then pull the fork cap/damper out of the fork tube as a unit. Take the fork out of the vise, invert it and remove the spring.
14   Clamp the flats of the fork cap in a vise, then unscrew the damper from it **(see illustration)**.

Caution: Don't squeeze the damper or place it in a vise, or it may be damaged.

15   Compress the fork tubes together, then yank them sharply apart, several times. The slide hammer-like motion is necessary to dislodge the guide bushing from the outer fork tube. Once this happens, separate the fork tubes.

Inspection

16   Clean all parts, except the fork damper, in solvent and blow them dry with compressed air (if available) **(see illustration)**. Clean the

damper with fresh fork oil (this is done because solvent is hard to remove from the damper). Check the inner and outer fork tubes and the damper rod for score marks, scratches, flaking of the chrome and excessive or abnormal wear. Look for dents in the tubes and replace them if any are found. Check the fork seal seat

for nicks, gouges and scratches. If damage is evident, leaks will occur around to seal-to-outer tube junction. Replace worn or defective parts with new ones.
17   Have the fork inner tube checked for runout at a dealer service department or other repair shop.

6.14 Secure the fork cap in a vise and unscrew the damper from it; it's tight, so be sure the wrench fits exactly

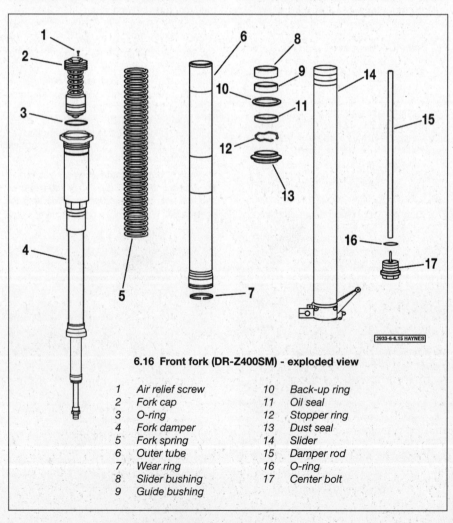

6.16 Front fork (DR-Z400SM) - exploded view

1	Air relief screw	10	Back-up ring
2	Fork cap	11	Oil seal
3	O-ring	12	Stopper ring
4	Fork damper	13	Dust seal
5	Fork spring	14	Slider
6	Outer tube	15	Damper rod
7	Wear ring	16	O-ring
8	Slider bushing	17	Center bolt
9	Guide bushing		

6.23 The wear ring at the bottom of the fork tube must protrude at least 1.5 mm (0.06 inch)

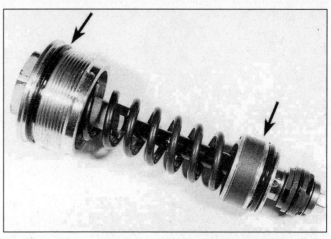

6.24 Replace the fork cap if the bushing is worn (right arrow); use a new O-ring on reassembly (left arrow)

6.27 Wrap the end of the fork tube with tape to protect the seals

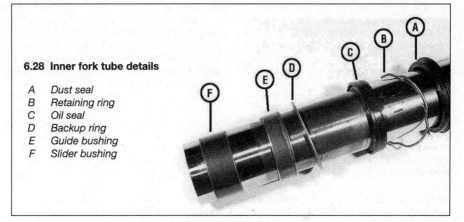

6.28 Inner fork tube details

A Dust seal
B Retaining ring
C Oil seal
D Backup ring
E Guide bushing
F Slider bushing

 Warning: If it is bent, it should not be straightened; replace it with a new one.

18 Measure the overall length of the spring and check it for cracks and other damage. Compare the length to the minimum length listed in this Chapter's Specifications. If it's defective or sagged, replace both fork springs with new ones. Never replace only one spring.
19 If it's necessary to replace the inner guide bushing (the one that won't come off that's on the bottom of the inner tube), pry it apart at the slit and slide it off **(see illustration 4.17a)**. Make sure the new one seats properly **(see illustration 4.17b)**.
20 Check the center bolt for wear or damage. Replace its O-rings and sealing washer whenever the fork is disassembled.
21 Check the bushing on the damper rod and replace it if it's worn.
22 Check the inner circumference of the back-up ring for distortion and replace it if any problems are found.
23 Check the wear ring on the fork tube

(see illustration). If it doesn't protrude more than 1.5 mm (0.6 inch) from the surface of the fork tube, replace it with a new one. **Note:** *The wear rings prevent the fork protectors from eroding the bottoms of the fork tubes.*
24 Inspect the fork cap bushing **(see illustration)**. The bushing can't be replaced separately; you'll need a new fork cap assembly if the bushing is worn or damaged. Remove the fork cap O-ring and use a new one on reassembly.
25 Compress and extend the damper rod and check for smooth movement. If it doesn't move smoothly, check its movements again after assembling the fork and bleeding the air from it. If there's visible wear or damage, replace the damper.
26 Clean all oil from the threads of the fork cap and damper.

Reassembly

27 Wrap the end of the inner fork tube with tape so it won't cut into the seals on reassembly **(see illustration)**.
28 Install the dust seal and retainer on the inner fork tube, then install the oil seal with its open end toward the dust seal. If the bushings were removed, make sure there aren't any burrs in the bushing seating areas on the fork tubes. Coat the bushings with the

recommended fork oil and install them **(see illustration)**.
29 Install the inner tube in the outer tube until the outer tube's bushing rests against its bore. Place the backup ring against the outer bushing, then tap on the backup ring with a seal driver to seat the bushing in its bore **(see illustration)**.

6.29 Drive the bushing into its bore in the outer fork tube with a seal driver; use the same tool to install the oil seal

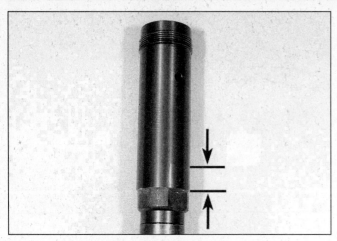

6.34 Measure the fork oil level in the damper

6.39 Pad the surface so you don't damage the damper rod and push up and down on the damper to pump it

30 Use the same driver to tap the oil seal into the outer fork just past the retaining ring groove **(see illustration 6.29)**. Install the retaining ring in the groove, making sure it seats securely.

31 Slide the dust seal down the inner fork tube and seat it in the outer fork tube.

32 Hold the damper in its upright position (rod down). Extend the rod all the way.

33 Pour the amount and type of fork oil listed in this Chapter's Specifications into the top of the damper, then slowly pump the damper rod up and down eight to ten times to bleed out air.

34 With the damper rod fully extended, measure the oil level in the damper **(see illustration)**. Add or remove oil as necessary to adjust the level. **Note:** *The fork cap will be difficult to install if the oil level is too high.*

35 Dip a new fork cap O-ring in fork oil and install it on the fork cap. Coat the fork cap bushing with fork oil.

36 While holding the damper rod in the fully extended position, thread the fork cap onto the damper and tighten it as firmly as possible with your fingers. Turn the damper over and place the fork cap in a padded vise. Place a wrench on the damper flats and tighten the damper onto the cap to the torque listed in this Chapter's Specifications.

37 Take the fork cap out of the vise. Turn the damper upright (rod down). Compress the damper rod all the way, then slowly pull it down 100 mm (3-7/8 inches). Do this several times.

38 Thread the locknut all the way onto the damper rod. Place the rebound and compression damping adjusters all the way counterclockwise (softest positions) if not already done.

39 Coat the damper rod surface with fork oil. With the damper upright, place the end of the damper rod on a rag or similar soft surface, then push down on the damper to pump the damper rod through its full stroke several times. This will force any extra fork oil in the spring chamber to the oil hole so it can be dumped out **(see illustration)**.

40 After dumping any extra oil, blow the remaining oil out the drain hole with compressed air **(see illustration 6.7)**. If you don't have a compressor, remove the air relief screw from the top of the fork cap, then prop the damper upside down for ten minutes (rod upward) so the oil can finish draining. Reinstall the air relief screw (if removed).

41 All the air should have been bled out of the damper at this point. If the damper rod doesn't move smoothly at this point, check the damper rod for bending or other damage. Replace the damper as an assembly if problems are found.

42 Hold the damper in a horizontal position and compress the damper rod all the way. It should extend fully by itself. If it doesn't, repeat Steps 39 and 40 to remove any remaining air.

43 Thoroughly clean any oil off the outside of the damper and rod. Place the damper in its upright position (rod down) and compress the rod 200 to 250 mm (eight to ten inches) from its fully extended position. Hold the damper like this for ten minutes and check for oil leaks form the spring chamber drain hole and the point where the damper rod enters the damper. If any oil leaks can be seen, replace the damper as an assembly.

44 Measure the length of the damper rod threads that protrude past the locknut **(see illustration)**. They should be within the range listed in this Chapter's Specifications.

45 Install the spring and damper assembly in the fork.

46 Place the fork in a vise, push in on the fork cap and install the support tool **(see illustration 6.10)**.

47 Recheck the thread protrusion from the damper rod locknut and make sure it's still within the Specifications.

48 Install the pushrod in the damper rod. Rotate it back and forth as you install it to make sure it goes in all the way.

49 Slip the adjusting rod on the center bolt into the pushrod, then tighten the center bolt as much as possible with your fingers **(see illustration)**.

50 Measure the gap between the locknut and center bolt **(see illustration)**. If it's not within the range listed in this Chapter's Specifications, make sure the locknut is installed the specified distance from the end of the damper rod.

51 Hold the center bolt with a wrench and tighten the locknut against it with your fingers. Then hold the locknut with a wrench and tighten the center bolt to the torque listed in this Chapter's Specifications.

52 Coat the threads of the center bolt with a non-permanent thread locking agent. Push in on the fork and pull out the support

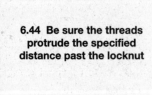

6.44 Be sure the threads protrude the specified distance past the locknut

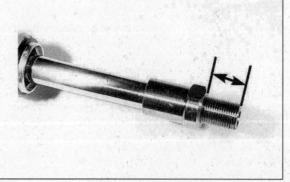

6.49 **The adjusting rod in the center bolt fits inside the pushrod, which fits inside the damper rod**

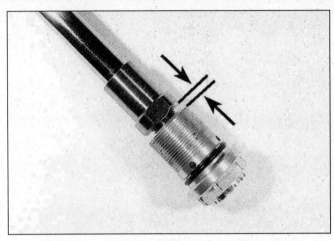

6.50 **Measure the gap between locknut and center bolt**

tool. Thread the center bolt into the fork and tighten it to the torque listed in this Chapter's Specifications.

53 Measure the distance from the dust seal to the axle holder **(see illustration 6.5)**. It should be the same distance it was before disassembly. If it isn't, recheck the installation of the locknut and center bolt.

54 Lower the upper fork tube away from the damper and pour the recommended amount of oil into the fork **(see illustration)**. **Note:** *Minimum oil level will make the suspension slightly softer near full compression; maximum oil level will make the suspension slightly stiffer near full compression.*

 Warning: To prevent unstable handling, make sure the oil level is exactly the same in both forks.

55 Pull the tube up to the damper, then thread the damper into the tube. Tighten the damper and fork cap to the specified torque

after installation, when it's held in the lower triple clamp. Use the special 50 mm hex wrench used on disassembly.

56 Return the compression and rebound adjusters to their original positions.

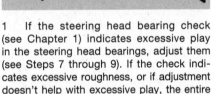

7 Steering head bearings - replacement and adjustment

1 If the steering head bearing check (see Chapter 1) indicates excessive play in the steering head bearings, adjust them (see Steps 7 through 9). If the check indicates excessive roughness, or if adjustment doesn't help with excessive play, the entire front end must be disassembled and the bearings and races replaced with new ones.

2 Remove the front wheel (see Chapter 7).

3 Remove the handlebar and front forks (see Sections 2 and 3).

4 Remove the headlight assembly and speedometer (if equipped) (see Chapter 5).

5 Disconnect the brake hose and wiring harness retainers from the triple clamps. If you're working on a DR-Z400S or SM, remove the front turn signal stalks from the triple clamps and disconnect the turn signal wiring connectors.

6 Remove the steering stem head nut and washer **(see illustration)**, then lift off the upper triple clamp (sometimes called the fork bridge or crown).

Adjustment

7 Tighten the steering stem adjusting nut to the torque listed in this Chapter's Specifications, using a special 4-point socket. These are available from aftermarket tool suppliers or Suzuki dealers. If you don't have the special tool, refer to Step 22 for a method to measure the torque accurately using a spanner wrench.

6.54 **Flattening the tip of an aluminum funnel will make it easier to pour oil into the fork tube**

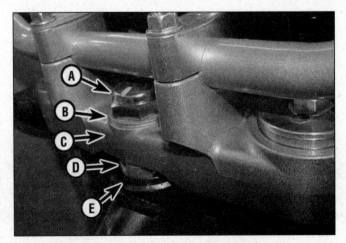

7.6 **Steering stem nut and related components**

A	Steering stem nut	D	Steering adjusting nut
B	Washer	E	Upper bearing with
C	Upper triple clamp		integral seal/cover

7.10a Unscrew the steering stem nut

7.10b Remove the washer, then lift off the upper triple clamp

8   Turn the lower triple clamp back and forth through its full travel 5 or 6 times to seat the bearings, then loosen the adjusting nut 1/4- to 1/2-turn.
9   Recheck play (see Chapter 1). If it's now acceptable, reverse Steps 2 through 6 to

7.10c Unscrew the adjusting nut

reinstall the removed components. If it's still loose or rough, proceed to Step 10 to continue with bearing removal.

Removal

10   Remove the stem adjusting nut and washer while supporting the steering head from the bottom, then lift off the upper triple clamp, unscrew the locknut and remove the upper bearing (see illustrations).
11   Remove the steering stem and lower triple clamp assembly together with the lower bearing (see illustration). If it's stuck, gently tap on the top of the steering stem with a plastic mallet or a hammer and a wood block.
12   Clean all the parts with solvent and dry them thoroughly, using compressed air, if available. If you do use compressed air, don't let the bearings spin as they're dried - it could ruin them. Wipe the old grease out of the frame steering head and bearing races.
13   Examine the races in the steering head for cracks, dents, and pits. If even the slightest amount of wear or damage is evident, the races should be replaced with new ones.

14   To remove the races, drive them out of the steering head with a bearing driver or a hammer and drift punch (see illustration). A slide hammer with the proper internal-jaw puller will also work. Since the races are an interference fit in the frame, installation will be easier if the new races are left overnight in a refrigerator. This will cause them to contract and slip into place in the frame with very little effort. When installing the races, tap them gently into place with a hammer and bearing driver or a large socket. Do not strike the bearing surface or the race will be damaged.

Inspection

15   Check the bearings for wear. Look for cracks, dents, and pits in the races and flat spots on the bearings. Replace any defective parts with new ones. If a new bearing is required, replace both of them as a set.
16   To remove the lower bearing and grease seal from the steering stem, use a hammer and chisel between the bearing cover and steering stem, taking care not to damage

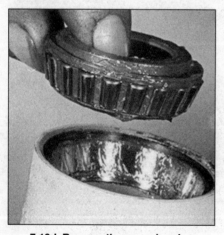

7.10d Remove the upper bearing

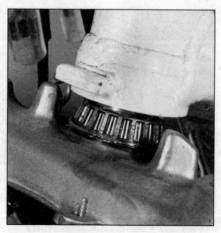

7.11 Lower the steering stem out of the steering head, together with the lower bearing and seal

7.14 Catch the edge of the inner race with a punch and tap it out

7.16 Tap a chisel under the seal to separate the seal and bearing from the steering stem

7.19 Work the grease completely into the bearing

the steering stem **(see illustration)**. Don't remove this bearing unless it, or the grease seal underneath, must be replaced.

17   Check the grease seals attached to the upper and lower bearings. The seals aren't available separately; if they're worn or damaged, the complete upper or lower bearing must be replaced. If you do replace the bearing, be sure to replace its outer race as well as the inner race and rollers.

18   Inspect the steering stem/lower triple clamp for cracks and other damage. Do not attempt to repair any steering components. Replace them with new parts if defects are found.

Installation

19   Pack the bearings and outer races with high-quality (preferably a moly-based) grease **(see illustration)**.

20   Install the grease seal and lower bearing onto the steering stem. Drive the lower bearing onto the steering stem using Suzuki stem bearing driver no. 09941-74910. If you don't have access to this tool, a section of pipe with a diameter the same as the inner

race of the bearing can be used. Drive the bearing on until it is fully seated.

21   Insert the steering stem/lower triple clamp into the frame head. Install the upper bearing **(see illustration 7.10d)**.

22   Install the adjusting nut with its notches upward. If you're using an adjustable spanner, tighten the nut while moving the lower triple clamp back and forth. Continue to tighten the nut to the torque listed in this Chapter's Specifications. You can calculate the torque by applying a measured amount

of force to the spanner handle at a measured distance from the center of the nut **(see illustration)**. Once the nut is tightened to the initial torque, make sure there is no more play (don't overtighten, though, or the steering will be too tight and the bearings may be damaged). Make sure the steering head turns smoothly.

23   Turn the steering stem from full left to full right lock 5 or 6 times to seat the bearings, then loosen it 1/4- to 1/2-turn.

24   Tighten the nut by hand, just enough to eliminate play in the bearing.

25   The remainder of installation is the reverse of removal.

8	Rear shock absorber - removal, inspection and installation	

Removal

1   Support the motorcycle securely upright.

2   Remove the rear subframe (see Chapter 8).

3   Unbolt the lower end of the shock absorber from the linkage **(see illustration)**. Unbolt the upper end from the frame and lift the shock out of the motorcycle **(see illustration)**.

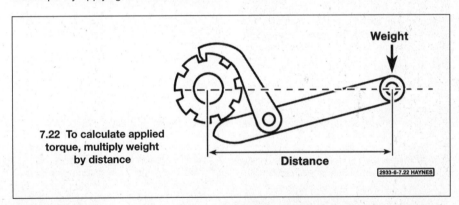

7.22 To calculate applied torque, multiply weight by distance

Weight

Distance

2933-6-7.22 HAYNES

8.3a Shock absorber lower bolt (lower arrow) and compression damping adjuster (upper arrow)

8.3b Shock absorber upper mounting bolt location

Inspection

4   The spherical bearing at the top of the shock can be replaced separately **(see illustration)**. If it's worn or damaged, remove the circlip that holds it in, then press it out with a hydraulic press or a drawbolt as described in *Tools and Workshop Tips* at the end of this manual. Use the same tool to install the new bearing and secure it with a new circlip.

5   Except for bearing replacement, the shock can't be repaired. If it's damaged, replace it with a new one.

6   The shock absorber oil can be changed on 2002 and later DR-Z400 and DR-Z400E models. This requires special equipment, including a nitrogen tank and regulator. Refer the procedure to a dealer service department or other qualified shop.

Installation

7   Installation is the reverse of removal. Be sure the bolt heads are facing in the proper directions. Tighten the bolts to the torque listed in this Chapter's Specifications.

9   Rear suspension linkage - removal, inspection and installation

Removal

1   Support the bike securely upright.

2   Unbolt the lower end of the shock absorber from the linkage (see Section 8).

3   Remove the linkage mounting bolts and nuts and remove the linkage **(see illustration)**.

Inspection

4   Remove the spacers from the rocker arm pivot points. Check the needle bearings in the rocker arm for wear or damage. If they're worn or damaged, replace them using a drawbolt (see Section 12).

5   Pull the shock absorber bearing in until it's centered in the bore of the rocker arm. At the other two pivot points of the rocker arm, pull the bearings (two per pivot point) in just far enough so the outer bearing and seal will fit into the bore.

6   If the bearings are good, lubricate them

8.4 The spherical bearing in the upper end can be replaced separately if it's worn or damaged

with molybdenum disulfide grease and reinstall the spacers.

Installation

7   Installation is the reverse of removal. Tighten the nuts and bolts to the torque listed in this Chapter's Specifications.

10 Swingarm bearings - check

1   Remove the rear wheel (see Chapter 7).

2   Grasp the rear of the swingarm with one hand and place your other hand at the junction of the swingarm and the frame. Try to move the rear of the swingarm from side-to-side. Any wear (play) in the bearings should be felt as movement between the swingarm and the frame at the front. The swingarm will actually be felt to move forward and backward at the front (not from side-to-side). If any play is noted, the bearings should be replaced with new ones (see Section 12).

3   Next, move the swingarm up and down through its full travel. It should move freely, without any binding or rough spots. If it does not move freely, refer to Section 12 for servicing procedures.

9.3 Rear shock linkage details

A   Rocker arm-to-frame bolt and nut
B   Tie rod-to-rocker arm bolt and nut
C   Tie rod-to-rocker arm bolt and nut
D   Shock absorber-to-tie rod bolt and nut

11 Swingarm - removal and installation

Removal

1   Raise the bike and support it securely so it can't be knocked over during this procedure.

2   Remove the rear wheel (see Chapter 7).

3   Unbolt the lower end of the rear shock absorber from the suspension linkage. If you're planning to remove the linkage together with the swingarm, unbolt the linkage from the frame (see Section 9). If you're not planning to remove the linkage, unbolt it from the swingarm.

4   Remove the retainers that secure the brake hose to the swingarm (see Chapter 7). Unbolt the caliper and support it out of the way. The hose can remain connected to the caliper.

5   Remove the upper and lower drive chain guards **(see illustrations)**.

6   Support the swingarm. Unscrew the

11.5a Remove the chain guard screws/bolts

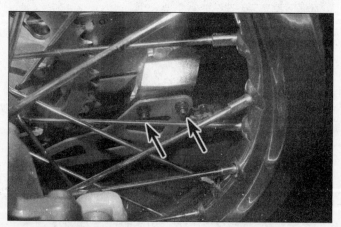

11.5b The long bolts on the lower chain guard have nuts

11.6a Unscrew the pivot nut and remove the washer

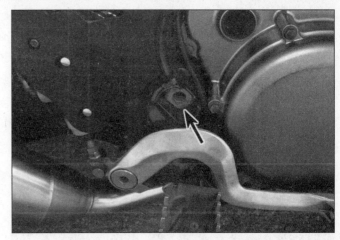

11.6b Tap the pivot bolt until its head protrudes from the recess

pivot shaft nut and remove its washer, then pull out the pivot shaft **(see illustrations)**.

7   Remove the swingarm to the rear of the vehicle.

8   Check the pivot bearings in the swingarm for dryness or deterioration. Lubricate them with molybdenum disulfide grease if necessary (see Section 12).

9   Check the pivot shaft for bending by rolling it on a piece of glass. If it's very slightly bent, check the amount of bend with a micrometer and V-blocks. If it exceeds the amount listed in this Chapter's Specifications, replace the pivot shaft.

Installation

10   Support the swing arm so its pivot holes are aligned with the holes in the frame. Install the pivot shaft, place the washer on the threaded end and tighten its nut to the torque listed in this Chapter's Specifications.

11   Raise and lower the swingarm to make sure it moves freely without binding or interference. Check swingarm bearing play (see Section 10).

12   The remainder of installation is the reverse of removal.

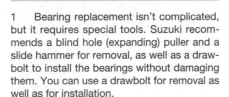

12 Swingarm bearings - replacement

1   Bearing replacement isn't complicated, but it requires special tools. Suzuki recommends a blind hole (expanding) puller and a slide hammer for removal, as well as a drawbolt to install the bearings without damaging them. You can use a drawbolt for removal as well as for installation.

 TOOL TiP *You can make a drawbolt from readily available hardware - a bolt, nut, washers and a pair of sockets or two pieces of metal tubing (see **Tools and Workshop** Tips at the end of this manual).*

The puller and slide hammer can be rented if you don't have them, but compare the cost

of having the bearings replaced by a dealer service department or other qualified shop to that of renting the equipment before you proceed.

2   Remove the swingarm (see Section 11).

3   Pry the bearing spacer out of each swingarm pivot hole (the spacers are removed toward the center of the swingarm) **(see illustration)**.

4   Remove the outer seal and outer bearing from the outer side of each pivot hole. Remove the inner seal from the inner side of each pivot hole.

5   Remove the bearings with one of the tools described in Step 1 **(see illustration)**.

6   Pull new bearings into the swingarm with a drawbolt. Pull the bearings in from the outside until there's just enough room in the bore to accept the outer bearing and outer seal.

7   Install the outer bearings and outer seals.

8   Pack the bearing with molybdenum disulfide grease.

9   Install the swingarm (see Section 11).

12.3 Pry the collar (left arrow) out to expose the seal (right arrow)

12.5 Inspect the needle roller bearings and replace them if they're worn or damaged

13.2 Engine sprocket cover bolt locations

13.4 Bend back the lockwasher tabs, unscrew the nut and remove the lockwasher from the transmission shaft

13 Drive chain - removal, cleaning, inspection and installation

1   These motorcycles come from the factory with an endless chain. They can be optionally equipped with a chain that has a removable master link. **Note:** *Suzuki recommends replacing the chain and sprockets as a set.*
2   Remove the engine sprocket cover and the spacer behind it **(see illustration)**.

Removal

Endless chain

3   Remove the chain guards (see Section 11).
4   If you plan to remove the engine sprocket, bend back the tab on the engine sprocket lockwasher **(see illustration)**. While an assistant holds the rear brake on, loosen the engine sprocket nut.
5   Remove the rear wheel (see Chapter 7).
6   Remove the swingarm (see Section 11).
7   Lift the chain off the engine sprocket and remove it from the bike.

8   Unscrew the engine sprocket nut and remove the sprocket.
9   Check the chain guard on the swingarm for wear or damage and replace it as necessary.

Master link chain

10   Locate the master link, referring to the chain breaking procedures in *Tools and Workshop Tips* at the end of this manual.
11   Remove the master link from the chain with a chain breaker tool (available from motorcycle dealerships and parts suppliers).
12   Disengage the chain from the sprockets and free it from the chain guards to remove it from the bike,

Cleaning and inspection

13   Soak the chain in a high flash point solvent for approximately five minutes. Use a brush to work the solvent into the spaces between the links and plates.

Caution: Do not use gasoline or trichloroethylene to clean the chain. They will dissolve the grease inside the rollers.

14   Wipe the chain dry, then check it carefully for worn or damaged links. Replace

the chain if wear or damage is found at any point.
15   Stretch the chain taut and measure its length between the number of pins listed in this Chapter's Specifications. Compare the measured length to the specified value replace the chain if it's beyond the limit. If the chain needs to be replaced, check the sprockets, replacing them if they are worn (see Section 14). If a new chain is installed on worn sprockets, it will wear out quickly.
16   Lubricate the chain with heavy engine oil or a spray chain lube compatible with O-ring chains.

Installation

17   Installation is the reverse of removal. If you used a chain breaker, refer to *Tools and Workshop Tips* at the end of this manual for installation instructions.
18   Adjust the chain (see Chapter 1).

14 Sprockets - check and replacement

1   Support the bike securely so it can't be knocked over during this procedure.
2   Whenever the sprockets are inspected, the chain should also be inspected, and replaced if it's worn. Installing a worn chain on new sprockets will cause them to wear quickly.
3   Remove the engine sprocket cover (see Section 13). Check the teeth on the engine sprocket and rear sprocket for wear.
4   If the sprockets are worn, remove the rear wheel (see Chapter 7) and the chain (see Section 13).
5   Remove the collar from the center of the rear wheel hub on the sprocket side. Remove the Allen bolts and nuts and detach the sprocket from the rear wheel hub **(see illustration)**.
6   Bend back the lockwasher, then unscrew the nut from the transmission shaft

14.5 The rear sprocket is secured by self-locking nuts (arrows, lower nuts hidden) and Allen bolts

14.7 These components are located behind the drive sprocket

A *Countershaft spacer*
B *Seal*
C *Bearing retainer screws*

15.5 Loosen the locknut (upper arrow) and turn the adjusting nut (lower arrow) to set spring preload

and remove the lockwasher **(see illustration 13.4)**. Pull the sprocket off the transmission shaft, together with the chain.

7   Inspect the seal behind the engine sprocket **(see illustration)**. If it has been leaking, remove the seal retainer. Pull out the output shaft spacer and its internal O-ring. Pry out the seal (taking care not to scratch the seal bore) and tap in a new seal with a socket the same diameter as the seal. Reinstall the output shaft spacer, using a new O-ring, then install the seal retainer.

8   Installation is the reverse of removal, with the following additions:

a) *Use a new lockwasher on the engine sprocket nut. Tighten the sprocket nut to the torque listed in this Chapter's Specifications.*

b) *Adjust the chain (see Chapter 1).*

c) *If you removed the output shaft spacer, check the engine oil level and add some if necessary (see Chapter 1).*

15 Suspension adjustments

Front suspension
2001 and earlier DR-Z400S

1   Adjust the spring preload with the adjuster at the top of the fork leg. Turn the adjuster in or out to change the number of grooves exposed. The standard position is three grooves.

2   Adjust the compression damping with the adjuster at the bottom of the fork leg **(see illustration 4.7)**. The standard setting is 7 clicks out from the fully clockwise position.

DR-Z400, DR-Z400E, 2002 and later DR-Z400S, DR-Z400SM

3   Adjust rebound damping with the adjuster at the top of the fork leg. Turn it all the way in to the hardest setting, then back it out to the standard setting listed in this Chapter's Specifications.

4   Adjust compression damping (see Step 2). Settings are listed in this Chapter's Specifications.

Rear suspension

5   Adjust spring preload by loosening the lock ring and turning the adjusting nut **(see illustration)**. Shortening the spring makes it harder; lengthening the spring makes it softer.

6   Rebound damping is adjustable on all except 2001 and earlier DR-Z400S models. To make the adjustment, turn the adjuster all the way clockwise (hard), then back it out to the standard setting listed in this Chapter's Specifications **(see illustration 8.3a)**.

7   Compression damping is adjustable on all models, using the adjuster at the top of the shock absorber **(see illustration)**. Early models have only one compression damping

15.7 The compression damping adjuster is located at the top of the shock

adjustment, obtained by turning the screw. Later models have separate adjustments for high-speed and low-speed damping. Adjust high-speed damping by turning the nut all the way in, then backing it out the number of turns listed in this Chapter's Specifications. Adjust low-speed damping by turning the screw all the way in, then backing it out the number of clicks listed in this Chapter's Specifications.

Notes

Chapter 7
Brakes, wheels and tires

Contents

Degrees of difficulty

| **Easy,** suitable for novice with little experience | | **Fairly easy,** suitable for beginner with some experience | | **Fairly difficult,** suitable for competent DIY mechanic | | **Difficult,** suitable for experienced DIY mechanic | | **Very difficult,** suitable for expert DIY or professional | |

Specifications

Disc brakes

Brake fluid type .... See Chapter 1
Brake pad minimum thickness.. See Chapter 1
Front disc thickness
    Standard .... 3.5 +/- 0.2 mm (0.138 +/- 0.008 inch)
    Limit* .... 3.0 mm (0.118 inch)
Rear disc thickness
    Standard .... 4.5 +/- 0.2 mm (0.18 +/- 0.008 inch)
    Limit* .... 4.0 mm (0.16 inch)
Disc runout limit (front and rear)... 0.3 mm (0.012 inch)
Refer to marks stamped into the disc (they supersede information printed here)

Wheels and tires

Tire pressures	See Chapter 1
Tire tread depth	See Chapter 1
Axle runout limit (front and rear)	0.25 mm (0.010 inch)
Wheel out-of-round and lateral runout limit (front and rear)	2.0 mm (0.08 inch)

Torque specifications

Front axle	42 Nm (30.5 ft-lbs)
Front axle pinch bolts	18 Nm (159 inch-lbs)
Rear axle nut	
US and Canada	100 Nm (72.5 ft-lbs)
All others	110 Nm (79.5 ft-lbs)
Brake caliper	
Front caliper bracket bolts	26 Nm (19 ft-lbs)
Pad retaining pins (front and rear)	18 Nm (159 inch-lbs)
Pad pin plugs	2.5 Nm (22 inch-lbs)
Brake hose union bolts	23 Nm (16.5 ft-lbs)
Brake disc-to-wheel bolts*	10 Nm (84 inch-lbs)
Front master cylinder mounting bolts	10 Nm (84 inch-lbs)
Rear master cylinder mounting bolts	10 Nm (84 inch-lbs)
Pedal pivot bolt	29 Nm (21 ft-lbs)

*Apply non-permanent thread locking agent to the threads.

2.2a Front caliper details

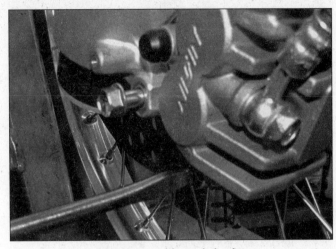

2.2b Unscrew the pad pin plug

A   Pad pin plug   D   Bleed valve
B   Caliper mounting bolts   E   Brake hose banjo bolt
C   Slide pins

1 General information

The front wheel on all motorcycles covered by this manual is equipped with a hydraulic disc brake using a pin slider caliper and dual pistons. The rear wheel on all models is equipped with a hydraulic disc brake using a pin slider caliper and a single piston.

Caution: Disc brake components rarely require disassembly. Do not disassemble components unless absolutely necessary. If any hydraulic brake line connection in the system is loosened, the entire system should be disassembled, drained and cleaned, then properly filled and bled upon reassembly. Do not use solvents on internal brake components; they will cause seals to swell and distort. Use only clean brake fluid or alcohol for cleaning. Use care when working with brake fluid as it can injure your eyes and it will damage painted surfaces and plastic parts.

2 Front brake pads - replacement

⚠️ *Warning: The dust created by the brake system is harmful to your health. Never blow it out* with compressed air and don't inhale any of it. An approved filtering mask should be worn when working on the brakes.

Removal

1   Support the bike securely upright.
2   Unscrew the plug from the pad pin **(see illustrations)**. Loosen the pad pin while the caliper is still bolted to the bracket **(see illustration)**.
3   Remove the caliper mounting bolts and lift off the caliper **(see illustration 2.2a and the accompanying illustration)**. Leave the brake hose connected and support the caliper so the hose won't be strained.

2.2c Loosen the pad with an Allen wrench while the caliper is still bolted to the bracket

2.3 Remove the caliper mounting bolts

2.4a Unscrew the pin with an Allen wrench after lifting off the caliper

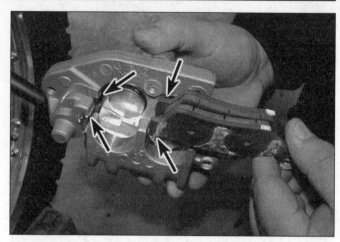

2.4b Slide out the pads; on installation, position the tabs in the caliper notches

4   Unscrew the pad pin the rest of the way and remove the pads from the caliper (see illustrations).

2.5 Check the pad spring for rust, wear and damage, and look for fluid leaks past the pistons

Inspection

5   Inspect the pad spring (see illustration). Replace the spring it if it's rusted or damaged.
6   Inspect the pads (see Chapter 1).
7   Look for signs of fluid leakage past the pistons (see illustration 2.5). If this has occurred, overhaul the caliper (see Section 4).
8   Check the condition of the brake disc (see Section 5). If it's in need of machining or replacement, remove it (see Section 5). If it's okay, deglaze it with sandpaper or emery cloth, using a swirling motion.

Installation

9   Remove the cover from the master cylinder reservoir and siphon out some fluid. Push the piston(s) into the caliper as far as possible, while checking the master cylinder reservoir to make sure it doesn't overflow. If you can't depress the pistons with thumb pressure, try using a C-clamp. If the pistons

stick, remove the caliper and overhaul it (see Section 4).
10   Install the spring, caliper shield and new pads. Coat the threads of the retaining pin(s) with non-permanent thread locking agent and install the retaining pins. Tighten the retaining pins to the torque listed in this Chapter's Specifications.
11   Install the plug over the retaining pin and tighten it to the torque listed in this Chapter's Specifications.
12   Operate the brake lever or pedal several times to bring the pads into contact with the disc. Check the operation of the brake carefully before riding the motorcycle.

3 Rear brake pads - replacement

1   Unscrew the plug that covers the pad retaining pin (see illustrations).

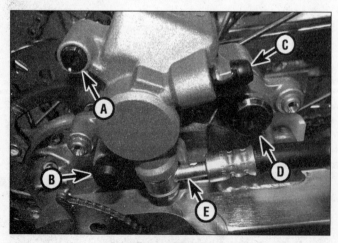

3.1a Rear caliper details

3.1b Unscrew the pad pin plug

A   Pad pin plug
B   Slide pin
C   Bleed valve
D   Slide pin/mounting bolt
E   Brake hose fitting

3.2 Loosen the pad pin with an Allen wrench

3.3a Lift the pad spring to relieve pressure on the pin and pull out the pin

2   Unscrew the pad retaining pin with an Allen wrench **(see illustration)**.
3   Lift the spring, pull out the pin and pull out the pads and shims **(see illustrations)**.
4   Inspection is the same as for front pads (see Section 2). Look inside the caliper to inspect the pad spring. If it's worn, corroded or damaged, replace it (on some models, you'll need to remove the caliper for access - see Section 4).
5   Installation is the reverse of removal. Lubricate the pad pin with high temperature grease before installing it. Note how the spring engages the pin **(see illustration 3.3b)**.

4   Brake caliper - removal, overhaul and installation

⚠ *Warning: If a caliper indicates the need for an overhaul (usually due to leaking fluid or sticky operation), all old brake fluid must be flushed from the*

system. Also, the dust created by the brake system is harmful to your health. Never blow it out with compressed air and don't inhale any of it. An approved filtering mask should be worn when working on the brakes. Do not, under any circumstances, use petroleum-based solvents to clean brake parts. Use clean brake fluid or denatured alcohol only!

Note: *If you are removing the caliper only to remove the front or rear wheel, don't disconnect the hose from the caliper.*

Removal

1   Support the bike securely upright. **Note:** *If you're planning to disassemble the caliper, read through the overhaul procedure, paying particular attention to the steps involved in removing the pistons with compressed air. If you don't have access to an air compressor, you can use the bike's hydraulic system to force the pistons out instead. To do this, remove the pads and pump the brake lever or pedal. If one piston in a dual-piston caliper comes out before the other, push it back*

into its bore and hold it in with a C-clamp while pumping the brake lever to remove the remaining piston.

Front caliper

2   Disconnect the brake hose from the caliper. Remove the brake hose banjo fitting bolt and separate the hose from the caliper **(see illustration 2.2a)**. Discard the sealing washers. Plug the end of the hose or wrap a plastic bag tightly around it to prevent excessive fluid loss and contamination.
3   Unscrew the caliper mounting bolts and lift the caliper off the fork leg, being careful not to strain or twist the brake hose if it's still connected.

Rear caliper

4   If you're planning to overhaul the caliper, loosen the brake hose union bolt (it's easier to loosen the bolts while the caliper is mounted on the bike) **(see illustration 3.1a)**.
5   Remove the rear wheel (see Section 11). Slide the caliper bracket backward off its rail **(see illustration)**. Support the caliper so it doesn't hang by the brake hose.

3.3b Remove the pads and their shims

4.5 Slide the caliper backward off its rail on the swingarm

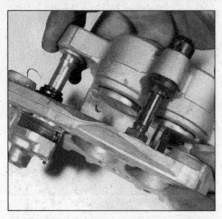

4.8 Slide the caliper off the bracket

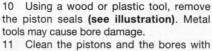
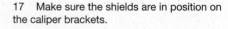

4.10 **Brake caliper details (typical rear shown, front similar but with an additional piston)**

1   Pin boot
2   Caliper body
3   Pad spring
4   Piston seal
5   Dust seal
6   Piston

6   Disconnect the brake hose from the caliper if you haven't already done so. Remove the brake hose banjo fitting bolt and separate the hose from the caliper. Discard the sealing washers. Plug the end of the hose or wrap a plastic bag tightly around it to prevent excessive fluid loss and contamination.

Overhaul

7   Remove the brake pads and anti-rattle spring from the caliper (see Section 2 or 3, if necessary). Clean the exterior of the caliper with denatured alcohol or brake system cleaner.
8   Slide the caliper off the bracket **(see illustration)**.
9   Pack a shop rag into the space that holds the brake pads. Use compressed air, directed into the caliper fluid inlet, to remove the piston(s). Use only enough air pressure to ease the piston(s) out of the bore. If a piston is blown out forcefully, even with the rag in place, it may be damaged.

⚠ **Warning: Never place your fingers in front of the piston in an attempt to catch or protect it when applying compressed air, as serious injury could occur.**

10   Using a wood or plastic tool, remove the piston seals **(see illustration)**. Metal tools may cause bore damage.
11   Clean the pistons and the bores with denatured alcohol, clean brake fluid or brake system cleaner and blow dry them with filtered, unlubricated compressed air. Inspect the surfaces of the pistons for nicks and burrs and loss of plating. Check the caliper bores, too. If surface defects are present, the caliper must be replaced.
12   If the caliper is in bad shape, the master cylinder should also be checked.
13   Lubricate the piston seals with clean brake fluid and install them in their grooves in the caliper bore **(see illustration)**. Make sure they seat completely and aren't twisted.
14   Lubricate the dust seals with clean brake fluid and install them in their grooves, making sure they seat correctly.
15   Lubricate the piston (both pistons on front calipers) with clean brake fluid and install it into the caliper bore. Using your thumbs, push the piston all the way in, making sure it doesn't get cocked in the bore.
16   Pull the old pin boots out of the caliper and bracket. Coat new ones with silicone grease and install them, making sure they seat completely **(see illustration)**.

17   Make sure the shields are in position on the caliper brackets.

Installation

18   Installation is the reverse of removal, with the following additions:

a) Apply silicone grease to the slider pins on the caliper bracket and caliper.
b) Use new sealing washers on the brake hose fitting. Position the brake hose fitting in the caliper notch or against the stop.
c) Tighten the caliper mounting bolts (if equipped), rear caliper shield bolts and brake line union bolt to the torque listed in this Chapter's Specifications.
d) If you're working on a rear caliper, adjust chain slack (see Chapter 1).
e) Fill the master cylinder with the recommended brake fluid (see Chapter 1) and bleed the system (see Section 10). Check for leaks.
f) Check the operation of the brakes carefully before riding the motorcycle.

---

5   Brake discs - inspection, removal and installation

Inspection

1   Support the bike securely upright. Place a jack beneath the bike and raise the wheel being checked off the ground. Be sure the bike is securely supported so it can't be knocked over.
2   Visually inspect the surface of the disc(s) for score marks and other damage. Light scratches are normal after use and won't affect brake operation, but deep grooves and heavy score marks will reduce braking efficiency and accelerate pad wear. If the discs are badly grooved they must be machined or replaced.
3   To check disc runout, mount a dial indicator to a fork leg or the swingarm, with the plunger on the indicator touching the surface of the disc about 1/2-inch from the outer edge **(see illustration)**. Slowly turn the

4.13 Fit the seals all the way into their grooves

4.16 Install the boot in the front caliper with its wide end facing the same direction as the pistons

wheel and watch the indicator needle, comparing your reading with the limit listed in this Chapter's Specifications. If the runout is greater than allowed, check the hub bearings for play (see Chapter 1). If the bearings are worn, replace them and repeat this check. If the disc runout is still excessive, the disc will have to be replaced.

4   The disc must not be machined or allowed to wear down to a thickness less than the minimum allowable thickness, listed in this Chapter's Specifications. The thickness of the disc can be checked with a micrometer. If the thickness of the disc is less than the minimum allowable, it must be replaced. The minimum thickness is also stamped into the disc **(see illustration)**.

Removal

5   Remove the wheel (see Section 11). Set the wheel on wood blocks so the disc doesn't support the weight of the wheel.

Caution: Don't lay the wheel down and allow it to rest on the disc - the disc could become warped.

6   Mark the relationship of the disc to the wheel, so it can be installed in the same position. Remove the bolts that retain the disc to the wheel **(see illustration)**. Loosen the bolts a little at a time, in a criss-cross pattern, to avoid distorting the disc.

Installation

7   Position the disc on the wheel, aligning the previously applied matchmarks (if you're reinstalling the original disc). On models so equipped, make sure the arrow (stamped on the disc) marking the direction of rotation is pointing in the proper direction.

8   Install the bolts, tightening them a little at a time in a criss-cross pattern, until the torque listed in this Chapter's Specifications is reached. Clean off all grease from the brake disc using acetone or brake system cleaner.

9   Install the wheel.

5.3 Set up a dial indicator against the brake disc and turn the wheel in its normal direction of rotation to measure runout

10   Operate the brake lever or pedal several times to bring the pads into contact with the disc. Check the operation of the brakes carefully before riding the motorcycle.

---

6   Front brake master cylinder - removal, overhaul and installation

Caution: Disassembly, overhaul and reassembly of the brake master cylinder must be done in a spotlessly clean work area to avoid contamination and possible failure of the brake hydraulic system components.

1   If the master cylinder is leaking fluid, or if the lever doesn't produce a firm feel when the brake is applied, and bleeding the brakes doesn't help, master cylinder overhaul is recommended.

2   Before disassembling the master cylinder, read through the entire procedure and

5.4 Marks on the disc indicate the minimum thickness and direction of rotation

make sure that you have the correct rebuild kit. You will need new, clean brake fluid of the recommended type, clean rags and internal snap-ring pliers. **Note:** *To prevent damage to the paint from spilled brake fluid, always cover the gas tank when working on the master cylinder.*

Removal

3   Place rags beneath the master cylinder to protect the paint in case of brake fluid spills.

4   Brake fluid will run out of the upper brake hose during this step, so either have a container handy to place the end of the hose in, or have a plastic bag and rubber band handy to cover the end of the hose. The objective is to prevent excess loss of brake fluid, fluid spills and system contamination.

5   Remove the banjo fitting bolt and sealing washers from the master cylinder **(see illustration)**. If the bike is equipped with a brake light, remove the brake light switch (see Chapter 5).

5.6 Brake disc hub bolt locations (rear disc shown)

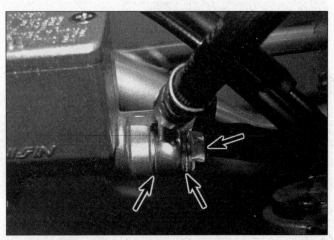

6.5 Unscrew the banjo bolt (upper arrow) and remove the seals (lower arrows)

6.6 Make an alignment mark for the clamp if there isn't one, then remove the bolts - the UP mark and arrow face upward on installation

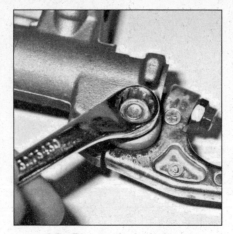

6.8a Remove the locknut . . .

6.8b . . . and unscrew the pivot bolt to detach the lever

6   Remove the master cylinder mounting bolts **(see illustration)**. Remove the master cylinder from the handlebar.

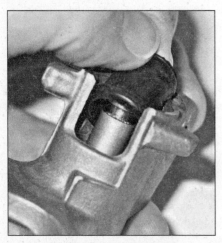

6.9 Remove the dust boot

Overhaul

7   Remove the master cylinder cover, retainer (if equipped) and diaphragm (see Chapter 1).
8   Remove the locknut from the underside of the lever pivot bolt, then unscrew the bolt **(see illustrations)**. Remove the lever pivot cover (it's held on by the pivot bolt).
9   Remove the dust boot **(see illustration)**.
10   Using snap-ring pliers, remove the snap-ring **(see illustration)**.
11   Slide out the piston assembly and the spring **(see illustration)**. Lay the parts out in the proper order to prevent confusion during reassembly.
12   Clean all of the parts with brake system cleaner (available at auto parts stores), isopropyl alcohol or clean brake fluid.

Caution: Do not, under any circumstances, use a petroleum-based solvent to clean brake parts. If compressed air is available, use it to dry the parts thoroughly (make sure it's filtered and unlubricated).

13   Check the master cylinder bore and piston for corrosion, scratches, nicks and score marks. If damage or wear can be seen, the master cylinder must be replaced with a new one. If you have a bore gauge and micrometer, check the bore and piston diameters and compare them to the values listed in this Chapter's Specifications. If the master cylinder is in poor condition, then the caliper should be checked as well.
14   If there's a baffle plate in the bottom of the reservoir, make sure it's securely held by its retainer.
15   Suzuki supplies a new piston in its rebuild kits. If the cup seals are not installed on the new piston, install them, making sure the lips face away from the lever end of the piston **(see illustration 6.11)**. Use the new piston regardless of the condition of the old one.
16   Before reassembling the master cylinder, soak the piston and the rubber cup seals in clean brake fluid for ten or fifteen minutes. Lubricate the master cylinder bore with clean brake fluid, then carefully insert the piston

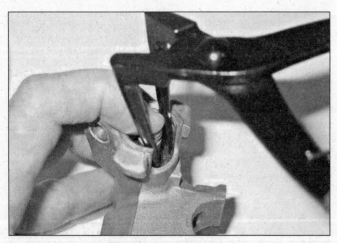

6.10 Remove the snap-ring from the master cylinder bore

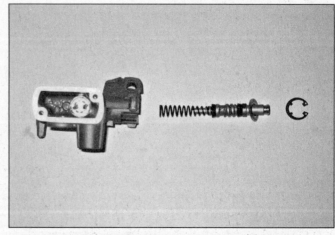

6.11 Remove the piston assembly from the bore

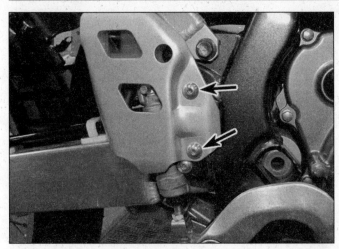

7.3 Remove the Allen bolts and remove the protective cover from the master cylinder

7.4 Remove the cotter pin and pull out the clevis pin to detach the master cylinder from the brake pedal

A   *Master cylinder pushrod clevis pin*
B   *Brake pedal pivot pin*
C   *Fluid reservoir hose clamp*

and related parts in the reverse order of disassembly. Make sure the lips on the cup seals do not turn inside out when they are slipped into the bore.

17   Depress the piston, then install the snap-ring (make sure the snap-ring is properly seated in the groove with the sharp edge facing out). Install the rubber dust boot (make sure the lip is seated properly in the piston groove).

18   Install the brake lever, pivot cover and pivot bolt. Tighten the pivot bolt locknut.

Installation

19   Installation is the reverse of removal, with the following additions:

a) *Attach the master cylinder to the handlebar. Align the upper gap between the master cylinder and clamp with the punch mark on the handlebar (see illustration 6.6).*

b) *Make sure the arrow and the word UP on the master cylinder clamp are pointing up, then tighten the bolts to the torque listed in this Chapter's Specifications.*

c) *Use new sealing washers at the brake hose banjo fitting. Tighten the union bolt to the torque listed in this Chapter's Specifications.*

d) *Install the dust cover over the lever and pivot.*

e) *Bleed the air from the system (see Section 10).*

f) *Check the operation of the brakes carefully before riding the motorcycle.*

7 Rear brake master cylinder - removal, overhaul and installation

Caution: Disassembly, overhaul and reassembly of the brake master cylinder

must be done in a spotlessly clean work area to avoid contamination and possible failure of the brake hydraulic system components.

1   If the master cylinder is leaking fluid, or if the pedal does not produce a firm feel when the brake is applied, and bleeding the brake does not help, master cylinder overhaul is recommended.

2   Before disassembling the master cylinder, read through the entire procedure and make sure that you have the correct rebuild kit. You will need new, clean brake fluid of the recommended type, clean rags and internal snap-ring pliers.

Removal

3   Support the bike securely upright. Remove the master cylinder cover (see illustration).

4   Remove the cotter pin from the clevis pin on the master cylinder pushrod (see

illustration). Remove the clevis pin.

5   Have a container and some rags ready to catch spilling brake fluid. Using a six-point box wrench, unscrew the banjo fitting bolt from the top of the master cylinder. Discard the sealing washers on either side of the fitting.

6   Squeeze the fluid feed hose clamp with pliers and slide the clamp up the hose (see illustration 7.4). Disconnect the hose from the fitting on the master cylinder. If necessary, unbolt the reservoir from the frame and remove it.

7   Remove the two master cylinder mounting bolts and detach the cylinder from the frame.

Overhaul

8   Use a pair of snap-ring pliers to remove the snap-ring from the fluid inlet fitting (see illustration) and detach the fitting from the master cylinder. Remove the O-ring from the bore (see illustration).

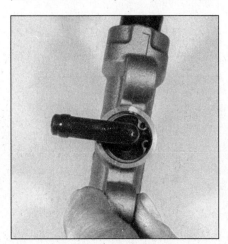

7.8a Remove the snap-ring

7.8b Work the fluid feed fitting free of its bore and remove the O-ring

7.9a Measure the length of the pushrod

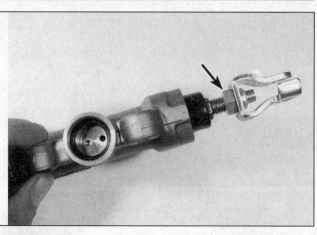

7.9b Loosen the locknut and unscrew the locknut and clevis from the pushrod

9   Measure and record the length of the exposed pushrod inside the clevis **(see illustration)**. Hold the clevis with a pair of pliers and loosen the locknut, then unscrew the clevis and locknut from the pushrod **(see illustration)**.

10   Remove the rubber dust boot from the master cylinder bore **(see illustration)**. Depress the pushrod and, using snap-ring pliers, remove the snap-ring **(see illustration)**. Slide out the piston, the cup seal and spring. Lay the parts out in the proper order to prevent confusion during reassembly **(see illustration)**.

11   Clean all of the parts with isopropyl alcohol or clean brake fluid.

Caution: Do not, under any circumstances, use a petroleum-based solvent to clean brake parts. If compressed air is available, use it to dry the parts thoroughly (make sure it's filtered and unlubricated).

12   Check the master cylinder bore for corrosion, scratches, nicks and score marks. If damage is evident, the master cylinder must be replaced with a new one. If the master cylinder is in poor condition, then the caliper should be checked as well.

13   Suzuki supplies a new piston in its rebuild kits. If the cup seals are not installed on the new piston, install them, making sure the lips face away from the lever end of the

7.10a Remove the dust boot from the pushrod

7.10b Remove the snap-ring from the master cylinder bore and withdraw the piston assembly and spring

piston. Use the new piston regardless of the condition of the old one.

14   Before reassembling the master cylinder, soak the piston and the rubber cup seals in clean brake fluid for ten or fifteen minutes. Lubricate the master cylinder bore with clean brake fluid, then carefully insert the parts in the reverse order of disassembly. Make sure the lips on the cup seals do not turn inside out when they are slipped into the bore.

15   Lubricate the end of the pushrod with PBC (poly butyl cuprysil) grease, or silicone grease designed for brake applications, and install the pushrod and stop washer into the

cylinder bore. Depress the pushrod, then install the snap-ring (make sure the snap-ring is properly seated in the groove with the sharp edge facing out) **(see illustration)**. Install the rubber dust boot (make sure the lip is seated properly in the groove in the piston stop nut).

16   Install the locknut and clevis to the end of the pushrod, leaving the same number of exposed threads inside the clevis as was

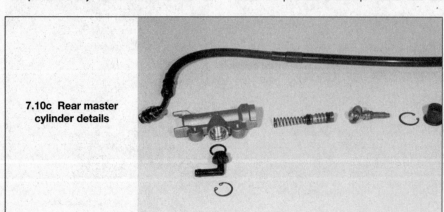

7.10c Rear master cylinder details

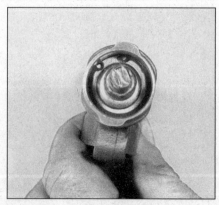

7.15 Make sure the snap-ring is securely seated in its groove

written down during removal. Tighten the locknut. This will ensure the brake pedal will be positioned correctly.

17   Install the feed hose fitting, using a new O-ring. Install the snap-ring, making sure it seats properly in its groove.

Installation

18   Install the fluid reservoir if it was removed. Connect the fluid feed hose to the fitting on the master cylinder and secure it with the clamp.

19   Position the master cylinder on the frame and install the bolts, tightening them securely.

20   Connect the banjo fitting to the top of the master cylinder, using new sealing washers on each side of the fitting. Tighten the banjo fitting bolt to the torque listed in this Chapter's Specifications.

21   Connect the clevis to the brake pedal and secure the clevis pin with a new cotter pin.

22   Fill the fluid reservoir with the specified fluid (see Chapter 1) and bleed the system (see Section 10).

23   Check the position of the brake pedal (see Chapter 1) and adjust it if necessary. Check the operation of the brakes carefully before riding the motorcycle.

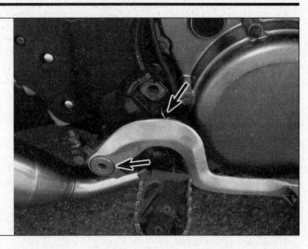

8.2 Brake pedal reurn spring (upper arrow) and pivot pin (lower arrow)

---

8   Brake pedal - removal and installation

1   Support the bike securely upright so it can't be knocked over during this procedure.

2   Unhook the pedal return spring from the frame **(see illustration)**.

3   Remove the cotter pin and clevis pin to detach the master cylinder pushrod from the pedal (see Section 7).

4   Remove the cotter pin and washer from the inner end of the pivot shaft **(see illustration 7.4)**. Unscrew the brake pedal pivot

shaft and remove the pedal **(see illustration 8.2)**.

5   Inspect the pedal pivot shaft seals. If they're worn, damaged or appear to have been leaking, pry them out and press in new ones.

6   Installation is the reverse of removal, with the following additions:

a) *Lubricate the pedal shaft or pivot bolt O-rings and the pivot hole with multipurpose grease.*

b) *Tighten the pedal pivot shaft to the torque listed in this Chapter's Specifications.*

c) *Use a new cotter pin.*

d) *Adjust brake pedal height (see Chapter 1).*

---

9   Brake hoses and lines - inspection and replacement

Inspection

1   Check the condition of the brake hoses at the intervals specified in Chapter 1.

2   Twist and flex the rubber hoses while looking for cracks, bulges and seeping fluid. Check extra carefully around the areas where

the hoses connect with the metal fittings, as these are common areas for hose failure.

Replacement

3   The pressurized brake hoses have banjo fittings on each end of the hose. The fluid feed hose that connects the rear master cylinder reservoir to the master cylinder is secured by spring clamps.

4   Cover the surrounding area with plenty of rags and unscrew the banjo bolt on either end of the hose. Detach the hose or line from any clips that may be present and remove the hose **(see illustrations)**.

5   Position the new hose or line, making sure it isn't twisted or otherwise strained. On hoses equipped with banjo fittings, make sure the metal tube portion of the banjo fitting is located against the stop on the component it's connected to, if equipped. Install the banjo bolts, using new sealing washers on both sides of the fittings, and tighten them to the torque listed in this Chapter's Specifications.

6   Flush the old brake fluid from the system. Refill the system with the recommended fluid (see Chapter 1) and bleed the air from the system (see Section 10). Check the operation of the brakes carefully before riding the motorcycle.

9.4a Make sure the front brake hose retainers are securely attached

9.4b The rear brake hose runs along the swingarm - make sure its retainers are securely attached

11.8 Front axle details (left side shown)

11.9 Right side front axle internal seal pinch bolts - the seal is integral with the speedometer drive unit

A	Locknut	D	Spacer
B	Washer	E	Seal
C	Pinch bolts		

10 Brake system bleeding

1   Bleeding the brake is simply the process of removing all the air bubbles from the brake fluid reservoir, the lines and the brake caliper. Bleeding is necessary whenever a brake system hydraulic connection is loosened, when a component or hose is replaced, or when the master cylinder or caliper is overhauled. Leaks in the system may also allow air to enter, but leaking brake fluid will reveal their presence and warn you of the need for repair.
2   To bleed the brake, you will need some new, clean brake fluid of the recommended type (see Chapter 1), a length of clear vinyl or plastic tubing, a small container partially filled with clean brake fluid, some rags and a wrench to fit the brake caliper bleeder valve.
3   Cover the fuel tank and other painted components to prevent damage in the event that brake fluid is spilled.
4   Remove the reservoir cover or cap and slowly pump the brake lever or pedal a few times, until no air bubbles can be seen floating up from the holes at the bottom of the reservoir. Doing this bleeds the air from the master cylinder end of the line. Reinstall the reservoir cover or cap.
5   Attach one end of the clear vinyl or plastic tubing to the brake caliper bleeder valve and submerge the other end in the brake fluid in the container (see illustrations 2.2a and 3.1a).
6   Check the fluid level in the reservoir. Do not allow the fluid level to drop below the lower mark during the bleeding process.
7   Carefully pump the brake lever or pedal three or four times and hold it while opening the caliper bleeder valve. When the valve is opened, brake fluid will flow out of the caliper into the clear tubing and the lever will move toward the handlebar or the pedal will move down.

8   Retighten the bleeder valve, then release the brake lever or pedal gradually. Repeat the process until no air bubbles are visible in the brake fluid leaving the caliper and the lever or pedal is firm when applied. Remember to add fluid to the reservoir as the level drops. Use only new, clean brake fluid of the recommended type. Never reuse the fluid lost during bleeding.
9   Be sure to check the fluid level in the master cylinder reservoir frequently.
10 Replace the reservoir cover or cap, wipe up any spilled brake fluid and check the entire system for leaks. **Note:** *If bleeding is difficult, it may be necessary to let the brake fluid in the system stabilize for a few hours (it may be aerated). Repeat the bleeding procedure when the tiny bubbles in the system have settled out.*

11 Wheels - inspection, removal and installation

Inspection

1   Clean the wheels thoroughly to remove mud and dirt that may interfere with the inspection procedure or mask defects. Make a general check of the wheels and tires as described in Chapter 1.
2   Support the motorcycle securely upright with the wheel to be checked in the air, then attach a dial indicator to the fork slider or the swingarm and position the stem against the side of the rim. Spin the wheel slowly and check the side-to-side (axial) runout of the rim, then compare your readings with the value listed in this Chapter's Specifications. In order to accurately check radial runout with the dial indicator, the wheel would have to be removed from the machine and the tire removed from the wheel. With the axle clamped in a vise, the wheel can be rotated to check the runout.

3   An easier, though slightly less accurate, method is to attach a stiff wire pointer to the outer fork tube or the swingarm and position the end a fraction of an inch from the wheel (where the wheel and tire join). If the wheel is true, the distance from the pointer to the rim will be constant as the wheel is rotated. Repeat the procedure to check the runout of the rear wheel. **Note:** *If wheel runout is excessive, check the wheel bearings very carefully before replacing the wheel (see Section 13).*
4   The wheels should also be visually inspected for cracks, flat spots on the rim and other damage. Individual spokes can be replaced. If other damage is evident, the wheel will have to be replaced with a new one. Never attempt to repair a damaged wheel.
5   Before installing the wheel, check the axle for straightness. If the axle is corroded, first remove the corrosion with fine emery cloth. Set the axle on V-blocks and check it for runout with a dial indicator. If the axle exceeds the maximum allowable runout limit listed in this Chapter's Specifications, it must be replaced.

Removal

Front wheel

6   Support the bike from below with a jack beneath the engine. Securely prop the bike upright so it can't fall over when the wheel is removed.
7   Remove the cap (if equipped) from the axle nut. On later DR-Z400SM models, remove the Allen bolts that secure the slider to each end of the axle. On the left side, remove the slider and its nut. On the right side, remove the Allen bolt, slider, washer, spacer, second washer, expander spacer, expander and nut.
8   Loosen the axle nut while the axle is held securely by the pinch bolts (see illustration).
9   Unscrew the axle pinch bolts (see illustration 11.8 and the accompanying illustration).

11.13 Rear axle details (all except DR-Z400SM models) - right side

A Locknut (with cotter pin on some models)
B Drive chain adjuster
C Brake caliper bracket
D Spacer
E Wheel bearing seal

10 Hold the axle from turning by placing a hex bit in the hex, then remove the axle nut from the left side **(see illustration 11.8)**. Unscrew the axle from the left fork leg, again using the hex bit.
11 Remove the axle from the right fork leg. Support the wheel and pull the axle out. Lower the wheel away from the motorcycle, sliding the brake disc out from between the pads. Collect the wheel bearing spacers.

Rear wheel

12 Support the bike from below with a jack beneath the swingarm. Securely prop the bike upright so it can't fall over when the wheel is removed.
13 Remove the cotter pin (if equipped), loosen the rear axle nut **(see illustration)** and back off the chain adjusters all the way (see Chapter 1). Disengage the drive chain from the rear sprocket.

DR-Z400, DR-Z400E, DR-Z400S

14 Hold the axle with a wrench or socket **(see illustration)**. Remove the axle nut, washer and chain adjusters from the right side of the swingarm.
15 Support the wheel and pull the axle out, together with the left chain adjuster (it's welded to the axle). Slide the wheel back until the axle clears the swingarm, then lower the wheel away from the motorcycle.

DR-Z400SM

16 If the bike is equipped with sliders on the outer ends of the axle, remove their Allen bolts, then remove the sliders and their nuts from the axle. Remove the cotter pin (if equipped), unscrew the nut and remove the washer and chain adjuster block from the right end of the axle (the axle head fits into a recess in the swingarm, so it doesn't need to be held while the nut is unscrewed).
17 Push the axle out of the swingarm and wheel until you can grab its head and pull on it. Support the wheel, pull out the axle and remove the chain adjuster block.
18 Lower the wheel away from the motorcycle.

Installation

19 Installation is the reverse of removal, with the following additions:
a) *If you're working on a front wheel, tighten the axle nut to the torque listed in this Chapter's Specifications, then tighten the pinch bolts to the torque listed in this Chapter's Specifications.*
b) *If you're working on a rear wheel, tighten the axle nut to the torque listed in this Chapter's Specifications. If the nut is equipped with a cotter pin, install a new one.*
c) *Adjust the drive chain slack (see Chapter 1).*

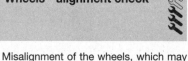

12 Wheels - alignment check

1 Misalignment of the wheels, which may be due to a cocked rear wheel or a bent frame or triple clamps, can cause strange and possibly serious handling problems. If the frame or triple clamps are at fault, repair by a frame specialist or replacement with new parts are the only alternatives.
2 To check the alignment you will need an assistant, a length of string or a perfectly straight piece of wood and a ruler graduated in 1/64 inch increments. A plumb bob or other suitable weight will also be required.
3 Support the motorcycle securely upright, then measure the width of both tires at their widest points. Subtract the smaller measurement from the larger measurement, then divide the difference by two. The result is the amount of offset that should exist between the front and rear tires on both sides.
4 If a string is used, have your assistant hold one end of it about half way between the floor and the rear axle, touching the rear sidewall of the tire.
5 Run the other end of the string forward and pull it tight so that it is roughly parallel to the floor. Slowly bring the string into contact with the front sidewall of the rear tire, then

11.14 On the left side (all except DR-Z400SM models), the axle has a hex head and is integral with the drive chain adjuster

turn the front wheel until it is parallel with the string. Measure the distance from the front tire sidewall to the string.
6 Repeat the procedure on the other side of the motorcycle. The distance from the front tire sidewall to the string should be equal on both sides.
7 As was previously pointed out, a perfectly straight length of wood may be substituted for the string. The procedure is the same.
8 If the distance between the string and tire is greater on one side, or if the rear wheel appears to be cocked, make sure the swingarm is tight (see Chapter 6).
9 If the front-to-back alignment is correct, the wheels still may be out of alignment vertically.
10 Using the plumb bob, or other suitable weight, and a length of string, check the rear wheel to make sure it is vertical. To do this, hold the string against the tire upper sidewall and allow the weight to settle just off the floor. When the string touches both the upper and lower tire sidewalls and is perfectly straight, the wheel is vertical. If it is not, place thin spacers under one leg of the centerstand.
11 Once the rear wheel is vertical, check the front wheel in the same manner. If both wheels are not perfectly vertical, the frame and/or major suspension components are bent.

13 Wheel bearings - inspection and maintenance

Front wheel bearings

1 Support the bike securely and remove the front wheel (see Section 11).
2 Set the wheel on blocks so as not to allow the weight of the wheel to rest on the brake disc.

13.6a If you can't position a metal rod against the bearings, this tool can be used instead - place the split portion inside the bearing and pass the wedged rod through the hub into the split; tapping on the end of the rod will spread the split portion, locking it to the bearing, so the split portion and bearing can be driven out together

13.6b The split portion fits into the bearing like this - if it keeps slipping out when you tap on it, coat it with valve grinding compound

13.17 Pull out the collar and pry the seal out of its bore

3   Remove the spacers (if you haven't already done so) from the wheel (see Section 11).

4   Remove the speedometer drive unit from the right side of the wheel.

5   Turn the wheel over. Pry the grease seal out of the left side.

 TOOL TiP *You can make the tool described in the next step by cutting a slot in the shaft of a bolt that just fits inside the bearings, and grinding a wedge shape on the end of a metal rod.*

6   A common method of removing front wheel bearings is to insert a metal rod (preferably a brass drift punch) through the center of one hub bearing and tap evenly around the inner race of the opposite bearing to drive it from the hub. The bearing spacer will also come out. On these motorcycles, it may not be possible to tilt the rod enough to catch the edge of the opposite bearing's inner race. In this case, use a bearing puller or use a bearing remover tool consisting of a shaft and remover head **(see illustration)**. The head fits inside the bearing **(see illustration)**, then the wedge end of the shaft is tapped into the groove in the head to expand the head and lock it inside the bearing. Tapping on the shaft from this point will force the bearing out of the hub.

7   Lay the wheel on its other side and remove the remaining bearing using the same technique. **Note:** *The bearings must be replaced with new ones whenever they're removed, as they're almost certain to be damaged during removal.*

8   If you're installing bearings that aren't sealed on both sides, pack the new bearings with grease from the open side. Rotate the

bearing to work the grease in between the bearing balls.

9   Thoroughly clean the hub area of the wheel. Install the bearing into the recess in the left side of the hub, with the sealed side facing out. Using a bearing driver or a socket large enough to contact the outer race of the bearing, drive it in until it seats.

10   Turn the wheel over and install the bearing spacer and the other bearing, driving the bearing into place as described in Step 9.

11   Coat the lip of a new grease seal with grease.

12   Install the grease seal; it should go in with thumb pressure but if not, use a seal driver, large socket or a flat piece of wood to drive it into place.

13   Install the grease seal on the other side as described in Step 12.

14   Clean off all grease from the brake disc using acetone or brake system cleaner. Install the wheel.

Rear wheel bearings

15   Remove the rear wheel (see Section 11).

16   These motorcycles use three rear wheel bearings. There are two bearings on the left side and one on the right.

17   Pull the collars out of the seals and pry out the seals **(see illustration)**.

18   Remove the bearings from the hub (see Step 6).

19   Thoroughly clean the hub area of the wheel.

20   Pack the single bearing with grease and install it into the recess in the hub, with the sealed side (if equipped) facing out. Using a bearing driver or a socket large enough to contact the outer race of the bearing, drive it in until it seats.

21   Turn the wheel over. Apply a coat of multi-purpose grease to the inside of the spacer and install it in the hub.

22   Pack the remaining bearings from the open side with grease, then install them in

the hub (one at a time), driving the bearing in with a socket or bearing driver large enough to contact the outer race of the bearing. Drive the bearing in until it seats.

23   Install a new grease seal in each side of the hub. It may go in with thumb pressure, but if not, use a seal driver, large socket or a flat piece of wood to drive it into place.

24   Install the collars in the grease seals.

25   Clean off all grease from the brake disc using acetone or brake system cleaner. Install the wheel.

14 Tires - removal and installation

1   To properly remove and install tires, you will need at least two motorcycle tire irons, some water and a tire pressure gauge.

2   Begin by removing the wheel from the motorcycle. If the tire is going to be re-used, mark it next to the valve stem, wheel balance weight or rim lock.

3   Deflate the tire by removing the valve stem core. When it is fully deflated, push the bead of the tire away from the rim on both sides. In some extreme cases, this can only be accomplished with a bead breaking tool, but most often it can be carried out with tire irons. Riding on a deflated tire to break the bead is not recommended, as damage to the rim and tire will occur.

4   Dismounting a tire is easier when the tire is warm, so an indoor tire change is recommended in cold climates. The rubber gets very stiff and is difficult to manipulate when cold.

5   Place the wheel on a thick pad or old blanket. This will help keep the wheel and tire from slipping around.

6   Once the bead is completely free of the rim, lubricate the inside edge of the rim and the tire bead with water only. The manufac-

TIRE CHANGING SEQUENCE - TUBED TIRES

1 Deflate the tire and loosen the rim lock nut. After pushing the tire beads away from the rim flanges push the tire bead into the well of the rim at the point opposite the valve. Insert the tire lever adjacent to the valve and work the bead over the edge of the rim.

2 Use two levers to work the bead over the edge of the rim. Note the use of rim protectors

3 Remove the inner tube from the tire

4 When the first bead is clear, remove the tire as shown. If the bead isn't too tight, rim protectors won't be necessary

5 To install, partially inflate the inner tube and insert it in the tire. Make sure there's a nut on the valve stem

6 Work the first bead over the rim and feed the valve through the hole in the rim. Partially screw on the retaining nut to hold the valve in place. (The nut should be removed after the tire has been inflated)

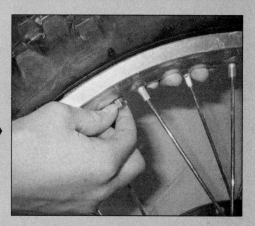

7 Check that the inner tube is positioned correctly and work the second bead over the rim using the tire levers. Start at a point between the valve stem and the rim lock

8 Work final area of the bead over the rim while pushing the valve inwards to ensure that the inner tube is not trapped. Also push the rim lock inwards and, if necessary, pry the tire bead over the rim lock. After inflating the tire, tighten the rim lock nut securely

turer recommends against the use of soap or other tire mounting lubricants, as the tire may shift on the rim. Remove the locknut and push the tire valve through the rim.

7   Insert one of the tire irons under the bead of the tire at the valve stem and lift the bead up over the rim. This should be fairly easy. Take care not to pinch the tube as this is done. If it is difficult to pry the bead up, make sure that the rest of the bead opposite the valve stem is in the dropped center section of the rim.

8   Hold the tire iron down with the bead over the rim, then move about 1 or 2 inches to either side and insert the second tire iron. Be careful not to cut or slice the bead or the tire may split when inflated. Also, take care not to catch or pinch the inner tube as the second tire iron is levered over. For this reason, tire irons are recommended over screwdrivers or other implements.

9   With a small section of the bead up over the rim, one of the levers can be removed and reinserted 1 or 2 inches farther around the rim until about 1/4 of the tire bead is above the rim edge. Make sure that the rest of the bead is in the dropped center of the rim. At this point, the bead can usually be pulled up over the rim by hand.

10   Once all of the first bead is over the rim, the inner tube can be withdrawn from the tire and rim. Push in on the valve stem, lift up on the tire next to the stem, reach inside the tire and carefully pull out the tube. It is usually not necessary to completely remove the tire from the rim to repair the inner tube. It is sometimes recommended though, because checking for foreign objects in the tire is difficult while it is still mounted on the rim.

11   To remove the tire completely, make sure the bead is broken all the way around on the remaining edge, then stand the tire and wheel up on the tread and grab the wheel with one hand. Push the tire down over the same edge of the rim while pulling the rim away from the tire. If the bead is correctly positioned in the dropped center of the rim, the tire should roll off and separate from the rim very easily. If tire irons are used to work this last bead over the rim, the outer edge of

the rim may be marred. If a tire iron is necessary, be sure to pad the rim as described earlier.

12   Refer to Section 15 for inner tube repair procedures.

13   Mounting a tire is basically the reverse of removal. Some tires have a balance mark and/or directional arrows molded into the tire sidewall. Look for these marks so that the tire can be installed properly. The dot should be aligned with the valve stem.

14   If the tire was not removed completely to repair or replace the inner tube, the tube should be inflated just enough to make it round. Sprinkle it with talcum powder, which acts as a dry lubricant, then carefully lift up the tire edge and install the tube with the valve stem next to the hole in the rim. Once the tube is in place, push the valve stem through the rim and start the locknut on the stem.

15   Lubricate the tire bead, then push it over the rim edge and into the dropped center section opposite the inner tube valve stem. Work around each side of the rim, carefully pushing the bead over the rim. The last section may have to be levered on with tire irons. If so, take care not to pinch the inner tube as this is done.

16   Once the bead is over the rim edge, check to see that the inner tube valve stem and the rim lock are pointing to the center of the hub. If they're angled slightly in either direction, rotate the tire on the rim to straighten it out. Run the locknut the rest of the way onto the stem and rim lock but don't tighten them completely.

17   Inflate the tube to approximately 1-1/2 times the pressure listed in the Chapter 1 Specifications and check to make sure the guidelines on the tire sidewalls are the same distance from the rim around the circumference of the tire.

 Warning: Do not over inflate the tube or the tire may burst, causing serious injury.

18   After the tire bead is correctly seated on the rim, allow the tire to deflate. Replace

the valve core and inflate the tube to the recommended pressure, then tighten the valve stem locknut securely and tighten the cap. Tighten the locknut on the rim locknut to the torque listed in the Chapter 1 Specifications.

15 Tubes - repair

1   Tire tube repair requires a patching kit that's usually available from motorcycle dealers, accessory stores or auto parts stores. Be sure to follow the directions supplied with the kit to ensure a safe repair. Patching should be done only when a new tube is unavailable. Replace the tube as soon as possible. Sudden deflation can cause loss of control and an accident.

2   To repair a tube, remove it from the tire, inflate and immerse it in a sink or tub full of water to pinpoint the leak. Mark the position of the leak, then deflate the tube. Dry it off and thoroughly clean the area around the puncture.

3   Most tire patching kits have a buffer to rough up the area around the hole for proper adhesion of the patch. Roughen an area slightly larger than the patch, then apply a thin coat of the patching cement to the roughened area. Allow the cement to dry until tacky, then apply the patch.

4   It may be necessary to remove a protective covering from the top surface of the patch after it has been attached to the tube. Keep in mind that tubes made from synthetic rubber may require a special patch and adhesive if a satisfactory bond is to be achieved.

5   Before replacing the tube, check the inside of the tire to make sure the object that caused the puncture is not still inside. Also check the outside of the tire, particularly the tread area, to make sure nothing is projecting through the tire that may cause another puncture. Check the rim for sharp edges or damage. Make sure the rubber trim band is in good condition and properly installed before inserting the tube.

Chapter 8
Frame and bodywork

Contents

Degrees of difficulty

Easy, suitable for novice with little experience	**Fairly easy,** suitable for beginner with some experience	**Fairly difficult,** suitable for competent DIY mechanic	**Difficult,** suitable for experienced DIY mechanic	**Very difficult,** suitable for expert DIY or professional

Specifications

Torque specifications
Sub-frame mounting bolts .... 35 Nm (25.5 ft-lbs)

---

1 General information

This Chapter covers the procedures necessary to remove and install the fenders and other body parts. Since many service and repair operations on these motorcycles require removal of the fenders and/or other body parts, the procedures are grouped here and referred to from other Chapters.

In the case of damage to plastic body parts, it is usually necessary to remove the broken component and replace it with a new (or used) one. The material that the fenders and other plastic body parts are composed of doesn't lend itself to conventional repair techniques. There are, however, some shops that specialize in plastic welding, so it would be advantageous to check around before throwing the damaged part away.

Note: *When attempting to remove any body panel, first study the panel closely, noting any fasteners and associated fittings, to be sure of returning everything to its correct place on installation. In some cases, the aid of an assistant will be required when removing panels, to help avoid damaging the paint. Once the visible fasteners have been removed, try to lift off the panel as described but DO NOT FORCE the panel - if it will not release, check that all fasteners have been removed and try again. Where a panel engages another by means of lugs and grommets, be careful not to break the lugs or damage the bodywork. Remember that a few moments of patience at this stage will save you a lot of money in replacing broken panels!*

2.2a Remove the right frame cover bolts (the upper bolt also secures the seat)

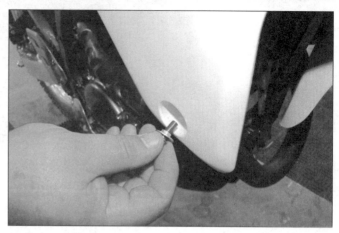

2.2b Remove the collar from the lower bolt

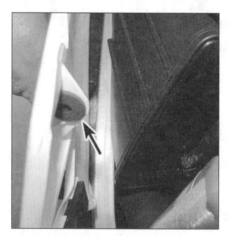

2.2c Pull the panel backward to disengage the grommet from the post

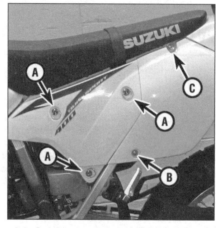

2.3 Quick-release fasteners (A), battery cover screws (B) and battery cover/seat bolt (C)

2 Frame and battery covers - removal and installation

1   There's a frame cover on the right-hand side of the bike, between the fuel tank and the rear fender. There's also a frame cover on the left side of the bike, with a battery cover behind it.

2   To remove the right frame cover, remove the cover bolts, pull it backward to disengage the grommet from the post and remove it **(see illustrations)**.

3   To remove the left frame cover, twist its quick-release fasteners 1/4 turn counter-clockwise to release them and remove the cover **(see illustration)**.

4   To remove the battery cover, unscrew its bolts and remove them, together with the collar on the lower bolt **(see illustrations)**. Disengage the rear edge of the cover from the fender and remove the cover.

5   Installation is the reverse of removal.

3 Seat - removal and installation

1   On all models, remove the bolt from the rear of the seat on each side of the bike **(see illustrations 2.2a and 2.3)**.

2   If you're working on a DR-Z400S or SM, remove the right frame cover (see Section 2) for access to the seat strap bolt. Remove the bolt, together with its collar **(see illustrations)**. Lift the seat strap off the seat and let it hang down on the left side of the bike.

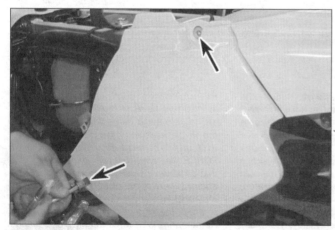

2.4a Remove the battery cover bolts (the upper bolt also secures the seat)

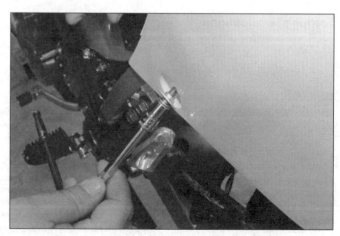

2.4b The battery cover lower bolt has a collar

3.2a Remove the right seat strap bolt . . .

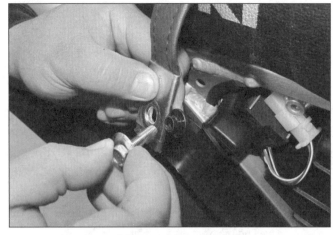

3.2b . . . and its collar

3   Pull the seat back and down to detach its center hook and the slot that engages the tab on the fuel tank **(see illustration 3.4)**. Lift off the seat.
4   Installation is the reverse of removal. Be sure to engage the hook and slot **(see illustration)**.

4   Footpegs - removal and installation

1   Support the bike securely so it can't be knocked over during this procedure.
2   To detach a front footpeg from the pivot, note how the spring is installed, then remove the cotter pin, washer and pivot pin **(see illustration)**. Separate the footpeg from the motorcycle. The front footpeg pivots are integral with the frame.
3   To detach a rubber pad from a front footpeg, remove its mounting bolt from the underside and remove the pad **(see illustration 4.2)**.

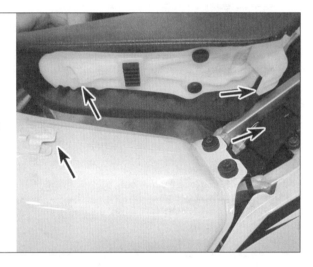

3.4 On installation, be sure to engage the slot with the tab (left arrows) and the hook with the slot (right arrows)

4   To remove a rear footpeg from its bracket, remove the circlip from the underside **(see illustration)**. Carefully pull the footpeg out, being ready to catch the spring-loaded ball that holds the peg in the Up and Down positions. Remove the ball and dump the spring out of the hole.

4.2 The front pedal pads are secured by a bolt (left arrow); to remove the footpeg, remove the cotter pin and pivot pin (right arrow)

4.4 To remove a rear footpeg, remove the circlip (right arrow); pull the footpeg out and be ready to catch the spring-loaded ball (left arrow)

4.5a Left rear footpeg mounting bracket bolts

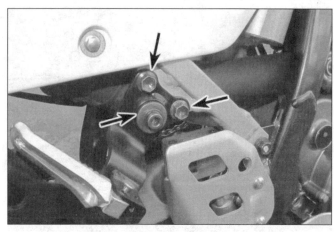

4.5b Right rear footpeg mounting bracket bolts

5   To remove a rear mounting bracket, unbolt it from the frame and remove it **(see illustrations)**.
6   Installation is the reverse of removal. If you removed a cotter pin, use a new one and wrap its ends around the pivot pin.

5 Headlight cover - removal and installation

1   Remove the screws - one at the front and one on each side **(see illustrations)**.
2   Remove the headlight cover.
3   Installation is the reverse of removal.

6 Side covers - removal and installation

1   Remove the bolts and remove the side covers **(see illustration)**.
2   Installation is the reverse of removal.

7 Front fender - removal and installation

1   Remove the front wheel (see Chapter 7).
2   Remove the fender bolts and detach

the speedometer cable retainer **(see illustration)**. Lower the fender clear of the lower triple clamp and remove the washers.
3   Installation is the reverse of removal. Be sure to reinstall the grommets in their correct locations. Tighten the bolts securely, but don't overtighten them and strip the threads.

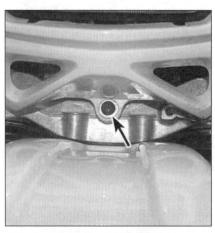

5.1a Remove the screw from the front of the headlight housing . . .

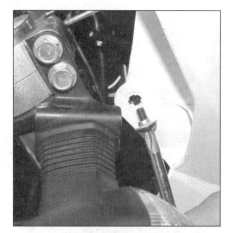

5.1b . . . and one from each side - all three screws have collars

6.1 Side cover bolts (right side shown)

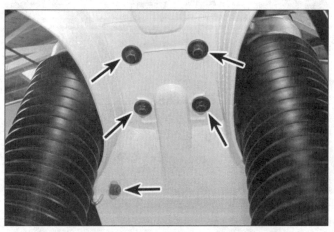

7.2 Remove the mounting bolts (upper arrows) and detach the speedometer cable retainer (lower arrow)

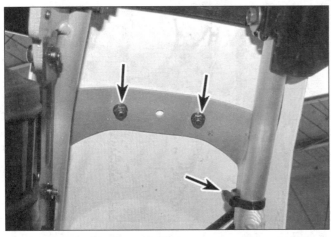

8.3a Free the wiring harness (lower arrow) and the nuts (upper arrows) from inside the fender

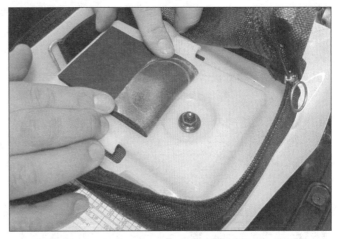

8.3b The top bolts secure the tool kit (one bolt hidden)

8 Rear fender - removal and installation

1   Remove the frame covers, battery cover and seat (see Sections 2 and 3).
2   Follow the wiring harness from the tail-light to the connector and disconnect it **(see illustration 8.3a)**. Free the harness from any retainers.
3   Remove the fender mounting bolts (and grommets if equipped) and remove the fender **(see illustrations)**.
4   If necessary, unbolt the fender extension from the rear of the fender and remove it.
5   Installation is the reverse of removal. Tighten the bolts securely, but don't over-tighten them and strip the threads.

8.3c Remove the bolt from the left side . . .

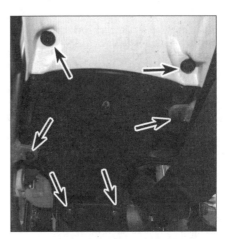

8.3d . . . and the bolts from the inside

9 Subframe - removal and installation

1   Remove the frame covers, battery cover

and seat (see Sections 2 and 3).
2   Remove the battery (see Chapter 5).
3   Remove the muffler (see Chapter 4).
4   Disconnect the wiring connectors for the taillight, rear brake light and turn signals

(if equipped) and the starter relay (except kickstart models). Also disconnect the battery cables from the starter relay **(see illustration)**.

8.3e Disengage the fender from the frame and lift it out

9.4 Subframe details

A   Brake/taillight connector (general location)
B   Rear turn signal connector (general location)
C   Starter relay connector
D   Starter relay battery cables
E   Subframe mounting bolts and nuts

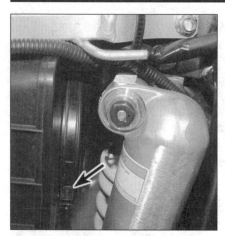

9.5 Loosen the clamping band on the air cleaner housing

9.6 Note which way the bolts face and remove them (lower right shown)

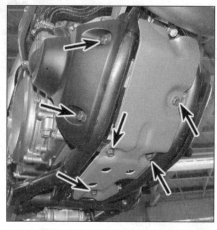

10.1 Skid plate mounting bolt locations

5   Loosen the clamping band that secures the carburetor to the air cleaner housing **(see illustration)**.
6   Unbolt the subframe from the main frame and lift it off, together with the air cleaner housing and rear fender **(see illustration)**.
7   Installation is the reverse of removal.

10 Skid plates - removal and installation

1   Remove the mounting bolts and remove the skid plate **(see illustration)**.
2   Installation is the reverse of removal.

11 Frame - general information, inspection and repair

1   All models use a semi-double cradle frame made of round-section steel tubing. All models have a detachable sub-frame at the rear.
2   The frame shouldn't require attention unless accident damage has occurred. In most cases, frame replacement is the only satisfactory remedy for such damage. A few frame specialists have the jigs and other equipment necessary for straightening the frame to the required standard of accuracy, but even then there is no simple way of assessing to what extent the frame may have been overstressed.
3   After the motorcycle has accumulated a lot of running time, the frame should be examined closely for signs of cracking or splitting at the welded joints. Corrosion can also cause weakness at these joints. Loose engine mount bolts can cause ovaling or fracturing to the mounting bolt holes. Minor damage can often be repaired by welding, depending on the nature and extent of the damage.
4   Remember that a frame that is out of alignment will cause handling problems. If misalignment is suspected as the result of an accident, it will be necessary to strip the machine completely so the frame can be thoroughly checked.

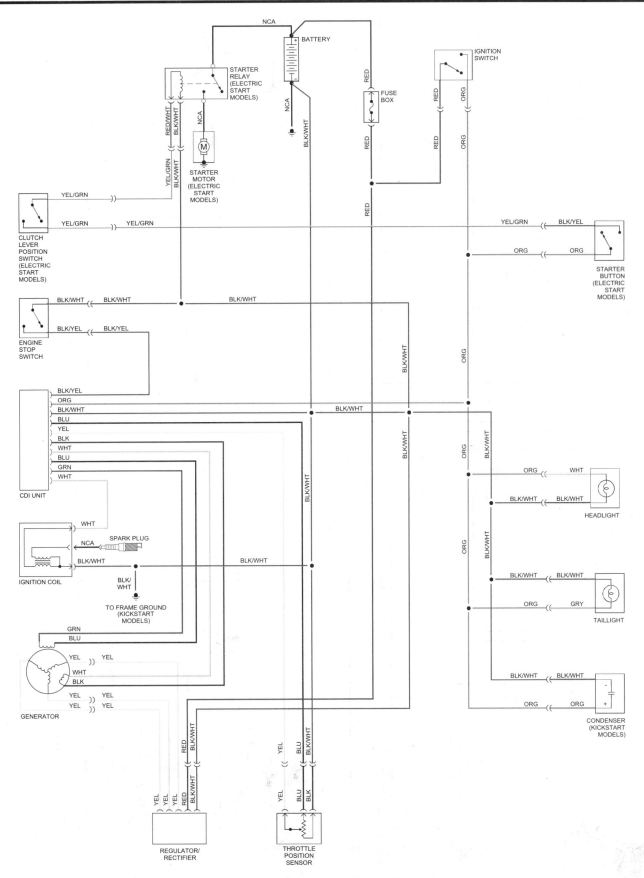

Wiring diagram - DR-Z400, DR-Z400E

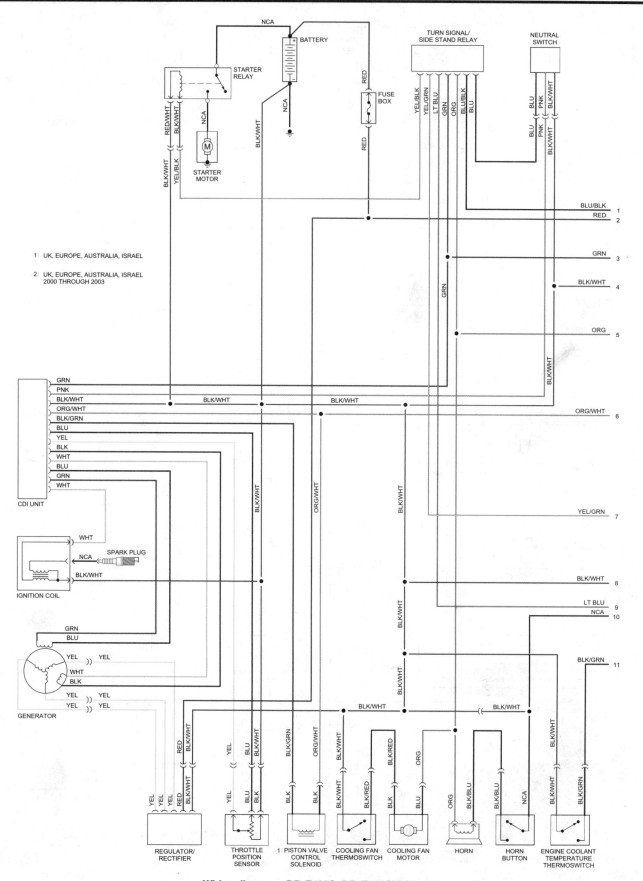

Wiring diagram - DR-Z400S, DR-Z400SM (1 of 2)

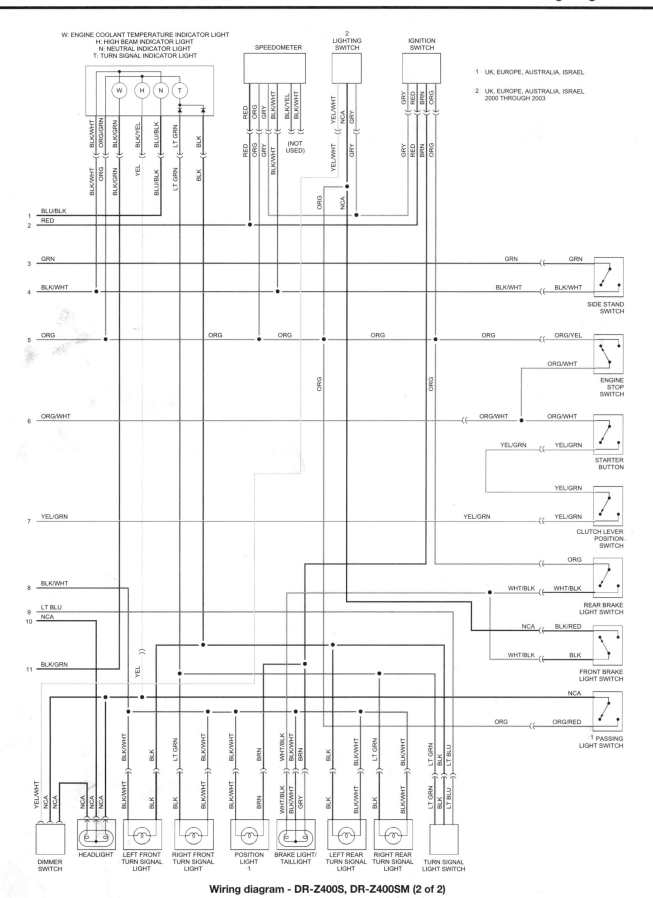

Wiring diagram - DR-Z400S, DR-Z400SM (2 of 2)

Notes

Dimensions and weights

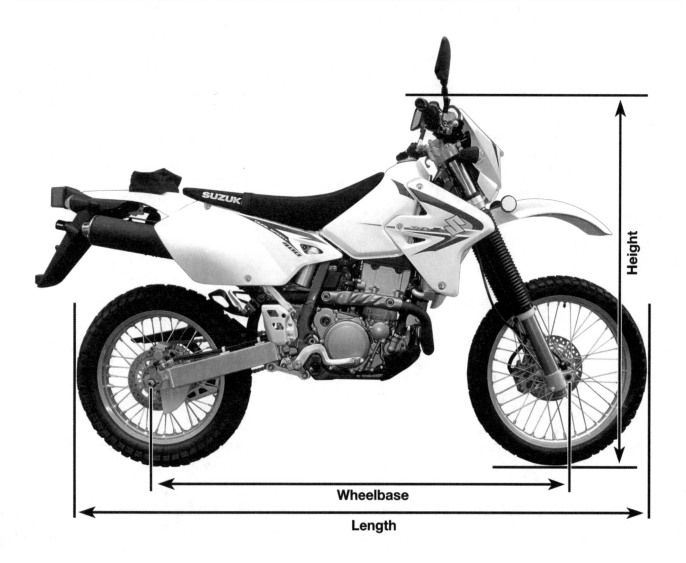

Height

Wheelbase

Length

DR-Z400, DR-Z400E

Wheelbase	1475 mm (58.1 inches)
Width	825 mm (32.5 inches)

Length

2000
Except Australia	2235 mm (88.0 inches)
Australia	2310 mm (90.9 inches)

2001 and later
Except Australia	2235 mm (88.0 inches)
Australia	2310 mm (90.9 inches)

Overall height
2000 and 2001	1245 mm (49.0 inches)
2002 and later	1235 mm (48.6 inches)

Ground clearance
2000	315 mm (12.4 inches)

2001
Except Australia	325 mm (12.8 inches)
Australia	315 mm (12.4 inches)

Seat height
Except Australia	945 mm (37.2 inches)
Australia	935 mm (36.8 inches)

Dry weight
DR-Z400	113 kg (249 lbs)

DR-Z400E
Except Australia	119 kg (262 lbs)

Australia
2007 and earlier (no 2008 model)	127 kg (279 lbs)
2009 and later	138 kg (304 lbs)

DR-Z400S

Wheelbase	1485 mm (58.5 inches)
Width	875 mm (34.4 inches)
Length	2310 mm (90.9 inches)
Overall height	1240 mm (48.8 inches)
Ground clearance	300 mm (11.8 inches)
Seat height	935 mm (36.8 inches)

Dry weight
2003 and earlier	132 kg (291 lbs)

2004 through 2008
US and Canada	132 kg (291 lbs)
All others	133 kg (293 lbs)

2009 and later
US and Canada	144 kg (317 lbs)
All others	145 kg (319 lbs)

DR-Z400SM

Wheelbase .... 1460 mm (57.5 inches)
Width
    2005 and 2006 .... 870 mm (34.3 inches)
    2007 and later .... 855 mm (33.7 inches)
Length .... 2225 mm (87.6 inches)
Overall height
    2005 and 2006 .... 1185 mm (46.7 inches)
    2007 and later .... 1200 mm (47.2 inches)
Ground clearance .... 260 mm (10.2 inches)
Seat height .... 890 mm (35.0 inches)
Dry weight
    2008 and earlier
        US and Canada .... 134 kg (295 lbs)
        All others... 135 kg (297 lbs)
    2009 and later .... 146 kg (321 lbs)

Buying tools

A good set of tools is a fundamental requirement for servicing and repairing a motorcycle. Although there will be an initial expense in building up enough tools for servicing, this will soon be offset by the savings made by doing the job yourself. As experience and confidence grow, additional tools can be added to enable the repair and overhaul of the motorcycle. Many of the special tools are expensive and not often used so it may be preferable to rent them, or for a group of friends or motorcycle club to join in the purchase.

As a rule, it is better to buy more expensive, good quality tools. Cheaper tools are likely to wear out faster and need to be replaced more often, nullifying the original savings.

> **Warning: To avoid the risk of a poor quality tool breaking in use, causing injury or damage to the component being worked on, always aim to purchase tools which meet the relevant national safety standards.**

The following lists of tools do not represent the manufacturer's service tools, but serve as a guide to help the owner decide which tools are needed for this level of work. In addition, items such as an electric drill, hacksaw, files, soldering iron and a workbench equipped with a vise, may be needed. Although not classed as tools, a selection of bolts, screws, nuts, washers and pieces of tubing always come in useful.

For more information about tools, refer to the Haynes *Motorcycle Workshop Practice Techbook* (Bk. No. 3470).

Manufacturer's service tools

Inevitably certain tasks require the use of a service tool. Where possible an alternative tool or method of approach is recommended, but sometimes there is no option if personal injury or damage to the component is to be avoided. Where required, service tools are referred to in the relevant procedure.

Service tools can usually only be purchased from a motorcycle dealer and are identified by a part number. Some of the commonly-used tools, such as rotor pullers, are available in aftermarket form from mail-order motorcycle tool and accessory suppliers.

Maintenance and minor repair tools

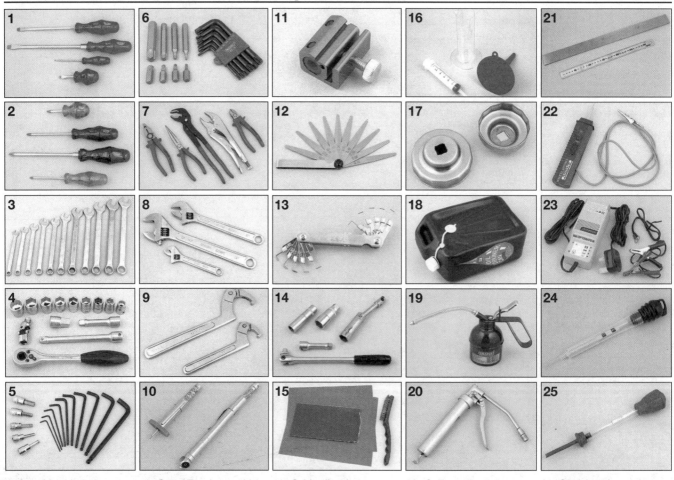

1 Set of flat-bladed screwdrivers
2 Set of Phillips head screwdrivers
3 Combination open-end and box wrenches
4 Socket set (3/8 inch or 1/2 inch drive)
5 Set of Allen keys or bits

6 Set of Torx keys or bits
7 Pliers, cutters and self-locking grips (vise grips)
8 Adjustable wrenches
9 C-spanners
10 Tread depth gauge and tire pressure gauge

11 Cable oiler clamp
12 Feeler gauges
13 Spark plug gap measuring tool
14 Spark plug wrench or deep plug sockets
15 Wire brush and emery paper

16 Calibrated syringe, measuring cup and funnel
17 Oil filter adapters
18 Oil drainer can or tray
19 Pump type oil can
20 Grease gun

21 Straight-edge and steel rule
22 Continuity tester
23 Battery charger
24 Hydrometer (for battery specific gravity check)
25 Anti-freeze tester (for liquid-cooled engines)

Repair and overhaul tools

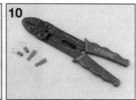

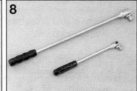

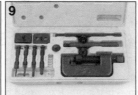

1 *Torque wrench (small and mid-ranges)*
2 *Conventional, plastic or soft-faced hammers*
3 *Impact driver set*
4 *Vernier caliper*
5 *Snap-ring pliers (internal and external, or combination)*
6 *Set of cold chisels and punches*
7 *Selection of pullers*
8 *Breaker bars*
9 *Chain breaking/ riveting tool set*
10 *Wire stripper and crimper tool*
11 *Multimeter (measures amps, volts and ohms)*
12 *Stroboscope (for dynamic timing checks)*
13 *Hose clamp (wingnut type shown)*
14 *Clutch holding tool*
15 *One-man brake/clutch bleeder kit*

Special tools

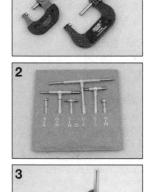
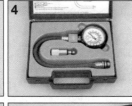

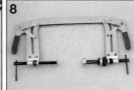
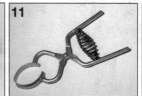

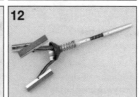

1 *Micrometers (external type)*
2 *Telescoping gauges*
3 *Dial gauge*
4 *Cylinder compression gauge*
5 *Vacuum gauges (left) or manometer (right)*
6 *Oil pressure gauge*
7 *Plastigage kit*
8 *Valve spring compressor (4-stroke engines)*
9 *Piston pin drawbolt tool*
10 *Piston ring removal and installation tool*
11 *Piston ring clamp*
12 *Cylinder bore hone (stone type shown)*
13 *Stud extractor*
14 *Screw extractor set*
15 *Bearing driver set*

1 Workshop equipment and facilities

The workbench

● Work is made much easier by raising the bike up on a ramp - components are much more accessible if raised to waist level. The hydraulic or pneumatic types seen in the dealer's workshop are a sound investment if you undertake a lot of repairs or overhauls **(see illustration 1.1)**.

1.1 Hydraulic motorcycle ramp

● If raised off ground level, the bike must be supported on the ramp to avoid it falling. Most ramps incorporate a front wheel locating clamp which can be adjusted to suit different diameter wheels. When tightening the clamp, take care not to mark the wheel rim or damage the tire - use wood blocks on each side to prevent this.
● Secure the bike to the ramp using tie-downs **(see illustration 1.2)**. If the bike has only a sidestand, and hence leans at a dangerous angle when raised, support the bike on an auxiliary stand.

1.2 Tie-downs are used around the passenger footrests to secure the bike

● Auxiliary (paddock) stands are widely available from mail order companies or motorcycle dealers and attach either to the wheel axle or swingarm pivot **(see illustration 1.3)**. If the motorcycle has a centerstand, you can support it under the crankcase to prevent it toppling while either wheel is removed **(see illustration 1.4)**.

1.3 This auxiliary stand attaches to the swingarm pivot

1.4 Always use a block of wood between the engine and jack head when supporting the engine in this way

Fumes and fire

● Refer to the Safety first! page at the beginning of the manual for full details. Make sure your workshop is equipped with a fire extinguisher suitable for fuel-related fires (Class B fire - flammable liquids) - it is not sufficient to have a water-filled extinguisher.
● Always ensure adequate ventilation is available. Unless an exhaust gas extraction system is available for use, ensure that the engine is run outside of the workshop.
● If working on the fuel system, make sure the workshop is ventilated to avoid a build-up of fumes. This applies equally to fume build-up when charging a battery. Do not smoke or allow anyone else to smoke in the workshop.

Fluids

● If you need to drain fuel from the tank, store it in an approved container marked as suitable for the storage of gasoline **(see illustration 1.5)**. Do not store fuel in glass jars

1.5 Use an approved can only for storing gasoline

or bottles.
● Use proprietary engine degreasers or solvents which have a high flash-point, such as kerosene, for cleaning off oil, grease and dirt - never use gasoline for cleaning. Wear rubber gloves when handling solvent and engine degreaser. The fumes from certain solvents can be dangerous - always work in a well-ventilated area.

Dust, eye and hand protection

● Protect your lungs from inhalation of dust particles by wearing a filtering mask over the nose and mouth. Many frictional materials still contain asbestos which is dangerous to your health. Protect your eyes from spouts of liquid and sprung components by wearing a pair of protective

1.6 A fire extinguisher, goggles, mask and protective gloves should be at hand in the workshop

goggles **(see illustration 1.6)**.
● Protect your hands from contact with solvents, fuel and oils by wearing rubber gloves. Alternatively apply a barrier cream to your hands before starting work. If handling hot components or fluids, wear suitable gloves to protect your hands from scalding and burns.

What to do with old fluids

● Old cleaning solvent, fuel, coolant and oils should not be poured down domestic drains or onto the ground. Package the fluid up in old oil containers, label it accordingly, and take it to a garage or disposal facility. Contact your local disposal company for location of such sites.

Note: It is illegal to dump oil down the drain. Check with your local auto parts store, disposal facility or environmental agency to see if they accept the oil for recycling.

2 Fasteners -
screws, bolts and nuts

Fastener types and applications

Bolts and screws

● Fastener head types are either of hexagonal, Torx or splined design, with internal and external versions of each type **(see illustrations 2.1 and 2.2)**; splined head fasteners are not in common use on motorcycles. The conventional slotted or Phillips head design is used for certain screws. Bolt or screw length is always measured from the underside of the head to the end of the item **(see illustration 2.11)**.

2.1 Internal hexagon/Allen (A), Torx (B) and splined (C) fasteners, with corresponding bits

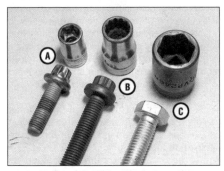

2.2 External Torx (A), splined (B) and hexagon (C) fasteners, with corresponding sockets

● Certain fasteners on the motorcycle have a tensile marking on their heads, the higher the marking the stronger the fastener. High tensile fasteners generally carry a 10 or higher marking. Never replace a high tensile fastener with one of a lower tensile strength.

Washers (see illustration 2.3)

● Plain washers are used between a fastener head and a component to prevent damage to the component or to spread the load when torque is applied. Plain washers can also be used as spacers or shims in certain assemblies. Copper or aluminum plain washers are often used as sealing washers on drain plugs.

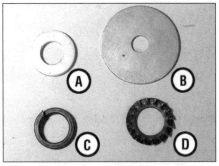

2.3 Plain washer (A), penny washer (B), spring washer (C) and serrated washer (D)

● The split-ring spring washer works by applying axial tension between the fastener head and component. If flattened, it is fatigued and must be replaced. If a plain (flat) washer is used on the fastener, position the spring washer between the fastener and the plain washer.

● Serrated star type washers dig into the fastener and component faces, preventing loosening. They are often used on electrical ground connections to the frame.

● Cone type washers (sometimes called Belleville) are conical and when tightened apply axial tension between the fastener head and component. They must be installed with the dished side against the component and often carry an OUTSIDE marking on their outer face. If flattened, they are fatigued and must be replaced.

● Tab washers are used to lock plain nuts or bolts on a shaft. A portion of the tab washer is bent up hard against one flat of the nut or bolt to prevent it loosening. Due to the tab washer being deformed in use, a new tab washer should be used every time it is removed.

● Wave washers are used to take up endfloat on a shaft. They provide light springing and prevent excessive side-to-side play of a component. Can be found on rocker arm shafts.

Nuts and cotter pins

● Conventional plain nuts are usually six-sided **(see illustration 2.4)**. They are sized by thread diameter and pitch. High tensile nuts carry a number on one end to denote their tensile strength.

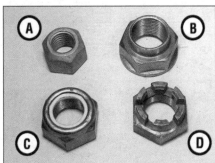

2.4 Plain nut (A), shouldered locknut (B), nylon insert nut (C) and castellated nut (D)

● Self-locking nuts either have a nylon insert, or two spring metal tabs, or a shoulder which is staked into a groove in the shaft - their advantage over conventional plain nuts is a resistance to loosening due to vibration. The nylon insert type can be used a number of times, but must be replaced when the friction of the nylon insert is reduced, i.e. when the nut spins freely on the shaft. The spring tab type can be reused unless the tabs are damaged. The shouldered type must be replaced every time it is removed.

● Cotter pins are used to lock a castellated nut to a shaft or to prevent loosening of a plain nut. Common applications are wheel axles and brake torque arms. Because the cotter pin arms are deformed to lock around the nut a new cotter pin must always be used on installation - always use the correct size cotter pin which will fit snugly in the shaft hole. Make sure the cotter pin arms are correctly located around the nut **(see illustrations 2.5 and 2.6)**.

2.5 Bend cotter pin arms as shown (arrows) to secure a castellated nut

2.6 Bend cotter pin arms as shown to secure a plain nut

Caution: If the castellated nut slots do not align with the shaft hole after tightening to the torque setting, tighten the nut until the next slot aligns with the hole - never loosen the nut to align its slot.

● R-pins (shaped like the letter R), or slip pins as they are sometimes called, are sprung and can be reused if they are otherwise in good condition. Always install R-pins with their closed end facing forwards **(see illustration 2.7)**.

**2.7 Correct fitting of R-pin.
Arrow indicates forward direction**

Snap-rings (see illustration 2.8)

● Snap-rings (sometimes called circlips) are used to retain components on a shaft or in a housing and have corresponding external or internal ears to permit removal. Parallel-sided (machined) snap-rings can be installed either way round in their groove, whereas stamped snap-rings (which have a chamfered edge on one face) must be installed with the chamfer facing away from the direction of thrust load **(see illustration 2.9)**.

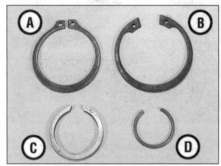

2.8 External stamped snap-ring (A), internal stamped snap-ring (B), machined snap-ring (C) and wire snap-ring (D)

● Always use snap-ring pliers to remove and install snap-rings; expand or compress them just enough to remove them. After installation, rotate the snap-ring in its groove to ensure it is securely seated. If installing a snap-ring on a splined shaft, always align its opening with a shaft channel to ensure the snap-ring ends are well supported and unlikely to catch **(see illustration 2.10)**.

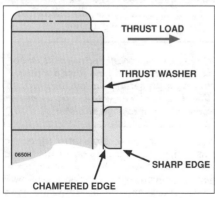

2.9 Correct fitting of a stamped snap-ring

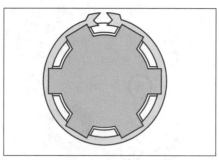

**2.10 Align snap-ring opening
with shaft channel**

● Snap-rings can wear due to the thrust of components and become loose in their grooves, with the subsequent danger of becoming dislodged in operation. For this reason, replacement is advised every time a snap-ring is disturbed.
● Wire snap-rings are commonly used as piston pin retaining clips. If a removal tang is provided, long-nosed pliers can be used to dislodge them, otherwise careful use of a small flat-bladed screwdriver is necessary. Wire snap-rings should be replaced every time they are disturbed.

Thread diameter and pitch

● Diameter of a male thread (screw, bolt or stud) is the outside diameter of the threaded portion **(see illustration 2.11)**. Most motor-cycle manufacturers use the ISO (International Standards Organization) metric system expressed in millimeters. For example, M6 refers to a 6 mm diameter thread. Sizing is the same for nuts, except that the thread diameter is measured across the valleys of the nut.
● Pitch is the distance between the peaks of the thread **(see illustration 2.11)**. It is expressed in millimeters, thus a common bolt size may be expressed as 6.0 x 1.0 mm (6 mm thread diameter and 1 mm pitch). Generally pitch increases in proportion to thread diameter, although there are always exceptions.
● Thread diameter and pitch are related for conventional fastener applications and the accompanying table can be used as a guide. Additionally, the AF (Across Flats), wrench or socket size dimension of the bolt or nut **(see illustration 2.11)** is linked to thread and pitch specification. Thread pitch can be measured with a thread gauge **(see illustration 2.12)**.

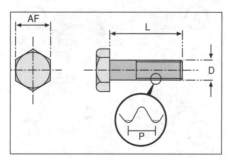

2.11 Fastener length (L), thread diameter (D), thread pitch (P) and head size (AF)

**2.12 Using a thread gauge
to measure pitch**

AF size	Thread diameter x pitch (mm)
8 mm	M5 x 0.8
8 mm	M6 x 1.0
10 mm	M6 x 1.0
12 mm	M8 x 1.25
14 mm	M10 x 1.25
17 mm	M12 x 1.25

● The threads of most fasteners are of the right-hand type, ie they are turned clockwise to tighten and counterclockwise to loosen. The reverse situation applies to left-hand thread fasteners, which are turned counter-clockwise to tighten and clockwise to loosen. Left-hand threads are used where rotation of a component might loosen a conventional right-hand thread fastener.

Seized fasteners

● Corrosion of external fasteners due to water or reaction between two dissimilar metals can occur over a period of time. It will build up sooner in wet conditions or in countries where salt is used on the roads during the winter. If a fastener is severely corroded it is likely that normal methods of removal will fail and result in its head being ruined. When you attempt removal, the fastener thread should be heard to crack free and unscrew easily - if it doesn't, stop there before damaging something.
● A smart tap on the head of the fastener will often succeed in breaking free corrosion which has occurred in the threads **(see illustration 2.13)**.
● An aerosol penetrating fluid (such as WD-40) applied the night beforehand may work its way down into the thread and ease removal. Depending on the location, you may be able to make up a modeling-clay well around the fastener head and fill it with penetrating fluid.

2.13 A sharp tap on the head of a fastener will often break free a corroded thread

● If you are working on an engine internal component, corrosion will most likely not be a problem due to the well lubricated environment. However, components can be very tight and an impact driver is a useful tool in freeing them **(see illustration 2.14)**.

2.14 Using an impact driver to free a fastener

● Where corrosion has occurred between dissimilar metals (e.g. steel and aluminum alloy), the application of heat to the fastener head will create a disproportionate expansion rate between the two metals and break the seizure caused by the corrosion. Whether heat can be applied depends on the location of the fastener - any surrounding components likely to be damaged must first be removed **(see illustration 2.15)**. Heat can be applied using a paint stripper heat gun or clothes iron, or by immersing the component in boiling water - wear protective gloves to prevent scalding or burns to the hands.

2.15 Using heat to free a seized fastener

● As a last resort, it is possible to use a hammer and cold chisel to work the fastener head unscrewed **(see illustration 2.16)**. This will damage the fastener, but more importantly extreme care must be taken not to damage the surrounding component.

> *Caution: Remember that the component being secured is generally of more value than the bolt, nut or screw - when the fastener is freed, do not unscrew it with force, instead work the fastener back and forth when resistance is felt to prevent thread damage.*

2.16 Using a hammer and chisel to free a seized fastener

Broken fasteners and damaged heads

● If the shank of a broken bolt or screw is accessible you can grip it with self-locking grips. The knurled wheel type stud extractor tool or self-gripping stud puller tool is particularly useful for removing the long studs which screw into the cylinder mouth surface of the crankcase or bolts and screws from which the head has broken off **(see illustration 2.17)**. Studs can also be removed by locking two nuts together on the threaded end of the stud and using a wrench on the lower nut **(see illustration 2.18)**.

2.17 Using a stud extractor tool to remove a broken crankcase stud

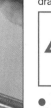

2.18 Two nuts can be locked together to unscrew a stud from a component

● A bolt or screw which has broken off below or level with the casing must be extracted using a screw extractor set. Centerpunch the fastener to centralize the drill bit, then drill a hole in the fastener **(see illustration 2.19)**. Select a drill bit which is approximately half

2.19 When using a screw extractor, first drill a hole in the fastener . . .

to three-quarters the diameter of the fastener and drill to a depth which will accommodate the extractor. Use the largest size extractor possible, but avoid leaving too small a wall thickness otherwise the extractor will merely force the fastener walls outwards wedging it in the casing thread.

● If a spiral type extractor is used, thread it counterclockwise into the fastener. As it is screwed in, it will grip the fastener and unscrew it from the casing **(see illustration 2.20)**.

2.20 . . . then thread the extractor counterclockwise into the fastener

● If a taper type extractor is used, tap it into the fastener so that it is firmly wedged in place. Unscrew the extractor (counter-clockwise) to draw the fastener out.

> ⚠ *Warning: Stud extractors are very hard and may break off in the fastener if care is not taken - ask a machine shop about spark erosion if this happens.*

● Alternatively, the broken bolt/screw can be drilled out and the hole retapped for an oversize bolt/screw or a diamond-section thread insert. It is essential that the drilling is carried out squarely and to the correct depth, otherwise the casing may be ruined - if in doubt, entrust the work to a machine shop.
● Bolts and nuts with rounded corners cause the correct size wrench or socket to slip when force is applied. Of the types of wrench/socket available always use a six-point type rather than an eight or twelve-point type - better grip

2.21 Comparison of surface drive box wrench (left) with 12-point type (right)

is obtained. Surface drive wrenches grip the middle of the hex flats, rather than the corners, and are thus good in cases of damaged heads **(see illustration 2.21)**.

● Slotted-head or Phillips-head screws are often damaged by the use of the wrong size screwdriver. Allen-head and Torx-head screws are much less likely to sustain damage. If enough of the screw head is exposed you can use a hacksaw to cut a slot in its head and then use a conventional flat-bladed screwdriver to remove it. Alternatively use a hammer and cold chisel to tap the head of the fastener around to loosen it. Always replace damaged fasteners with new ones, preferably Torx or Allen-head type.

HAYNES
HiNT

A dab of valve grinding compound between the screw head and screwdriver tip will often give a good grip.

Thread repair

● Threads (particularly those in aluminum alloy components) can be damaged by overtightening, being assembled with dirt in the threads, or from a component working loose and vibrating. Eventually the thread will fail completely, and it will be impossible to tighten the fastener.

● If a thread is damaged or clogged with old locking compound it can be renovated with a thread repair tool (thread chaser) **(see illustrations 2.22 and 2.23)**; special thread

2.22 A thread repair tool being used to correct an internal thread

2.23 A thread repair tool being used to correct an external thread

chasers are available for spark plug hole threads. The tool will not cut a new thread, but clean and true the original thread. Make sure that you use the correct diameter and pitch tool. Similarly, external threads can be cleaned up with a die or a thread restorer file **(see illustration 2.24)**.

2.24 Using a thread restorer file

● It is possible to drill out the old thread and retap the component to the next thread size. This will work where there is enough surrounding material and a new bolt or screw can be obtained. Sometimes, however, this is not possible - such as where the bolt/screw passes through another component which must also be suitably modified, also in cases where a spark plug or oil drain plug cannot be obtained in a larger diameter thread size.

● The diamond-section thread insert (often known by its popular trade name of Heli-Coil) is a simple and effective method of replacing the thread and retaining the original size. A kit can be purchased which contains the tap, insert and installing tool **(see illustration 2.25)**. Drill out the damaged thread with the size drill specified **(see illustration 2.26)**. Carefully retap the thread **(see illustration 2.27)**. Install the

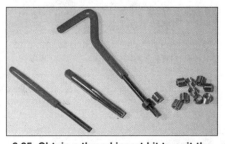

2.25 Obtain a thread insert kit to suit the thread diameter and pitch required

2.26 To install a thread insert, first drill out the original thread . . .

2.27 . . . tap a new thread . . .

2.28 . . . fit insert on the installing tool . . .

2.29 . . . and thread into the component . . .

2.30 . . . break off the tang when complete

insert on the installing tool and thread it slowly into place using a light downward pressure **(see illustrations 2.28 and 2.29)**. When positioned between a 1/4 and 1/2 turn below the surface withdraw the installing tool and use the break-off tool to press down on the tang, breaking it off **(see illustration 2.30)**.

● There are epoxy thread repair kits on the market which can rebuild stripped internal threads, although this repair should not be used on high load-bearing components.

Thread locking and sealing compounds

● Locking compounds are used in locations where the fastener is prone to loosening due to vibration or on important safety-related items which might cause loss of control of the motorcycle if they fail. It is also used where important fasteners cannot be secured by other means such as lockwashers or cotter pins.

● Before applying locking compound, make sure that the threads (internal and external) are clean and dry with all old compound removed. Select a compound to suit the component being secured - a non-permanent general locking and sealing type is suitable for most applications, but a high strength type is needed for permanent fixing of studs in castings. Apply a drop or two of the compound to the first few threads of the fastener, then thread it into place and tighten to the specified torque. Do not apply excessive thread locking compound otherwise the thread may be damaged on subsequent removal.

● Certain fasteners are impregnated with a dry film type coating of locking compound on their threads. Always replace this type of fastener if disturbed.

● Anti-seize compounds, such as copper-based greases, can be applied to protect threads from seizure due to extreme heat and corrosion. A common instance is spark plug threads and exhaust system fasteners.

3 Measuring tools and gauges

Feeler gauges

● Feeler gauges (or blades) are used for measuring small gaps and clearances (see illustration 3.1). They can also be used to measure endfloat (sideplay) of a component on a shaft where access is not possible with a dial gauge.

● Feeler gauge sets should be treated with care and not bent or damaged. They are etched with their size on one face. Keep them clean and very lightly oiled to prevent corrosion build-up.

3.1 Feeler gauges are used for measuring small gaps and clearances - thickness is marked on one face of gauge

● When measuring a clearance, select a gauge which is a light sliding fit between the two components. You may need to use two gauges together to measure the clearance accurately.

Micrometers

● A micrometer is a precision tool capable of measuring to 0.01 or 0.001 of a millimeter. It should always be stored in its case and not in the general toolbox. It must be kept clean and never dropped, otherwise its frame or measuring anvils could be distorted resulting in inaccurate readings.

● External micrometers are used for measuring outside diameters of components and have many more applications than internal micrometers. Micrometers are available in different size ranges, typically 0 to 25 mm, 25 to 50 mm, and upwards in 25 mm steps; some large micrometers have interchangeable anvils to allow a range of measurements to be taken. Generally the largest precision measurement you are likely to take on a motorcycle is the piston diameter.

● Internal micrometers (or bore micrometers) are used for measuring inside diameters, such as valve guides and cylinder bores. Telescoping gauges and small hole gauges are used in conjunction with an external micrometer, whereas the more expensive internal micrometers have their own measuring device.

External micrometer

Note: *The conventional analogue type instrument is described. Although much easier to read, digital micrometers are considerably more expensive.*

● Always check the calibration of the micrometer before use. With the anvils closed (0 to 25 mm type) or set over a test gauge

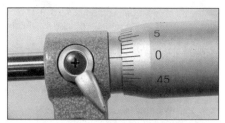

3.2 Check micrometer calibration before use

(for the larger types) the scale should read zero **(see illustration 3.2)**; make sure that the anvils (and test piece) are clean first. Any discrepancy can be adjusted by referring to the instructions supplied with the tool. Remember that the micrometer is a precision measuring tool - don't force the anvils closed, use the ratchet (4) on the end of the micrometer to close it. In this way, a measured force is always applied.

● To use, first make sure that the item being measured is clean. Place the anvil of the micrometer (1) against the item and use the thimble (2) to bring the spindle (3) lightly into contact with the other side of the item **(see illustration 3.3)**. Don't tighten the thimble down because this will damage the micrometer - instead use the ratchet (4) on the end of the micrometer. The ratchet mechanism applies a measured force preventing damage to the instrument.

● The micrometer is read by referring to the linear scale on the sleeve and the annular scale on the thimble. Read off the sleeve first to obtain the base measurement, then add the fine measurement from the thimble to obtain the overall reading. The linear scale on the sleeve represents the measuring range of the micrometer (eg 0 to 25 mm). The annular scale

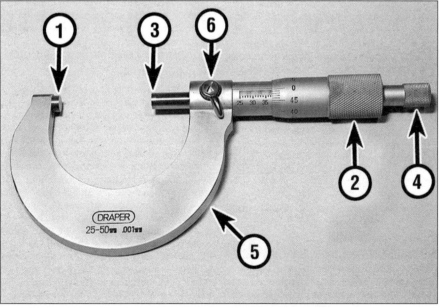

3.3 Micrometer component parts

1	Anvil	3	Spindle	5	Frame
2	Thimble	4	Ratchet	6	Locking lever

on the thimble will be in graduations of 0.01 mm (or as marked on the frame) - one full revolution of the thimble will move 0.5 mm on the linear scale. Take the reading where the datum line on the sleeve intersects the thimble's scale. Always position the eye directly above the scale otherwise an inaccurate reading will result.

In the example shown the item measures 2.95 mm **(see illustration 3.4)**:

Linear scale	2.00 mm
Linear scale	0.50 mm
Annular scale	0.45 mm
Total figure	**2.95 mm**

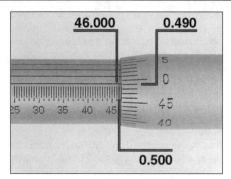
3.5 Micrometer reading of 46.99 mm on linear and annular scales . . .

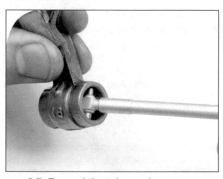
3.7 Expand the telescoping gauge in the bore, lock its position . . .

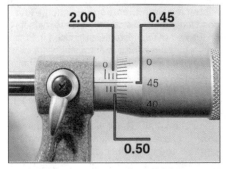
3.4 Micrometer reading of 2.95 mm

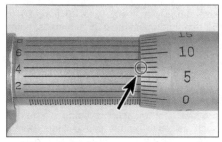
3.6 . . . and 0.004 mm on vernier scale

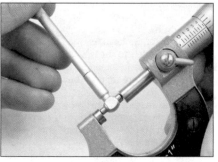
3.8 . . . then measure the gauge with a micrometer

Most micrometers have a locking lever (6) on the frame to hold the setting in place, allowing the item to be removed from the micrometer.
● Some micrometers have a vernier scale on their sleeve, providing an even finer measurement to be taken, in 0.001 increments of a millimeter. Take the sleeve and thimble measurement as described above, then check which graduation on the vernier scale aligns with that of the annular scale on the thimble **Note:** *The eye must be perpendicular to the scale when taking the vernier reading - if necessary rotate the body of the micrometer to ensure this.* Multiply the vernier scale figure by 0.001 and add it to the base and fine measurement figures.

In the example shown the item measures 46.994 mm **(see illustrations 3.5 and 3.6)**:

Linear scale (base)	46.000 mm
Linear scale (base)	00.500 mm
Annular scale (fine)	00.490 mm
Vernier scale	00.004 mm
Total figure	**46.994 mm**

Internal micrometer

● Internal micrometers are available for measuring bore diameters, but are expensive and unlikely to be available for home use. It is suggested that a set of telescoping gauges and small hole gauges, both of which must be used with an external micrometer, will suffice for taking internal measurements on a motorcycle.
● Telescoping gauges can be used to

measure internal diameters of components. Select a gauge with the correct size range, make sure its ends are clean and insert it into the bore. Expand the gauge, then lock its position and withdraw it from the bore **(see illustration 3.7)**. Measure across the gauge ends with a micrometer **(see illustration 3.8)**.
● Very small diameter bores (such as valve guides) are measured with a small hole gauge. Once adjusted to a slip-fit inside the component, its position is locked and the gauge withdrawn for measurement with a micrometer **(see illustrations 3.9 and 3.10)**.

Vernier caliper

Note: *The conventional linear and dial gauge type instruments are described. Digital types are easier to read, but are far more expensive.*
● The vernier caliper does not provide the precision of a micrometer, but is versatile in being able to measure internal and external diameters. Some types also incorporate a depth gauge. It is ideal for measuring clutch plate friction material and spring free lengths.
● To use the conventional linear scale vernier, loosen off the vernier clamp screws (1) and set its jaws over (2), or inside (3), the item to be measured **(see illustration 3.11)**. Slide the jaw into contact, using the thumb-wheel (4) for fine movement of the sliding scale (5) then tighten the clamp screws (1). Read off the main scale (6) where the zero on the sliding scale (5) intersects it, taking the whole number to the left of the zero; this provides the base measurement. View along the sliding scale and select the division which lines up exactly

3.9 Expand the small hole gauge in the bore, lock its position . . .

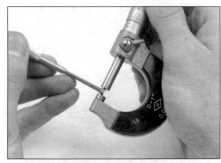
3.10 . . . then measure the gauge with a micrometer

with any of the divisions on the main scale, noting that the divisions usually represents 0.02 of a millimeter. Add this fine measurement to the base measurement to obtain the total reading.

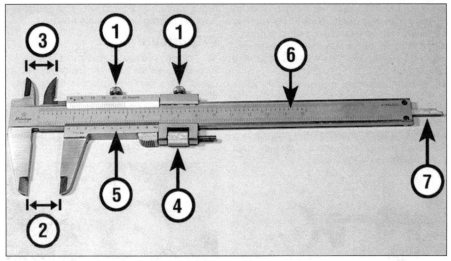

3.11 Vernier component parts (linear gauge)

1 Clamp screws
2 External jaws
3 Internal jaws
4 Thumbwheel
5 Sliding scale
6 Main scale
7 Depth gauge

In the example shown the item measures 55.92 mm **(see illustration 3.12)**:

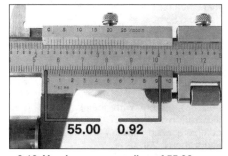

3.12 Vernier gauge reading of 55.92 mm

Base measurement	55.00 mm
Fine measurement	00.92 mm
Total figure	**55.92 mm**

● Some vernier calipers are equipped with a dial gauge for fine measurement. Before use, check that the jaws are clean, then close them fully and check that the dial gauge reads zero. If necessary adjust the gauge ring accordingly. Slacken the vernier clamp screw (1) and set its jaws over (2), or inside (3), the item to be measured **(see illustration 3.13)**. Slide the jaws into contact, using the thumbwheel (4) for fine movement. Read off the main scale (5) where the edge of the sliding scale (6) intersects it, taking the whole number to the left of the zero; this provides the base measurement. Read off the needle position on the dial gauge (7) scale to provide the fine measurement; each division represents 0.05 of a millimeter. Add this fine measurement to the base measurement to obtain the total reading.

In the example shown the item measures 55.95 mm **(see illustration 3.14)**:

Base measurement	55.00 mm
Fine measurement	00.95 mm
Total figure	**55.95 mm**

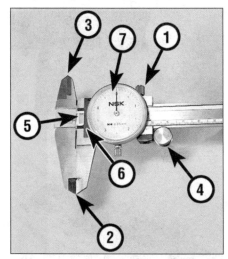

3.13 Vernier component parts (dial gauge)

1 Clamp screw
2 External jaws
3 Internal jaws
4 Thumbwheel
5 Main scale
6 Sliding scale
7 Dial gauge

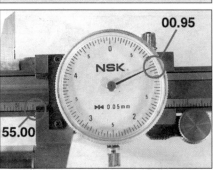

3.14 Vernier gauge reading of 55.95 mm

Plastigage

● Plastigage is a plastic material which can be compressed between two surfaces to measure the oil clearance between them. The width of the compressed Plastigage is measured against a calibrated scale to determine the clearance.

● Common uses of Plastigage are for measuring the clearance between crankshaft journal and main bearing inserts, between crankshaft journal and big-end bearing inserts, and between camshaft and bearing surfaces. The following example describes big-end oil clearance measurement.

● Handle the Plastigage material carefully to prevent distortion. Using a sharp knife, cut a length which corresponds with the width of the bearing being measured and place it carefully across the journal so that it is parallel with the shaft **(see illustration 3.15)**. Carefully install both bearing shells and the connecting rod. Without rotating the rod on the journal tighten its bolts or nuts (as applicable) to the specified torque. The connecting rod and bearings are then disassembled and the crushed Plastigage examined.

3.15 Plastigage placed across shaft journal

● Using the scale provided in the Plastigage kit, measure the width of the material to determine the oil clearance **(see illustration 3.16)**. Always remove all traces of Plastigage after use using your fingernails.

Caution: Arriving at the correct clearance demands that the assembly is torqued correctly, according to the settings and sequence (where applicable) provided by the motorcycle manufacturer.

3.16 Measuring the width of the crushed Plastigage

Dial gauge or DTI (Dial Test Indicator)

● A dial gauge can be used to accurately measure small amounts of movement. Typical uses are measuring shaft runout or shaft endfloat (sideplay) and setting piston position for ignition timing on two-strokes. A dial gauge set usually comes with a range of different probes and adapters and mounting equipment.

● The gauge needle must point to zero when at rest. Rotate the ring around its periphery to zero the gauge.

● Check that the gauge is capable of reading the extent of movement in the work. Most gauges have a small dial set in the face which records whole millimeters of movement as well as the fine scale around the face periphery which is calibrated in 0.01 mm divisions. Read off the small dial first to obtain the base measurement, then add the measurement from the fine scale to obtain the total reading.

Base measurement	1.00 mm
Fine measurement	0.48 mm
Total figure	**1.48 mm**

3.17 Dial gauge reading of 1.48 mm

In the example shown the gauge reads 1.48 mm **(see illustration 3.17)**:

● If measuring shaft runout, the shaft must be supported in vee-blocks and the gauge mounted on a stand perpendicular to the shaft. Rest the tip of the gauge against the center of the shaft and rotate the shaft slowly while watching the gauge reading **(see illustration 3.18)**. Take several measurements along the length of the shaft and record the

3.18 Using a dial gauge to measure shaft runout

maximum gauge reading as the amount of runout in the shaft. **Note:** *The reading obtained will be total runout at that point - some manufacturers specify that the runout figure is halved to compare with their specified runout limit.*

● Endfloat (sideplay) measurement requires that the gauge is mounted securely to the surrounding component with its probe touching the end of the shaft. Using hand pressure, push and pull on the shaft noting the maximum endfloat recorded on the gauge **(see illustration 3.19)**.

3.19 Using a dial gauge to measure shaft endfloat

● A dial gauge with suitable adapters can be used to determine piston position BTDC on two-stroke engines for the purposes of ignition timing. The gauge, adapter and suitable length probe are installed in the place of the spark plug and the gauge zeroed at TDC. If the piston position is specified as 1.14 mm BTDC, rotate the engine back to 2.00 mm BTDC, then slowly forwards to 1.14 mm BTDC.

Cylinder compression gauges

● A compression gauge is used for measuring cylinder compression. Either the rubber-cone type or the threaded adapter type can be used. The latter is preferred to ensure a perfect seal against the cylinder head. A 0 to 300 psi (0 to 20 Bar) type gauge (for gasoline engines) will be suitable for motorcycles.

● The spark plug is removed and the gauge either held hard against the cylinder head (cone type) or the gauge adapter screwed into the cylinder head (threaded type) **(see illustration 3.20)**. Cylinder compression is measured with the engine turning over, but not running - carry out the compression test as described in

3.20 Using a rubber-cone type cylinder compression gauge

Troubleshooting Equipment. The gauge will hold the reading until manually released.

Oil pressure gauge

● An oil pressure gauge is used for measuring engine oil pressure. Most gauges come with a set of adapters to fit the thread of the take-off point **(see illustration 3.21)**. If the take-off point specified by the motorcycle manufacturer is an external oil pipe union, make sure that the specified replacement union is used to prevent oil starvation.

3.21 Oil pressure gauge and take-off point adapter (arrow)

● Oil pressure is measured with the engine running (at a specific rpm) and often the manufacturer will specify pressure limits for a cold and hot engine.

Straight-edge and surface plate

● If checking the gasket face of a component for warpage, place a steel rule or precision straight-edge across the gasket face and measure any gap between the straight-edge and component with feeler gauges **(see illustration 3.22)**. Check diagonally across the component and between mounting holes **(see illustration 3.23)**.

3.22 Use a straight-edge and feeler gauges to check for warpage

3.23 Check for warpage in these directions

● Checking individual components for warpage, such as clutch plain (metal) plates, requires a perfectly flat plate or piece of plate glass and feeler gauges.

4 Torque and leverage

What is torque?

● Torque describes the twisting force around a shaft. The amount of torque applied is determined by the distance from the center of the shaft to the end of the lever and the amount of force being applied to the end of the lever; distance multiplied by force equals torque.

● The manufacturer applies a measured torque to a bolt or nut to ensure that it will not loosen in use and to hold two components securely together without movement in the joint. The actual torque setting depends on the thread size, bolt or nut material and the composition of the components being held.

● Too little torque may cause the fastener to loosen due to vibration, whereas too much torque will distort the joint faces of the component or cause the fastener to shear off. Always stick to the specified torque setting.

Using a torque wrench

● Check the calibration of the torque wrench and make sure it has a suitable range for the job. Torque wrenches are available in Nm (Newton-meters), kgf m (kilograms-force meter), lbf ft (pounds-feet), lbf in (inch-pounds). Do not confuse lbf ft with lbf in.

● Adjust the tool to the desired torque on the scale (see illustration 4.1). If your torque wrench is not calibrated in the units specified, carefully convert the figure (see Conversion Factors). A manufacturer sometimes gives a torque setting as a range (8 to 10 Nm) rather than a single figure - in this case set the tool midway between the two settings. The same torque may be expressed as 9 Nm ± 1 Nm. Some torque wrenches have a method of locking the setting so that it isn't inadvertently altered during use.

4.1 Set the torque wrench index mark to the setting required, in this case 12 Nm

● Install the bolts/nuts in their correct location and secure them lightly. Their threads must be clean and free of any old locking compound. Unless specified the threads and flange should be dry - oiled threads are necessary in certain circumstances and the manufacturer will take this into account in the specified torque figure. Similarly, the manufacturer may also specify the application of thread-locking compound.

● Tighten the fasteners in the specified sequence until the torque wrench clicks, indicating that the torque setting has been reached. Apply the torque again to double-check the setting. Where different thread diameter fasteners secure the component, as a rule tighten the larger diameter ones first.

● When the torque wrench has been finished with, release the lock (where applicable) and fully back off its setting to zero - do not leave the torque wrench tensioned. Also, do not use a torque wrench for loosening a fastener.

Angle-tightening

● Manufacturers often specify a figure in degrees for final tightening of a fastener. This usually follows tightening to a specific torque setting.

● A degree disc can be set and attached to the socket (see illustration 4.2) or a protractor can be used to mark the angle of movement on the bolt/nut head and the surrounding casting (see illustration 4.3).

4.2 Angle tightening can be accomplished with a torque-angle gauge . . .

4.3 . . . or by marking the angle on the surrounding component

Loosening sequences

● Where more than one bolt/nut secures a component, loosen each fastener evenly a little at a time. In this way, not all the stress of the joint is held by one fastener and the components are not likely to distort.

● If a tightening sequence is provided, work in the REVERSE of this, but if not, work from the outside in, in a criss-cross sequence (see illustration 4.4).

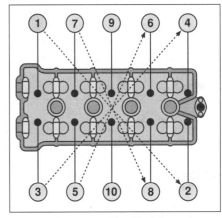

4.4 When loosening, work from the outside inwards

Tightening sequences

● If a component is held by more than one fastener it is important that the retaining bolts/nuts are tightened evenly to prevent uneven stress build-up and distortion of sealing faces. This is especially important on high-compression joints such as the cylinder head.

● A sequence is usually provided by the manufacturer, either in a diagram or actually marked in the casting. If not, always start in the center and work outwards in a criss-cross pattern (see illustration 4.5). Start off by securing all bolts/nuts finger-tight, then set the torque wrench and tighten each fastener by a small amount in sequence until the final torque is reached. By following this practice,

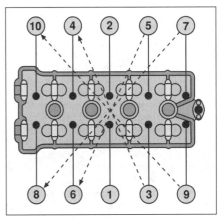

4.5 When tightening, work from the inside outwards

the joint will be held evenly and will not be distorted. Important joints, such as the cylinder head and big-end fasteners often have two- or three-stage torque settings.

Applying leverage

● Use tools at the correct angle. Position a socket or wrench on the bolt/nut so that you pull it towards you when loosening. If this can't be done, push the wrench without curling your fingers around it **(see illustration 4.6)** - the wrench may slip or the fastener loosen suddenly, resulting in your fingers being crushed against a component.

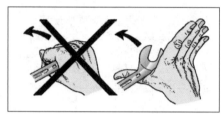

4.6 If you can't pull on the wrench to loosen a fastener, push with your hand open

● Additional leverage is gained by extending the length of the lever. The best way to do this is to use a breaker bar instead of the regular length tool, or to slip a length of tubing over the end of the wrench or socket.
● If additional leverage will not work, the fastener head is either damaged or firmly corroded in place (see *Fasteners*).

5 Bearings

Bearing removal and installation

Drivers and sockets

● Before removing a bearing, always inspect the casing to see which way it must be driven out - some casings will have retaining plates or a cast step. Also check for any identifying markings on the bearing and, if installed to a certain depth, measure this at this stage. Some roller bearings are sealed on one side - take note of the original installed position.
● Bearings can be driven out of a casing using a bearing driver tool (with the correct size head) or a socket of the correct diameter. Select the driver head or socket so that it contacts the outer race of the bearing, not the balls/rollers or inner race. Always support the casing around the bearing housing with wood blocks, otherwise there is a risk of fracture. The bearing is driven out with a few blows on the driver or socket from a heavy mallet. Unless access is severely restricted (as with wheel bearings), a pin-punch is not recommended unless it is moved around the bearing to keep it square in its housing.

● The same equipment can be used to install bearings. Make sure the bearing housing is supported on wood blocks and line up the bearing in its housing. Install the bearing as noted on removal - generally they are installed with their marked side facing outwards. Tap the bearing squarely into its housing using a driver or socket which bears only on the bearing's outer race - contact with the bearing balls/rollers or inner race will destroy it **(see illustrations 5.1 and 5.2)**.
● Check that the bearing inner race and balls/rollers rotate freely.

5.1 Using a bearing driver against the bearing's outer race

5.2 Using a large socket against the bearing's outer race

Pullers and slide-hammers

● Where a bearing is pressed on a shaft a puller will be required to extract it **(see illustration 5.3)**. Make sure that the puller clamp or legs fit securely behind the bearing and are unlikely to slip out. If pulling a bearing

5.3 This bearing puller clamps behind the bearing and pressure is applied to the shaft end to draw the bearing off

off a gear shaft for example, you may have to locate the puller behind a gear pinion if there is no access to the race and draw the gear pinion off the shaft as well **(see illustration 5.4)**.

> **Caution: Ensure that the puller's center bolt locates securely against the end of the shaft and will not slip when pressure is applied. Also ensure that puller does not damage the shaft end.**

5.4 Where no access is available to the rear of the bearing, it is sometimes possible to draw off the adjacent component

● Operate the puller so that its center bolt exerts pressure on the shaft end and draws the bearing off the shaft.
● When installing the bearing on the shaft, tap only on the bearing's inner race - contact with the balls/rollers or outer race will destroy the bearing. Use a socket or length of tubing as a drift which fits over the shaft end **(see illustration 5.5)**.

5.5 When installing a bearing on a shaft use a piece of tubing which bears only on the bearing's inner race

● Where a bearing locates in a blind hole in a casing, it cannot be driven or pulled out as described above. A slide-hammer with knife-edged bearing puller attachment will be required. The puller attachment passes through the bearing and when tightened expands to fit firmly behind the bearing **(see illustration 5.6)**. By operating the slide-hammer part of the tool the bearing is jarred out of its housing **(see illustration 5.7)**.
● It is possible, if the bearing is of reasonable weight, for it to drop out of its housing if the casing is heated as described opposite. If

5.6 Expand the bearing puller so that it locks behind the bearing . . .

5.7 . . . attach the slide hammer to the bearing puller

this method is attempted, first prepare a work surface which will enable the casing to be tapped face down to help dislodge the bearing - a wood surface is ideal since it will not damage the casing's gasket surface. Wearing protective gloves, tap the heated casing several times against the work surface to dislodge the bearing under its own weight **(see illustration 5.8)**.

5.8 Tapping a casing face down on wood blocks can often dislodge a bearing

● Bearings can be installed in blind holes using the driver or socket method described above.

Drawbolts

● Where a bearing or bushing is set in the eye of a component, such as a suspension linkage arm or connecting rod small-end, removal by drift may damage the component. Furthermore, a rubber bushing in a shock absorber eye cannot successfully be driven out of position. If access is available to a hydraulic press, the task is straightforward. If not, a drawbolt can be fabricated to extract the bearing or bushing.

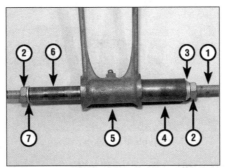

5.9 Drawbolt component parts assembled on a suspension arm

1   Bolt or length of threaded bar
2   Nuts
3   Washer (external diameter greater than tubing internal diameter)
4   Tubing (internal diameter sufficient to accommodate bearing)
5   Suspension arm with bearing
6   Tubing (external diameter slightly smaller than bearing)
7   Washer (external diameter slightly smaller than bearing)

5.10 Drawing the bearing out of the suspension arm

● To extract the bearing/bushing you will need a long bolt with nut (or piece of threaded bar with two nuts), a piece of tubing which has an internal diameter larger than the bearing/bushing, another piece of tubing which has an external diameter slightly smaller than the bearing/bushing, and a selection of washers **(see illustrations 5.9 and 5.10)**. Note that the pieces of tubing must be of the same length, or longer, than the bearing/bushing.
● The same kit (without the pieces of tubing) can be used to draw the new bearing/bushing back into place **(see illustration 5.11)**.

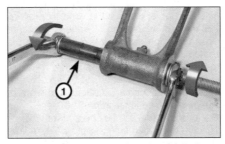

5.11 Installing a new bearing (1) in the suspension arm

Temperature change

● If the bearing's outer race is a tight fit in the casing, the aluminum casing can be heated to release its grip on the bearing. Aluminum will expand at a greater rate than the steel bearing outer race. There are several ways to do this, but avoid any localized extreme heat (such as a blow torch) - aluminum alloy has a low melting point.
● Approved methods of heating a casing are using a domestic oven (heated to 100°C/200°F) or immersing the casing in boiling water **(see illustration 5.12)**. Low temperature range localized heat sources such as a paint stripper heat gun or clothes iron can also be used **(see illustration 5.13)**. Alternatively, soak a rag in boiling water, wring it out and wrap it around the bearing housing.

> ⚠ **Warning: All of these methods require care in use to prevent scalding and burns to the hands. Wear protective gloves when handling hot components.**

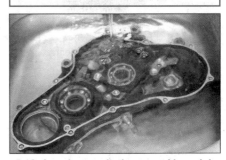

5.12 A casing can be immersed in a sink of boiling water to aid bearing removal

5.13 Using a localized heat source to aid bearing removal

● If heating the whole casing note that plastic components, such as the neutral switch, may suffer - remove them beforehand.
● After heating, remove the bearing as described above. You may find that the expansion is sufficient for the bearing to fall out of the casing under its own weight or with a light tap on the driver or socket.
● If necessary, the casing can be heated to aid bearing installation, and this is sometimes the recommended procedure if the motorcycle manufacturer has designed the housing and bearing fit with this intention.

● Installation of bearings can be eased by placing them in a freezer the night before installation. The steel bearing will contract slightly, allowing easy insertion in its housing. This is often useful when installing steering head outer races in the frame.

Bearing types and markings

● Plain shell bearings, ball bearings, needle roller bearings and tapered roller bearings will all be found on motorcycles (see illustrations 5.14 and 5.15). The ball and roller types are usually caged between an inner and outer race, but uncaged variations may be found.

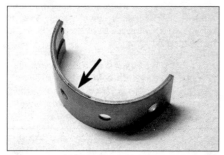

5.14 Shell bearings are either plain or grooved. They are usually identified by color code (arrow)

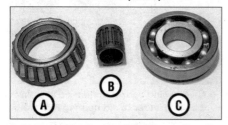

5.15 Tapered roller bearing (A), needle roller bearing (B) and ball journal bearing (C)

● Shell bearings (often called inserts) are usually found at the crankshaft main and connecting rod big-end where they are good at coping with high loads. They are made of a phosphor-bronze material and are impregnated with self-lubricating properties.

● Ball bearings and needle roller bearings consist of a steel inner and outer race with the balls or rollers between the races. They require constant lubrication by oil or grease and are good at coping with axial loads. Taper roller bearings consist of rollers set in a tapered cage set on the inner race; the outer race is separate. They are good at coping with axial loads and prevent movement along the shaft - a typical application is in the steering head.

● Bearing manufacturers produce bearings to ISO size standards and stamp one face of the bearing to indicate its internal and external diameter, load capacity and type (see illustration 5.16).

● Metal bushings are usually of phosphor-bronze material. Rubber bushings are used in suspension mounting eyes. Fiber bushings have also been used in suspension pivots.

5.16 Typical bearing marking

Bearing troubleshooting

● If a bearing outer race has spun in its housing, the housing material will be damaged. You can use a bearing locking compound to bond the outer race in place if damage is not too severe.

● Shell bearings will fail due to damage of their working surface, as a result of lack of lubrication, corrosion or abrasive particles in the oil (see illustration 5.17). Small particles of dirt in the oil may embed in the bearing material whereas larger particles will score the bearing and shaft journal. If a number of short journeys are made, insufficient heat will be generated to drive off condensation which has built up on the bearings.

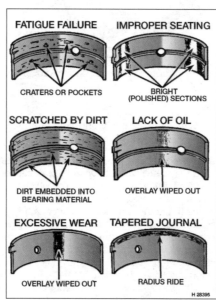

5.17 Typical bearing failures

● Ball and roller bearings will fail due to lack of lubrication or damage to the balls or rollers. Tapered-roller bearings can be damaged by overloading them. Unless the bearing is sealed on both sides, wash it in kerosene to remove all old grease then allow it to dry. Make a visual inspection looking to dented balls or rollers, damaged cages and worn or pitted races (see illustration 5.18).

● A ball bearing can be checked for wear by listening to it when spun. Apply a film of light oil to the bearing and hold it close to the ear - hold the outer race with one hand and spin the

5.18 Example of ball journal bearing with damaged balls and cages

5.19 Hold outer race and listen to inner race when spun

inner race with the other hand (see illustration 5.19). The bearing should be almost silent when spun; if it grates or rattles it is worn.

6 Oil seals

Oil seal removal and installation

● Oil seals should be replaced every time a component is dismantled. This is because the seal lips will become set to the sealing surface and will not necessarily reseal.

● Oil seals can be pried out of position using a large flat-bladed screwdriver (see illustration 6.1). In the case of crankcase seals, check first that the seal is not lipped on the inside, preventing its removal with the crankcases joined.

6.1 Pry out oil seals with a large flat-bladed screwdriver

● New seals are usually installed with their marked face (containing the seal reference code) outwards and the spring side towards the fluid being retained. In certain cases, such as a two-stroke engine crankshaft seal, a double lipped seal may be used due to there being fluid or gas on each side of the joint.

● Use a bearing driver or socket which bears only on the outer hard edge of the seal to install it in the casing - tapping on the inner edge will damage the sealing lip.

Oil seal types and markings

● Oil seals are usually of the single-lipped type. Double-lipped seals are found where a liquid or gas is on both sides of the joint.
● Oil seals can harden and lose their sealing ability if the motorcycle has been in storage for a long period - replacement is the only solution.
● Oil seal manufacturers also conform to the ISO markings for seal size - these are molded into the outer face of the seal (see illustration 6.2).

6.2 These oil seal markings indicate inside diameter, outside diameter and seal thickness

7 Gaskets and sealants

Types of gasket and sealant

● Gaskets are used to seal the mating surfaces between components and keep lubricants, fluids, vacuum or pressure contained within the assembly. Aluminum gaskets are sometimes found at the cylinder joints, but most gaskets are paper-based. If the mating surfaces of the components being joined are undamaged the gasket can be installed dry, although a dab of sealant or grease will be useful to hold it in place during assembly.
● RTV (Room Temperature Vulcanizing) silicone rubber sealants cure when exposed to moisture in the atmosphere. These sealants are good at filling pits or irregular gasket faces, but will tend to be forced out of the joint under very high torque. They can be used to replace a paper gasket, but first make sure that the width of the paper gasket is not essential to the shimming of internal components. RTV sealants should not be used on components containing gasoline.
● Non-hardening, semi-hardening and hard setting liquid gasket compounds can be used with a gasket or between a metal-to-metal joint. Select the sealant to suit the application: universal non-hardening sealant can be used on virtually all joints; semi-hardening on joint faces which are rough or damaged; hard setting sealant on joints which require a permanent bond and are subjected to high temperature and pressure. **Note:** Check first if the paper gasket has a bead of sealant

impregnated in its surface before applying additional sealant.
● When choosing a sealant, make sure it is suitable for the application, particularly if being applied in a high-temperature area or in the vicinity of fuel. Certain manufacturers produce sealants in either clear, silver or black colors to match the finish of the engine. This has a particular application on motorcycles where much of the engine is exposed.
● Do not over-apply sealant. That which is squeezed out on the outside of the joint can be wiped off, whereas an excess of sealant on the inside can break off and clog oilways.

Breaking a sealed joint

● Age, heat, pressure and the use of hard setting sealant can cause two components to stick together so tightly that they are difficult to separate using finger pressure alone. Do not resort to using levers unless there is a pry point provided for this purpose (see illustration 7.1) or else the gasket surfaces will be damaged.
● Use a soft-faced hammer (see illustration 7.2) or a wood block and conventional hammer to strike the component near the mating surface. Avoid hammering against cast extremities since they may break off. If this method fails, try using a wood wedge between the two components.

Caution: If the joint will not separate, double-check that you have removed all the fasteners.

7.1 If a pry point is provided, apply gentle pressure with a flat-bladed screwdriver

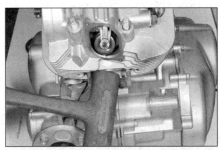

7.2 Tap around the joint with a soft-faced mallet if necessary - don't strike cooling fins

Removal of old gasket and sealant

● Paper gaskets will most likely come away complete, leaving only a few traces stuck

Most components have one or two hollow locating dowels between the two gasket faces. If a dowel cannot be removed, do not resort to gripping it with pliers - it will almost certainly be distorted. Install a close-fitting socket or Phillips screwdriver into the dowel and then grip the outer edge of the dowel to free it.

on the sealing faces of the components. It is imperative that all traces are removed to ensure correct sealing of the new gasket.
● Very carefully scrape all traces of gasket away making sure that the sealing surfaces are not gouged or scored by the scraper (see illustrations 7.3, 7.4 and 7.5). Stubborn deposits can be removed by spraying with an aerosol gasket remover. Final preparation of

7.3 Paper gaskets can be scraped off with a gasket scraper tool . . .

7.4 . . . a knife blade . . .

7.5 . . . or a household scraper

7.6 Fine abrasive paper is wrapped around a flat file to clean up the gasket face

7.7 A kitchen scourer can be used on stubborn deposits

the gasket surface can be made with very fine abrasive paper or a plastic kitchen scourer **(see illustrations 7.6 and 7.7)**.
● Old sealant can be scraped or peeled off components, depending on the type originally used. Note that gasket removal compounds are available to avoid scraping the components clean; make sure the gasket remover suits the type of sealant used.

8 Chains

Breaking and joining "endless" final drive chains

● Drive chains for many larger bikes are continuous and do not have a clip-type connecting link. The chain must be broken using a chain breaker tool and the new chain securely riveted together using a new soft rivet-type link. Never use a clip-type connecting link instead of a rivet-type link, except in an emergency. Various chain breaking and riveting tools are available, either as separate tools or combined as illustrated in the accompanying photographs - read the instructions supplied with the tool carefully.

> ⚠ **Warning: The need to rivet the new link pins correctly cannot be overstressed - loss of control of the motorcycle is very likely to result if the chain breaks in use.**

● Rotate the chain and look for the soft link. The soft link pins look like they have been

8.1 Tighten the chain breaker to push the pin out of the link . . .

8.2 . . . withdraw the pin, remove the tool . . .

8.3 . . . and separate the chain link

deeply center-punched instead of peened over like all the other pins **(see illustration 8.9)** and its sideplate may be a different color. Position the soft link midway between the sprockets and assemble the chain breaker tool over one of the soft link pins **(see illustration 8.1)**. Operate the tool to push the pin out through the chain **(see illustration 8.2)**. On an O-ring chain, remove the O-rings **(see illustration 8.3)**. Carry out the same procedure on the other soft link pin.

> *Caution: Certain soft link pins (particularly on the larger chains) may require their ends to be filed or ground off before they can be pressed out using the tool.*

● Check that you have the correct size and strength (standard or heavy duty) new soft link - do not reuse the old link. Look for the size marking on the chain sideplates **(see illustration 8.10)**.
● Position the chain ends so that they are

8.4 Insert the new soft link, with O-rings, through the chain ends . . .

8.5 . . . install the O-rings over the pin ends . . .

8.6 . . . followed by the sideplate

engaged over the rear sprocket. On an O-ring chain, install a new O-ring over each pin of the link and insert the link through the two chain ends **(see illustration 8.4)**. Install a new O-ring over the end of each pin, followed by the sideplate (with the chain manufacturer's marking facing outwards) **(see illustrations 8.5 and 8.6)**. On an unsealed chain, insert the link through the two chain ends, then install the sideplate with the chain manufacturer's marking facing outwards.
● Note that it may not be possible to install the sideplate using finger pressure alone. If using a joining tool, assemble it so that the plates of the tool clamp the link and press the sideplate over the pins **(see illustration 8.7)**. Otherwise, use two small sockets placed over

8.7 Push the sideplate into position using a clamp

8.8 Assemble the chain riveting tool over one pin at a time and tighten it fully

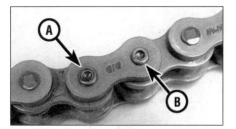

8.9 Pin end correctly riveted (A), pin end unriveted (B)

the rivet ends and two pieces of the wood between a C-clamp. Operate the clamp to press the sideplate over the pins.

● Assemble the joining tool over one pin (following the manufacturer's instructions) and tighten the tool down to spread the pin end securely **(see illustrations 8.8 and 8.9)**. Do the same on the other pin.

 Warning: Check that the pin ends are secure and that there is no danger of the sideplate coming loose. If the pin ends are cracked the soft link must be replaced.

Final drive chain sizing

● Chains are sized using a three digit number, followed by a suffix to denote the chain type **(see illustration 8.10)**. Chain type is either standard or heavy duty (thicker sideplates), and also unsealed or O-ring/X-ring type.

● The first digit of the number relates to the pitch of the chain, ie the distance from the center of one pin to the center of the next pin **(see illustration 8.11)**. Pitch is expressed in eighths of an inch, as follows:

8.10 Typical chain size and type marking

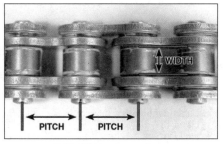

8.11 Chain dimensions

Sizes commencing with a 4 (for example 428) have a pitch of 1/2 inch (12.7 mm)

Sizes commencing with a 5 (for example 520) have a pitch of 5/8 inch (15.9 mm)

Sizes commencing with a 6 (for example 630) have a pitch of 3/4 inch (19.1 mm)

● The second and third digits of the chain size relate to the width of the rollers, for example the 525 shown has 5/16 inch (7.94 mm) rollers **(see illustration 8.11)**.

9 Hoses

Clamping to prevent flow

● Small-bore flexible hoses can be clamped to prevent fluid flow while a component is worked on. Whichever method is used, ensure that the hose material is not permanently distorted or damaged by the clamp.

a) A brake hose clamp available from auto parts stores **(see illustration 9.1)**.
b) A wingnut type hose clamp **(see illustration 9.2)**.

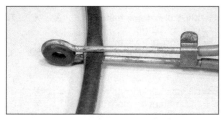

9.1 Hoses can be clamped with an automotive brake hose clamp . . .

9.2 . . . a wingnut type hose clamp . . .

c) Two sockets placed on each side of the hose and held with straight-jawed self-locking pliers **(see illustration 9.3)**.
d) Thick card stock on each side of the hose held between straight-jawed self-locking pliers **(see illustration 9.4)**.

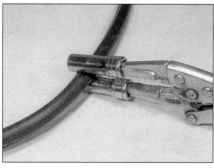

9.3 . . . two sockets and a pair of self-locking grips . . .

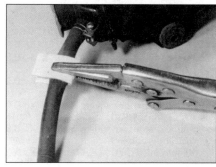

9.4 . . . or thick card and self-locking grips

Freeing and fitting hoses

● Always make sure the hose clamp is moved well clear of the hose end. Grip the hose with your hand and rotate it while pulling it off the union. If the hose has hardened due to age and will not move, slit it with a sharp knife and peel its ends off the union **(see illustration 9.5)**.

● Resist the temptation to use grease or soap on the unions to aid installation; although it helps the hose slip over the union it will equally aid the escape of fluid from the joint. It is preferable to soften the hose ends in hot water and wet the inside surface of the hose with water or a fluid which will evaporate.

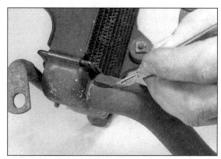

9.5 Cutting a coolant hose free with a sharp knife

Conversion Factors

Length (distance)
Inches (in)	X	25.4	= Millimeters (mm)	X 0.0394	= Inches (in)
Feet (ft)	X	0.305	= Meters (m)	X 3.281	= Feet (ft)
Miles	X	1.609	= Kilometers (km)	X 0.621	= Miles

Volume (capacity)
Cubic inches (cu in; in³)	X	16.387	= Cubic centimeters (cc; cm³)	X 0.061	= Cubic inches (cu in; in³)
Imperial pints (Imp pt)	X	0.568	= Liters (l)	X 1.76	= Imperial pints (Imp pt)
Imperial quarts (Imp qt)	X	1.137	= Liters (l)	X 0.88	= Imperial quarts (Imp qt)
Imperial quarts (Imp qt)	X	1.201	= US quarts (US qt)	X 0.833	= Imperial quarts (Imp qt)
US quarts (US qt)	X	0.946	= Liters (l)	X 1.057	= US quarts (US qt)
Imperial gallons (Imp gal)	X	4.546	= Liters (l)	X 0.22	= Imperial gallons (Imp gal)
Imperial gallons (Imp gal)	X	1.201	= US gallons (US gal)	X 0.833	= Imperial gallons (Imp gal)
US gallons (US gal)	X	3.785	= Liters (l)	X 0.264	= US gallons (US gal)

Mass (weight)
Ounces (oz)	X	28.35	= Grams (g)	X 0.035	= Ounces (oz)
Pounds (lb)	X	0.454	= Kilograms (kg)	X 2.205	= Pounds (lb)

Force
Ounces-force (ozf; oz)	X	0.278	= Newtons (N)	X 3.6	= Ounces-force (ozf; oz)
Pounds-force (lbf; lb)	X	4.448	= Newtons (N)	X 0.225	= Pounds-force (lbf; lb)
Newtons (N)	X	0.1	= Kilograms-force (kgf; kg)	X 9.81	= Newtons (N)

Pressure
Pounds-force per square inch (psi; lbf/in²; lb/in²)	X	0.070	= Kilograms-force per square centimeter (kgf/cm²; kg/cm²)	X 14.223	= Pounds-force per square inch (psi; lbf/in²; lb/in²)
Pounds-force per square inch (psi; lbf/in²; lb/in²)	X	0.068	= Atmospheres (atm)	X 14.696	= Pounds-force per square inch (psi; lbf/in²; lb/in²)
Pounds-force per square inch (psi; lbf/in²; lb/in²)	X	0.069	= Bars	X 14.5	= Pounds-force per square inch (psi; lbf/in²; lb/in²)
Pounds-force per square inch (psi; lbf/in²; lb/in²)	X	6.895	= Kilopascals (kPa)	X 0.145	= Pounds-force per square inch (psi; lbf/in²; lb/in²)
Kilopascals (kPa)	X	0.01	= Kilograms-force per square centimeter (kgf/cm²; kg/cm²)	X 98.1	= Kilopascals (kPa)

Torque (moment of force)
Pounds-force inches (lbf in; lb in)	X	1.152	= Kilograms-force centimeter (kgf cm; kg cm)	X 0.868	= Pounds-force inches (lbf in; lb in)
Pounds-force inches (lbf in; lb in)	X	0.113	= Newton meters (Nm)	X 8.85	= Pounds-force inches (lbf in; lb in)
Pounds-force inches (lbf in; lb in)	X	0.083	= Pounds-force feet (lbf ft; lb ft)	X 12	= Pounds-force inches (lbf in; lb in)
Pounds-force feet (lbf ft; lb ft)	X	0.138	= Kilograms-force meters (kgf m; kg m)	X 7.233	= Pounds-force feet (lbf ft; lb ft)
Pounds-force feet (lbf ft; lb ft)	X	1.356	= Newton meters (Nm)	X 0.738	= Pounds-force feet (lbf ft; lb ft)
Newton meters (Nm)	X	0.102	= Kilograms-force meters (kgf m; kg m)	X 9.804	= Newton meters (Nm)

Vacuum
Inches mercury (in. Hg)	X	3.377	= Kilopascals (kPa)	X 0.2961	= Inches mercury
Inches mercury (in. Hg)	X	25.4	= Millimeters mercury (mm Hg)	X 0.0394	= Inches mercury

Power
Horsepower (hp)	X	745.7	= Watts (W)	X 0.0013	= Horsepower (hp)

Velocity (speed)
Miles per hour (miles/hr; mph)	X	1.609	= Kilometers per hour (km/hr; kph)	X 0.621	= Miles per hour (miles/hr; mph)

Fuel consumption*
Miles per gallon, Imperial (mpg)	X	0.354	= Kilometers per liter (km/l)	X 2.825	= Miles per gallon, Imperial (mpg)
Miles per gallon, US (mpg)	X	0.425	= Kilometers per liter (km/l)	X 2.352	= Miles per gallon, US (mpg)

Temperature
Degrees Fahrenheit = (°C x 1.8) + 32

Degrees Celsius (Degrees Centigrade; °C) = (°F - 32) x 0.56

*It is common practice to convert from miles per gallon (mpg) to liters/100 kilometers (l/100km), where mpg (Imperial) x l/100 km = 282 and mpg (US) x l/100 km = 235

A number of chemicals and lubricants are available for use in motorcycle maintenance and repair. They include a wide variety of products ranging from cleaning solvents and degreasers to lubricants and protective sprays for rubber, plastic and vinyl.

• **Contact point/spark plug cleaner** is a solvent used to clean oily film and dirt from points, grim from electrical connectors and oil deposits from spark plugs. It is oil free and leaves no residue. It can also be used to remove gum and varnish from carburetor jets and other orifices.

• **Carburetor cleaner** is similar to contact point/spark plug cleaner but it usually has a stronger solvent and may leave a slight oily residue. It is not recommended for cleaning electrical components or connections.

• **Brake system cleaner** is used to remove brake dust, grease and brake fluid from the brake system, where clean surfaces are absolutely necessary. It leaves no residue and often eliminates brake squeal caused by contaminants.

• **Silicone-based lubricants** are used to protect rubber parts such as hoses and grommets, and are used as lubricants for hinges and locks.

• **Multi-purpose grease** is an all purpose lubricant used wherever grease is more practical than a liquid lubricant such as oil. Some multi-purpose grease is colored white and specially formulated to be more resistant to water than ordinary grease.

• **Gear oil** (sometimes called gear lube) is a specially designed oil used in transmissions and final drive units, as well as other areas where high friction, high temperature lubrication is required. It is available in a number of viscosities (weights) for various applications.

• **Motor oil** is the lubricant formulated for use in engines. It normally contains a wide variety of additives to prevent corrosion and reduce foaming and wear. Motor oil comes in various weights (viscosity ratings) from 0 to 50. The recommended weight of the oil depends on the season, temperature and the demands on the engine. Light oil is used in cold climates and under light load conditions. Heavy oil is used in hot climates and where high loads are encountered. Multi-viscosity oils are designed to have characteristics of both light and heavy oils and are available in a number of weights from 0W-20 to 20W-50.

• **Gasoline additives** perform several functions, depending on their chemical makeup. They usually contain solvents that help dissolve gum and varnish that build up on carburetor and inlet parts. They also serve to break down carbon deposits that form on the inside surfaces of the combustion chambers. Some additives contain upper cylinder lubricants for valves and piston rings.

• **Brake and clutch fluid** is a specially formulated hydraulic fluid that can withstand the heat and pressure encountered in break/clutch systems. Care must be taken that this fluid does not come in contact with painted surfaces or plastics. An opened container should always be resealed to prevent contamination by water or dirt.

• **Chain lubricants** are formulated especially for use on motorcycle final drive chains. A good chain lube should adhere well and have good penetrating qualities to be effective as a lubricant inside the chain and on the side plates, pins and rollers. Most chain lubes are either the foaming type or quick drying type and are usually marketed as sprays. Take care to use a lubricant marked as being suitable for O-ring chains.

• **Degreasers** are heavy duty solvents used to remove grease and grime that may accumulate on the engine and frame components. They can be sprayed or brushed on and, depending on the type, are rinsed with either water or solvent.

• **Solvents** are used alone or in combination with degreasers to clean parts and assemblies during repair and overhaul. The home mechanic should use only solvents that are non-flammable and that do not produce irritating fumes.

• **Gasket sealing compounds** may be used in conjunction with gaskets, to improve their sealing capabilities, or alone, to seal metal-to-metal joints. Many gasket sealers can withstand extreme heat, some are impervious to gasoline and lubricants, while others are capable of filling and sealing large cavities. Depending on the intended use, gasket sealers either dry hard or stay relatively soft and pliable. They are usually applied by hand, with a brush or are sprayed on the gasket sealing surfaces.

• **Thread locking compound** is an adhesive locking compound that prevents threaded fasteners from loosening because of vibration. It is available in a variety of types for different applications.

• **Moisture dispersants** are usually sprays that can be used to dry out electrical components such as the fuse block and wiring connectors. Some types an also be used as treatment for rubber and as a lubricant for hinges, cables and locks.

• **Waxes and polishes** are used to help protect painted and plated surfaces from the weather. Different types of pain may require the use of different types of wax polish. Some polishes utilize a chemical or abrasive cleaner to help remove the top layer of oxidized (dull) paint on older vehicles. In recent years, many non-wax polishes (that contain a wide variety of chemicals such as polymers and silicones) have been introduced. These non-wax polishes are usually easier to apply and last longer than conventional waxes and polishes.

Preparing for storage

Before you start

If repairs or an overhaul is needed, see that this is carried out now rather than left until you want to ride the bike again.

Give the bike a good wash and scrub all dirt from its underside. Make sure the bike dries completely before preparing for storage.

Engine

● Remove the spark plug(s) and lubricate the cylinder bores with approximately a teaspoon of motor oil using a spout-type oil can **(see illustration 1)**. Reinstall the spark plug(s). Crank the engine over a couple of times to coat the piston rings and bores with oil. If the bike has a kickstart, use this to turn the engine over. If not, flick the kill switch to the OFF position and crank the engine over on the starter **(see illustration 2)**. If the nature of the ignition system prevents the starter operating with the kill switch in the OFF position, remove the spark plugs and fit them back in their caps; ensure that the plugs are grounded against the cylinder head when the starter is operated **(see illustration 3)**.

> ⚠️ **Warning: It is important that the plugs are grounded away from the spark plug holes otherwise there is a risk of atomized fuel from the cylinders igniting.**

> **HAYNES HINT** On a single cylinder four-stroke engine, you can seal the combustion chamber completely by positioning the piston at TDC on the compression stroke.

● Drain the carburetor(s) otherwise there is a risk of jets becoming blocked by gum deposits from the fuel **(see illustration 4)**.

● If the bike is going into long-term storage, consider adding a fuel stabilizer to the fuel in the tank. If the tank is drained completely, corrosion of its internal surfaces may occur if left unprotected for a long period. The tank can be treated with a rust preventative especially for this purpose. Alternatively, remove the tank and pour half a liter of motor oil into it, install the filler cap and shake the tank to coat its internals with oil before draining off the excess. The same effect can also be achieved by spraying WD40 or a similar water-dispersant around the inside of the tank via its flexible nozzle.

● Make sure the cooling system contains the correct mix of antifreeze. Antifreeze also contains important corrosion inhibitors.

● The air intakes and exhaust can be sealed off by covering or plugging the openings. Ensure that you do not seal in any condensation; run the engine until it is hot, then switch off and allow to cool. Tape a

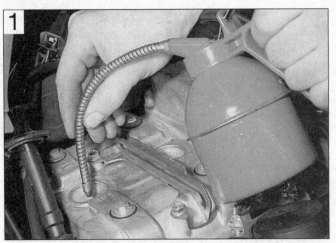

Squirt a drop of motor oil into each cylinder

Flick the kill switch to OFF . . .

. . . and ensure that the metal bodies of the plugs (arrows) are grounded against the cylinder head

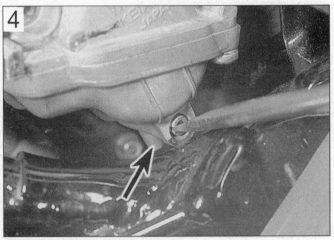

Connect a hose to the carburetor float chamber drain stub (arrow) and unscrew the drain screw

Exhausts can be sealed off with a plastic bag

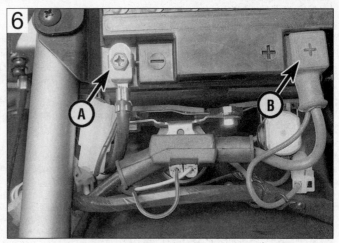

Disconnect the negative lead (A) first, followed by the positive lead (B)

piece of thick plastic over the silencer end(s) **(see illustration 5)**. Note that some advocate pouring a tablespoon of motor oil into the silencer(s) before sealing them off.

Battery

● Remove it from the bike - in extreme cases of cold the battery may freeze and crack its case **(see illustration 6)**.
● Check the electrolyte level and top up if necessary (conventional refillable batteries). Clean the terminals.
● Store the battery off the motorcycle and away from any sources of fire. Position a wooden block under the battery if it is to sit on the ground.
● Give the battery a trickle charge for a few hours every month **(see illustration 7)**.

Tires

● Place the bike on its centerstand or an auxiliary stand which will support the motorcycle in an upright position. Position wood blocks under the tires to keep them off the ground and to provide insulation from damp. If the bike is being put into long-term

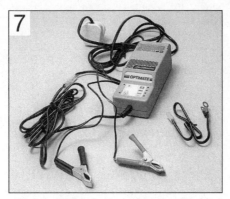

Use a suitable battery charger - this kit also assesses battery condition

storage, ideally both tires should be off the ground; not only will this protect the tires, but will also ensure that no load is placed on the steering head or wheel bearings.
● Deflate each tire by 5 to 10 psi, no more or the beads may unseat from the rim, making subsequent inflation difficult on tubeless tires.

Pivots and controls

● Lubricate all lever, pedal, stand and footrest pivot points. If grease nipples are fitted to the rear suspension components, apply lubricant to the pivots.
● Lubricate all control cables.

Cycle components

● Apply a wax protectant to all painted and plastic components. Wipe off any excess, but don't polish to a shine. Where fitted, clean the screen with soap and water.
● Coat metal parts with Vaseline (petroleum jelly). When applying this to the fork tubes, do not compress the forks otherwise the seals will rot from contact with the Vaseline.
● Apply a vinyl cleaner to the seat.

Storage conditions

● Aim to store the bike in a shed or garage which does not leak and is free from damp.
● Drape an old blanket or bedspread over the bike to protect it from dust and direct contact with sunlight (which will fade paint). Beware of tight-fitting plastic covers which may allow condensation to form and settle on the bike.

Getting back on the road

Engine and transmission

● Change the oil and replace the oil filter. If this was done prior to storage, check that the oil hasn't emulsified - a thick whitish substance which occurs through condensation.
● Remove the spark plugs. Using a spout-type oil can, squirt a few drops of oil into the cylinder(s). This will provide initial lubrication as the piston rings and bores comes back into contact. Service the spark plugs, or buy new ones, and install them in the engine.

● Check that the clutch isn't stuck on. The plates can stick together if left standing for some time, preventing clutch operation. Engage a gear and try rocking the bike back and forth with the clutch lever held against the handlebar. If this doesn't work on cable-operated clutches, hold the clutch lever back against the handlebar with a strong rubber band or cable tie for a couple of hours **(see illustration 8)**.
● If the air intakes or silencer end(s) were blocked off, remove the plug or cover used.
● If the fuel tank was coated with a rust

Hold the clutch lever back against the handlebar with rubber bands or a cable tie

preventative, oil or a stabilizer added to the fuel, drain and flush the tank and dispose of the fuel sensibly. If no action was taken with the fuel tank prior to storage, it is advised that the old fuel is disposed of since it will go bad over a period of time. Refill the fuel tank with fresh fuel.

Frame and running gear

● Oil all pivot points and cables.
● Check the tire pressures. They will definitely need inflating if pressures were reduced for storage.
● Lubricate the final drive chain (where applicable).
● Remove any protective coating applied to the fork tubes (stanchions) since this may well destroy the fork seals. If the fork tubes weren't protected and have picked up rust spots, remove them with very fine abrasive paper and refinish with metal polish.
● Check that both brakes operate correctly. Apply each brake hard and check that it's not possible to move the motorcycle forwards, then check that the brake frees off again once released. Brake caliper pistons can stick due to corrosion around the piston head, or on the sliding caliper types, due to corrosion of the slider pins. If the brake doesn't free after repeated operation, take the caliper off for examination. Similarly drum brakes can stick due to a seized operating cam, cable or rod linkage.
● If the motorcycle has been in long-term storage, replace the brake fluid and clutch fluid (where applicable).
● Depending on where the bike has been stored, the wiring, cables and hoses may have been nibbled by rodents. Make a visual check and investigate disturbed wiring loom tape.

Battery

● If the battery has been previously removed and given top up charges it can simply be reconnected. Remember to connect the positive cable first and the negative cable last.
● On conventional refillable batteries, if the battery has not received any attention, remove it from the motorcycle and check its electrolyte level. Top up if necessary then charge the battery. If the battery fails to hold a charge and a visual check show heavy white sulfation of the plates, the battery is probably defective and must be replaced. This is particularly likely if the battery is old. Confirm battery condition with a specific gravity check.
● On sealed (MF) batteries, if the battery has not received any attention, remove it from the motorcycle and charge it according to the information on the battery case - if the battery fails to hold a charge it must be replaced.

Starting procedure

● If a kickstart is fitted, turn the engine over a couple of times with the ignition OFF to distribute oil around the engine. If no kickstart is fitted, flick the engine kill switch OFF and the ignition ON and crank the engine over a couple of times to work oil around the upper cylinder components. If the nature of the ignition system is such that the starter won't work with the kill switch OFF, remove the spark plugs, fit them back into their caps and ground their bodies on the cylinder head. Reinstall the spark plugs afterwards.
● Switch the kill switch to RUN, operate the choke and start the engine. If the engine won't start don't continue cranking the engine - not only will this flatten the battery, but the starter motor will overheat. Switch the ignition off and try again later. If the engine refuses to start, go through the troubleshooting procedures in this manual. **Note:** *If the bike has been in storage for a long time, old fuel or a carburetor blockage may be the problem. Gum deposits in carburetors can block jets - if a carburetor cleaner doesn't prove successful the carburetors must be dismantled for cleaning.*
● Once the engine has started, check that the lights, turn signals and horn work properly.
● Treat the bike gently for the first ride and check all fluid levels on completion. Settle the bike back into the maintenance schedule.

This Section provides an easy reference-guide to the more common faults that are likely to afflict your machine. Obviously, the opportunities are almost limitless for faults to occur as a result of obscure failures, and to try and cover all eventualities would require a book. Indeed, a number have been written on the subject.

Successful troubleshooting is not a mysterious 'black art' but the application of a bit of knowledge combined with a systematic and logical approach to the problem. Approach any troubleshooting by first accurately identifying the symptom and then checking through the list of possible causes, starting with the simplest or most obvious and progressing in stages to the most complex. Take nothing for granted, but above all apply liberal quantities of common sense.

The main symptom of a fault is given in the text as a major heading below which are listed the various systems or areas which may contain the fault. Details of each possible cause for a fault and the remedial action to be taken are given. Further information should be sought in the relevant Chapter.

1 Engine doesn't start or is difficult to start

- [ ] Starter motor doesn't rotate
- [ ] Starter motor rotates but engine does not turn over
- [ ] Starter works but engine won't turn over (seized)
- [ ] No fuel flow
- [ ] Engine flooded
- [ ] No spark or weak spark
- [ ] Compression low
- [ ] Stalls after starting
- [ ] Rough idle

2 Poor running at low speed

- [ ] Spark weak
- [ ] Fuel/air mixture incorrect
- [ ] Compression low
- [ ] Poor acceleration

3 Poor running or no power at high speed

- [ ] Firing incorrect
- [ ] Fuel/air mixture incorrect
- [ ] Compression low
- [ ] Knocking or pinging
- [ ] Miscellaneous causes

4 Overheating

- [ ] Engine overheats
- [ ] Firing incorrect
- [ ] Fuel/air mixture incorrect
- [ ] Compression too high
- [ ] Engine load excessive
- [ ] Lubrication inadequate
- [ ] Miscellaneous causes

5 Clutch problems

- [ ] Clutch slipping
- [ ] Clutch not disengaging completely

6 Gearchanging problems

- [ ] Doesn't go into gear, or lever doesn't return
- [ ] Jumps out of gear
- [ ] Overselects

7 Abnormal engine noise

- [ ] Knocking or pinging
- [ ] Piston slap or rattling
- [ ] Valve noise
- [ ] Other noise

8 Abnormal driveline noise

- [ ] Clutch noise
- [ ] Transmission noise
- [ ] Final drive noise

9 Abnormal frame and suspension noise

- [ ] Front end noise
- [ ] Shock absorber noise
- [ ] Brake noise

10 Coolant temperature warning light comes on

- [ ] Engine cooling system
- [ ] Electrical system

11 Excessive exhaust smoke

- [ ] White smoke
- [ ] Black smoke

12 Poor handling or stability

- [ ] Handlebar hard to turn
- [ ] Handlebar shakes or vibrates excessively
- [ ] Handlebar pulls to one side
- [ ] Poor shock absorbing qualities

13 Braking problems

- [ ] Brakes are spongy, don't hold
- [ ] Brake lever or pedal pulsates
- [ ] Brakes drag

14 Electrical problems

- [ ] Battery dead or weak
- [ ] Battery overcharged

1 Engine doesn't start or is difficult to start

Starter motor doesn't rotate

☐ Engine kill switch OFF.
☐ Fuse blown. Check main fuse and starter circuit fuse (Chapter 5).
☐ Battery voltage low. Check and recharge battery (Chapter 5).
☐ Starter motor defective. Make sure the wiring to the starter is secure. Make sure the starter relay clicks when the start button is pushed. If the relay clicks, then the fault is in the wiring or motor.
☐ Starter relay faulty. Check it according to the procedure in Chapter 5.
☐ Starter switch not contacting. The contacts could be wet, corroded or dirty. Disassemble and clean the switch (Chapter 5).
☐ Wiring open or shorted. Check all wiring connections and harnesses to make sure that they are dry, tight and not corroded. Also check for broken or frayed wires that can cause a short to ground (see wiring diagram, Chapter 5).
☐ Ignition (main) switch defective. Check the switch according to the procedure in Chapter 5. Replace the switch with a new one if it is defective.
☐ Engine kill switch defective. Check for wet, dirty or corroded contacts. Clean or replace the switch as necessary (Chapter 5).
☐ Faulty neutral, sidestand or clutch switch. Check the wiring to each switch and the switch itself according to the procedures in Chapter 5.

Starter motor rotates but engine does not turn over

☐ Starter motor clutch defective. Inspect and repair or replace (Chapter 5).
☐ Damaged idler or starter gears. Inspect and replace the damaged parts (Chapter 5).

Starter works but engine won't turn over (seized)

☐ Seized engine caused by one or more internally damaged components. Failure due to wear, abuse or lack of lubrication. Damage can include seized valves, followers/rocker arms, camshafts, pistons, crankshaft, connecting rod bearings, or transmission gears or bearings. Refer to Chapter 2 for engine disassembly.

No fuel flow

☐ No fuel in tank.
☐ Fuel tank breather hose obstructed.
☐ Fuel strainer is blocked (see Chapter 1).

Engine flooded

☐ Starting technique incorrect. Under normal circumstances the machine should start with little or no throttle. When the engine is cold, the choke should be operated and the engine started without opening the throttle. When the engine is at operating temperature, only a very slight amount of throttle should be necessary.

No spark or weak spark

☐ Ignition switch OFF.
☐ Engine kill switch turned to the OFF position.
☐ Battery voltage low. Check and recharge the battery as necessary (Chapter 5).
☐ Spark plugs dirty, defective or worn out. Locate reason for fouled plugs using spark plug condition chart and follow the plug maintenance procedures (Chapter 1).
☐ Spark plug caps or secondary (HT) wiring faulty. Check condition. Replace either or both components if cracks or deterioration are evident (Chapter 5).
☐ Spark plug caps not making good contact. Make sure that the plug caps fit snugly over the plug ends.
☐ Ignition coil defective. Check the coil, referring to Chapter 5.
☐ CDI igniter unit defective. Refer to Chapter 5 for details.
☐ Pick-up coil defective. Check the unit, referring to Chapter 5 for details.
☐ Ignition or kill switch shorted. This is usually caused by water, corrosion, damage or excessive wear. The switches can be disassembled and cleaned with electrical contact cleaner. If cleaning does not help, replace the switches (Chapter 5).
☐ Wiring shorted or broken between:

   a) *Ignition (main) switch and engine kill switch (or blown fuse)*
   b) *CDI unit and engine kill switch*
   c) *CDI unit and ignition coil*
   d) *Ignition coil and spark plugs*
   e) *CDI unit and ignition pick-up coil.*

☐ Make sure that all wiring connections are clean, dry and tight. Look for chafed and broken wires (Chapters 5 and 9).

Compression low

☐ Spark plugs loose. Remove the plugs and inspect their threads. Reinstall and tighten to the specified torque (Chapter 1).
☐ Cylinder head not sufficiently tightened down. If the cylinder head is suspected of being loose, then there's a chance that the gasket or head is damaged if the problem has persisted for any length of time. The head bolts should be tightened to the proper torque in the correct sequence (Chapter 2).
☐ Improper valve clearance. This means that the valve is not closing completely and compression pressure is leaking past the valve. Check and adjust the valve clearances (Chapter 1).
☐ Cylinder and/or piston worn. Excessive wear will cause compression pressure to leak past the rings. This is usually accompanied by worn rings as well. A top-end overhaul is necessary (Chapter 2).
☐ Piston rings worn, weak, broken, or sticking. Broken or sticking piston rings usually indicate a lubrication or fuelling problem that causes excess carbon deposits or seizures to form on the pistons and rings. Top-end overhaul is necessary (Chapter 2).
☐ Piston ring-to-groove clearance excessive. This is caused by excessive wear of the piston ring lands. Piston replacement is necessary (Chapter 2).
☐ Cylinder head gasket damaged. If a head is allowed to become loose, or if excessive carbon build-up on the piston crown and combustion chamber causes extremely high compression, the head gasket may leak. Retorquing the head is not always sufficient to restore the seal, so gasket replacement is necessary (Chapter 2).
☐ Cylinder head warped. This is caused by overheating or improperly tightened head bolts. Machine shop resurfacing or head replacement is necessary (Chapter 2).
☐ Valve spring broken or weak. Caused by component failure or wear; the springs must be replaced (Chapter 2).
☐ Valve not seating properly. This is caused by a bent valve (from over-revving or improper valve adjustment), burned valve or seat (improper fuelling) or an accumulation of carbon deposits on the seat (from fuelling or lubrication problems). The valves must be cleaned and/or replaced and the seats serviced if possible (Chapter 2).

1 Engine doesn't start or is difficult to start (continued)

Stalls after starting

- ☐ Improper choke action. Make sure the choke knob is getting a full stroke and staying in the out position (Chapter 4).
- ☐ Ignition malfunction. See Chapter 5.
- ☐ Carburetor malfunction. See Chapter 4.
- ☐ Fuel contaminated. The fuel can be contaminated with either dirt or water, or can change chemically if the machine is allowed to sit for several months or more. Drain the tank (Chapter 4).
- ☐ Intake air leak. Check for loose intake manifold retaining clips and damaged/disconnected vacuum hoses (Chapter 4).
- ☐ Engine idle speed incorrect. See Chapter 1 to adjust the idle speed.

Rough idle

- ☐ Ignition malfunction. See Chapter 5.
- ☐ Idle speed incorrect. See Chapter 1.
- ☐ Carburetor malfunction. See Chapter 4.
- ☐ Fuel contaminated. The fuel can be contaminated with either dirt or water, or can change chemically if the machine is allowed to sit for several months or more. Drain the tank (Chapter 4).
- ☐ Intake air leak. Check for loose intake manifold retaining clips and damaged/disconnected vacuum hoses. Replace the intake ducts if they are split or deteriorated (Chapter 4).
- ☐ Air filter clogged. Replace the air filter element (Chapter 1).

2 Poor running at low speeds

Spark weak

- ☐ Battery voltage low. Check and recharge battery (Chapter 5).
- ☐ Spark plugs fouled, defective or worn out. Refer to Chapter 1 for spark plug maintenance.
- ☐ Spark plug cap or HT wiring defective. Refer to Chapters 1 and 5 for details on the ignition system.
- ☐ Spark plug caps not making contact.
- ☐ Incorrect spark plugs. Wrong type, heat range or cap configuration. Check and install correct plugs listed in Chapter 1.
- ☐ CDI unit faulty. See Chapter 5.
- ☐ Pick-up coil defective. See Chapter 5.
- ☐ Ignition coils defective. See Chapter 5.

Fuel/air mixture incorrect

- ☐ Pilot screw incorrectly set (Chapter 4)
- ☐ Pilot jet or air passage blocked. Remove and overhaul the carburetor (Chapter 4).
- ☐ Air filter clogged, poorly sealed or missing (Chapter 1).
- ☐ Air filter housing poorly sealed. Look for cracks, holes or loose clamps and replace or repair defective parts.
- ☐ Fuel tank breather hose obstructed.
- ☐ Intake air leak. Check for loose intake manifold retaining clips and damaged/disconnected vacuum hoses. Replace the intake ducts if they are split or deteriorated (Chapter 4).

Compression low

- ☐ Spark plugs loose. Remove the plugs and inspect their threads. Reinstall and tighten to the specified torque (Chapter 1).
- ☐ Cylinder head not sufficiently tightened down. If the cylinder head is suspected of being loose, then there's a chance that the gasket and head are damaged if the problem has persisted for any length of time. The head bolts should be tightened to the proper torque in the correct sequence (Chapter 2).
- ☐ Improper valve clearance. This means that the valve is not closing completely and compression pressure is leaking past the valve. Check and adjust the valve clearances (Chapter 1).

- ☐ Cylinder and/or piston worn. Excessive wear will cause compression pressure to leak past the rings. This is usually accompanied by worn rings as well. A top-end overhaul is necessary (Chapter 2).
- ☐ Piston rings worn, weak, broken, or sticking. Broken or sticking piston rings usually indicate a lubrication or fuelling problem that causes excess carbon deposits or seizures to form on the pistons and rings. Top-end overhaul is necessary (Chapter 2).
- ☐ Piston ring-to-groove clearance excessive. This is caused by excessive wear of the piston ring lands. Piston replacement is necessary (Chapter 2).
- ☐ Cylinder head gasket damaged. If a head is allowed to become loose, or if excessive carbon build-up on the piston crown and combustion chamber causes extremely high compression, the head gasket may leak. Retorquing the head is not always sufficient to restore the seal, so gasket replacement is necessary (Chapter 2).
- ☐ Cylinder head warped. This is caused by overheating or improperly tightened head bolts. Machine shop resurfacing or head replacement is necessary (Chapter 2).
- ☐ Valve spring broken or weak. Caused by component failure or wear; the springs must be replaced (Chapter 2).
- ☐ Valve not seating properly. This is caused by a bent valve (from over-revving or improper valve adjustment), burned valve or seat (improper fuelling) or an accumulation of carbon deposits on the seat (from fuelling, lubrication problems). The valves must be cleaned and/or replaced and the seats serviced if possible (Chapter 2).

Poor acceleration

- ☐ Fuel system fault. Remove and overhaul the carburetor (Chapter 4).
- ☐ Engine oil viscosity too high. Using a heavier oil than that recommended in Chapter 1 can damage the oil pump or lubrication system and cause drag on the engine.
- ☐ Brakes dragging. Usually caused by debris which has entered the brake piston seals, or from a warped disc or bent axle. Repair as necessary (Chapter 7).

3 Poor running or no power at high speed

Firing incorrect

- ☐ Air filter restricted. Clean or replace filter (Chapter 1).
- ☐ Spark plugs fouled, defective or worn out. See Chapter 1 for spark plug maintenance.
- ☐ Spark plug caps or HT wiring defective. See Chapters 1 and 5 for details of the ignition system.
- ☐ Spark plug caps not in good contact. See Chapter 5.
- ☐ Incorrect spark plugs. Wrong type, heat range or cap configuration. Check and install correct plugs listed in Chapter 1.
- ☐ CDI unit defective. See Chapter 5.
- ☐ Pick-up coil defective. See Chapter 5.
- ☐ Ignition coil defective. See Chapter 5.

Fuel/air mixture incorrect

- ☐ Fuel system fault. Remove and overhaul the carburetor (Chapter 4).
- ☐ Air filter clogged, poorly sealed, or missing (Chapter 1).
- ☐ Air filter housing poorly sealed. Look for cracks, holes or loose clamps, and replace or repair defective parts.
- ☐ Fuel tank breather hose obstructed.
- ☐ Intake air leak. Check for loose intake manifold retaining clips and damaged/disconnected vacuum hoses. Replace the intake ducts if they are split or deteriorated (Chapter 4).

Compression low

- ☐ Spark plug loose. Remove the plug and inspect its threads. Reinstall and tighten to the specified torque (Chapter 1).
- ☐ Cylinder head not sufficiently tightened down. If the cylinder head is suspected of being loose, then there's a chance that the gasket and head are damaged if the problem has persisted for any length of time. The head bolts should be tightened to the proper torque in the correct sequence (Chapter 2).
- ☐ Improper valve clearance. This means that the valve is not closing completely and compression pressure is leaking past the valve. Check and adjust the valve clearances (Chapter 1).
- ☐ Cylinder and/or piston worn. Excessive wear will cause compression pressure to leak past the rings. This is usually accompanied by worn rings as well. A top-end overhaul is necessary (Chapter 2).
- ☐ Piston rings worn, weak, broken, or sticking. Broken or sticking piston rings usually indicate a lubrication or fueling problem that causes excess carbon deposits or seizures to form on the pistons and rings. Top-end overhaul is necessary (Chapter 2).
- ☐ Piston ring-to-groove clearance excessive. This is caused by excessive wear of the piston ring lands. Piston replacement is necessary (Chapter 2).
- ☐ Cylinder head gasket damaged. If a head is allowed to become loose, or if excessive carbon build-up on the piston crown and combustion chamber causes extremely high compression, the head gasket may leak. Retorquing the head is not always sufficient to restore the seal, so gasket replacement is necessary (Chapter 2).
- ☐ Cylinder head warped. This is caused by overheating or improperly tightened head bolts. Machine shop resurfacing or head replacement is necessary (Chapter 2).
- ☐ Valve spring broken or weak. Caused by component failure or wear; the springs must be replaced (Chapter 2).
- ☐ Valve not seating properly. This is caused by a bent valve (from over-revving or improper valve adjustment), burned valve or seat (improper fuelling) or an accumulation of carbon deposits on the seat (from fuelling or lubrication problems). The valves must be cleaned and/or replaced and the seats serviced if possible (Chapter 2).

Knocking or pinging

- ☐ Carbon build-up in combustion chamber. Use of a fuel additive that will dissolve the adhesive bonding the carbon particles to the crown and chamber is the easiest way to remove the build-up. Otherwise, the cylinder head will have to be removed and decarbonized (Chapter 2).
- ☐ Incorrect or poor quality fuel. Old or improper grades of fuel can cause detonation. This causes the piston to rattle, thus the knocking or pinging sound. Drain old fuel and always use the recommended fuel grade (Chapter 4).
- ☐ Spark plug heat range incorrect. Uncontrolled detonation indicates the plug heat range is too hot. The plug in effect becomes a glow plug, raising cylinder temperatures. Install the proper heat range plug (Chapter 1).
- ☐ Improper air/fuel mixture. This will cause the cylinder to run hot, which leads to detonation. An intake air leak can cause this imbalance. Refer to the carburetor and air cleaner housing removal and installation procedures in Chapter 4 and make sure the air intake ducts (between the air cleaner housing and carburetor, and between the carburetor and engine) are securely clamped and in good condition.

Miscellaneous causes

- ☐ Throttle valve doesn't open fully. Adjust the throttle grip freeplay (Chapter 1).
- ☐ Clutch slipping. May be caused by loose or worn clutch components. Refer to Chapter 2 for clutch overhaul procedures.
- ☐ Engine oil viscosity too high. Using a heavier oil than the one recommended in Chapter 1 can damage the oil pump or lubrication system and cause drag on the engine.
- ☐ Brakes dragging. Usually caused by debris which has entered the brake piston seals, or from a warped disc or bent axle. Repair as necessary.

4 Overheating

Engine overheats

- [ ] Coolant level low. Check and add coolant (Chapter 1).
- [ ] Leak in cooling system. Check cooling system hoses and radiator for leaks and other damage. Repair or replace parts as necessary (Chapter 3).
- [ ] Thermostat sticking open or closed. Check and replace as described in Chapter 3.
- [ ] Faulty pressure cap. Remove the cap and have it pressure tested (Chapter 3).
- [ ] Coolant passages clogged. Have the entire system drained and flushed, then refill with fresh coolant.
- [ ] Water pump defective. Remove the pump and check the components (Chapter 3).
- [ ] Clogged radiator fins. Clean them by blowing compressed air through the fins from the backside.
- [ ] Cooling fan or fan switch fault (Chapter 3).

Firing incorrect

- [ ] Spark plugs fouled, defective or worn out. See Chapter 1 for spark plug maintenance.
- [ ] Incorrect spark plugs.
- [ ] CDI unit defective. See Chapter 5.
- [ ] Pick-up coil faulty. See Chapter 5.
- [ ] Faulty ignition coil. See Chapter 5.

Fuel/air mixture incorrect

- [ ] Fuel system fault. Remove and overhaul the carburetor (Chapter 4).
- [ ] Air filter clogged, poorly sealed, or missing (Chapter 1).
- [ ] Air filter housing poorly sealed. Look for cracks, holes or loose clamps, and replace or repair defective parts.
- [ ] Fuel tank breather hose obstructed.
- [ ] Intake air leak. Check for loose intake manifold retaining clips and damaged/disconnected vacuum hoses. Replace the intake ducts if they are split or deteriorated (Chapter 4).

Compression too high

- [ ] Carbon build-up in combustion chamber. Use of a fuel additive that will dissolve the adhesive bonding the carbon particles to the piston crown and chamber is the easiest way to remove the build-up. Otherwise, the cylinder head will have to be removed and decarbonized (Chapter 2).
- [ ] Improperly machined head surface or installation of incorrect gasket during engine assembly.

Engine load excessive

- [ ] Clutch slipping. Can be caused by damaged, loose or worn clutch components. Refer to Chapter 2 for overhaul procedures.
- [ ] Engine oil level too high. The addition of too much oil will cause pressurization of the crankcase and inefficient engine operation. Check Specifications and drain to proper level (Chapter 1).
- [ ] Engine oil viscosity too high. Using a heavier oil than the one recommended in Chapter 1 can damage the oil pump or lubrication system as well as cause drag on the engine.
- [ ] Brakes dragging. Usually caused by debris which has entered the brake piston seals, or from a warped disc or bent axle. Repair as necessary.

Lubrication inadequate

- [ ] Engine oil level too low. Friction caused by intermittent lack of lubrication or from oil that is overworked can cause overheating. The oil provides a definite cooling function in the engine. Check the oil level (Chapter 1).
- [ ] Poor quality engine oil or incorrect viscosity or type. Oil is rated not only according to viscosity but also according to type. Some oils are not rated high enough for use in this engine. Check the Specifications section and change to the correct oil (Chapter 1).

Miscellaneous causes

- [ ] Modification to exhaust system. Most aftermarket exhaust systems cause the engine to run leaner, which makes it run hotter.

5 Clutch problems

Clutch slipping

- [ ] Clutch lever freeplay incorrectly adjusted (lever clutch models) (Chapter 1).
- [ ] Friction plates worn or warped. Overhaul the clutch assembly (Chapter 2).
- [ ] Metal plates warped (Chapter 2).
- [ ] Clutch springs broken or weak. Old or heat-damaged (from slipping clutch) springs should be replaced with new ones (Chapter 2).
- [ ] Clutch pushrod bent. Check and, if necessary, replace (Chapter 2).
- [ ] Clutch center or housing unevenly worn. This causes improper engagement of the plates. Replace the damaged or worn parts (Chapter 2).
- [ ] Wrong type of oil used. DO NOT use oil with anti-friction additives (such as molybdenum disulfide) in an engine/transmission with a wet clutch.

Clutch not disengaging completely

- [ ] Clutch lever freeplay incorrectly adjusted (Chapter 1).

- [ ] Clutch plates warped or damaged. This will cause clutch drag, which in turn will cause the machine to creep. Overhaul the clutch assembly (Chapter 2).
- [ ] Clutch spring tension uneven. Usually caused by a sagged or broken spring. Check and replace the springs as a set (Chapter 2).
- [ ] Engine oil deteriorated. Old, thin, worn out oil will not provide proper lubrication for the plates, causing the clutch to drag. Replace the oil and filter (Chapter 1).
- [ ] Engine oil viscosity too high. Using a heavier oil than recommended in Chapter 1 can cause the plates to stick together, putting a drag on the engine. Change to the correct weight oil (Chapter 1).
- [ ] Clutch housing bearing seized. Lack of lubrication, severe wear or damage can cause the bearing to seize on the input shaft. Overhaul of the clutch, and perhaps transmission, may be necessary to repair the damage (Chapter 2).
- [ ] Loose clutch center nut. Causes housing and center misalignment putting a drag on the engine. Engagement adjustment continually varies. Overhaul the clutch assembly (Chapter 2).

6 Gearchanging problems

Doesn't go into gear or lever doesn't return

- [ ] Clutch not disengaging. See Section 5.
- [ ] Shift fork(s) bent or seized. Often caused by dropping the machine or from lack of lubrication. Overhaul the transmission (Chapter 2).
- [ ] Gear(s) stuck on shaft. Most often caused by a lack of lubrication or excessive wear in transmission bearings and bushings. Overhaul the transmission (Chapter 2).
- [ ] Gear shift drum binding. Caused by lubrication failure or excessive wear. Replace the drum and bearing (Chapter 2).
- [ ] Gear shift lever pawl spring weak or broken (Chapter 2).
- [ ] Gear shift lever broken. Splines stripped out of lever or shaft, caused by allowing the lever to get loose or from dropping the machine. Replace necessary parts (Chapter 2).
- [ ] Gear shift mechanism stopper arm broken or worn. Full engagement and rotary movement of shift drum results. Replace the arm (Chapter 2).

- [ ] Stopper arm spring broken. Allows arm to float, causing sporadic shift operation. Replace spring (Chapter 2).

Jumps out of gear

- [ ] Shift fork(s) worn. Overhaul the transmission (Chapter 2).
- [ ] Gear groove(s) worn. Overhaul the transmission (Chapter 2).
- [ ] Gear dogs or dog slots worn or damaged. The gears should be inspected and replaced. No attempt should be made to service the worn parts (Chapter 2, Section 28).

Overselects

- [ ] Stopper arm spring weak or broken (Chapter 2).
- [ ] Return spring post broken or distorted (Chapter 2).

7 Abnormal engine noise

Knocking or pinging

- [ ] Carbon build-up in combustion chamber. Use of a fuel additive that will dissolve the adhesive bonding the carbon particles to the piston crown and chamber is the easiest way to remove the build-up. Otherwise, the cylinder head will have to be removed and decarbonized (Chapter 2).
- [ ] Incorrect or poor quality fuel. Old or improper fuel can cause detonation. This causes the pistons to rattle, thus the knocking or pinging sound. Drain the old fuel and always use the recommended grade fuel (Chapter 4).
- [ ] Spark plug heat range incorrect. Uncontrolled detonation indicates that the plug heat range is too hot. The plug in effect becomes a glow plug, raising cylinder temperatures. Install the proper heat range plug (Chapter 1).
- [ ] Improper air/fuel mixture. This will cause the cylinders to run hot and lead to detonation. Blocked carburetor jets or an air leak can cause this imbalance. See Chapter 4.

Piston slap or rattling

- [ ] Cylinder-to-piston clearance excessive. Caused by improper assembly. Inspect and overhaul top-end parts (Chapter 2).
- [ ] Connecting rod bent. Caused by over-revving, trying to start a badly flooded engine or from ingesting a foreign object into the combustion chamber. Replace the damaged parts (Chapter 2).
- [ ] Piston pin or piston pin bore worn or seized from wear or lack of lubrication. Replace damaged parts (Chapter 2).
- [ ] Piston ring(s) worn, broken or sticking. Overhaul the top-end (Chapter 2).
- [ ] Piston seizure damage. Usually from lack of lubrication or overheating. Replace the pistons and cylinders, as necessary (Chapter 2).

- [ ] Connecting rod bearing clearance excessive. Caused by excessive wear or lack of lubrication. Replace worn parts.

Valve noise

- [ ] Incorrect valve clearances. Adjust the clearances by referring to Chapter 1.
- [ ] Valve spring broken or weak. Check and replace weak valve springs (Chapter 2).
- [ ] Camshaft or cylinder head worn or damaged. Lack of lubrication at high rpm is usually the cause of damage. Insufficient oil or failure to change the oil at the recommended intervals are the chief causes. Since there are no replaceable bearings in the head, the head itself will have to be replaced if there is excessive wear or damage (Chapter 2).

Other noise

- [ ] Cylinder head gasket leaking.
- [ ] Exhaust pipe leaking at cylinder head connection. Caused by improper fit of pipe(s) or loose exhaust nuts. All exhaust fasteners should be tightened evenly and carefully. Failure to do this will lead to a leak.
- [ ] Crankshaft runout excessive. Caused by a bent crankshaft (from over-revving) or damage from an upper cylinder component failure. Can also be attributed to dropping the machine on either of the crankshaft ends.
- [ ] Engine mounting bolts loose. Tighten all engine mount bolts (Chapter 2).
- [ ] Crankshaft bearings worn (Chapter 2).
- [ ] Cam chain, tensioner or guides worn. Replace according to the procedure in Chapter 2.

8 Abnormal driveline noise

Clutch noise

- [ ] Clutch outer drum/friction plate clearance excessive (Chapter 2).
- [ ] Loose or damaged clutch pressure plate and/or bolts (Chapter 2).

Transmission noise

- [ ] Bearings worn. Also includes the possibility that the shafts are worn. Overhaul the transmission (Chapter 2).
- [ ] Gears worn or chipped (Chapter 2).
- [ ] Metal chips jammed in gear teeth. Probably pieces from a broken clutch, gear or shift mechanism that were picked up by the gears. This will cause early bearing failure (Chapter 2).

- [ ] Engine oil level too low. Causes a howl from transmission. Also affects engine power and clutch operation (Chapter 1).

Final drive noise

- [ ] Drive chain not adjusted properly (Chapter 1).
- [ ] Front or rear sprocket loose. Tighten fasteners (Chapter 6).
- [ ] Sprockets worn. Replace sprockets (Chapter 6).
- [ ] Rear sprocket warped. Replace sprockets (Chapter 6).

9 Abnormal frame and suspension noise

Front end noise

- [ ] Low fluid level or improper viscosity oil in forks. This can sound like spurting and is usually accompanied by irregular fork action (Chapter 6).
- [ ] Spring weak or broken. Makes a clicking or scraping sound. Fork oil, when drained, will have a lot of metal particles in it (Chapter 6).
- [ ] Steering head bearings loose or damaged. Clicks when braking. Check and adjust or replace as necessary (Chapters 1 and 6).
- [ ] Triple clamps loose. Make sure all clamp bolts are tightened to the specified torque (Chapter 6).
- [ ] Fork tube bent. Good possibility if machine has been dropped. Replace tube with a new one (Chapter 6).
- [ ] Front axle bolt or axle pinch bolts loose. Tighten them to the specified torque (Chapter 7).
- [ ] Loose or worn wheel bearings. Check and replace as needed (Chapter 7).

Shock absorber noise

- [ ] Fluid level incorrect. Indicates a leak caused by defective seal. Shock will be covered with oil. Replace shock or seek advice on repair from a dealer (Chapter 6).
- [ ] Defective shock absorber with internal damage. This is in the body of the shock and can't be remedied. The shock must be replaced with a new one (Chapter 6).

- [ ] Bent or damaged shock body. Replace the shock with a new one (Chapter 6).
- [ ] Loose or worn suspension linkage components. Check and replace as necessary (Chapter 6).

Brake noise

- [ ] Squeal caused by dust on brake pads. Usually found in combination with glazed pads. Clean using brake cleaning solvent (Chapter 7).
- [ ] Contamination of brake pads. Oil, brake fluid or dirt causing brake to chatter or squeal. Clean or replace pads (Chapter 7).
- [ ] Pads glazed. Caused by excessive heat from prolonged use or from contamination. Do not use sandpaper/emery cloth or any other abrasive to roughen the pad surfaces as abrasives will stay in the pad material and damage the disc. A very fine flat file can be used, but pad replacement is suggested (Chapter 7).
- [ ] Disc warped. Can cause a chattering, clicking or intermittent squeal. Usually accompanied by a pulsating lever and uneven braking. Replace the disc (Chapter 7).
- [ ] Loose or worn wheel bearings. Check and replace as needed (Chapter 7).

10 Coolant temperature warning light comes on

Engine cooling system

- [ ] Coolant level low. Refer to *Daily (pre-ride) checks* at the front of this manual to check coolant level, then check the cooling system for leaks (Chapter 3).
- [ ] Thermostat defective (models so equipped). Remove and test the thermostat (Chapter 3).
- [ ] Coolant passages clogged. Drain and flush the entire system, then fill with fresh coolant (Chapter 1).
- [ ] Water pump defective. Remove the pump and check the components (Chapter 3).

- [ ] Clogged radiator fins. Clean them by blowing compressed air through them from the rear of the radiator.

Electrical system

- [ ] Cooling fan or thermoswitch fault (Chapter 3).
- [ ] Warning light switch fault (Chapter 5).

11 Excessive exhaust smoke

White smoke

☐ Piston oil ring worn. The ring may be broken or damaged, causing oil from the crankcase to be pulled past the piston into the combustion chamber. Replace the rings with new ones (Chapter 2).

☐ Cylinders worn, cracked, or scored. Caused by overheating or oil starvation. Install a new cylinder block (Chapter 2).

☐ Valve oil seal damaged or worn. Replace oil seals with new ones (Chapter 2).

☐ Valve guide worn. Perform a complete valve job (Chapter 2).

☐ Engine oil level too high, which causes the oil to be forced past the rings. Drain oil to the proper level (Chapter 1).

☐ Head gasket broken between oil return and cylinder. Causes oil to be pulled into the combustion chamber. Replace the head gasket and check the head for warpage (Chapter 2).

☐ Abnormal crankcase pressurization, which forces oil past the rings. Clogged breather is usually the cause.

Black smoke

☐ Air filter clogged. Clean or replace the element (Chapter 1).

☐ Carburetor flooding. Remove and overhaul the carburetor (Chapter 4).

☐ Main jet too large. Remove and overhaul the carburetor (Chapter 4).

☐ Choke knob stuck (Chapter 4).

☐ Fuel level too high. Check the float level (Chapter 4).

12 Poor handling or stability

Handlebar hard to turn

☐ Steering head bearing adjuster nut too tight. Check adjustment as described in Chapter 6.

☐ Bearings damaged. Roughness can be felt as the bars are turned from side-to-side. Replace bearings and races (Chapter 6).

☐ Races dented or worn. Denting results from wear in only one position (e.g., straight ahead), from a collision or hitting a pothole or from dropping the machine. Replace races and bearings (Chapter 6).

☐ Steering stem lubrication inadequate. Causes are grease getting hard from age or being washed out by high pressure car washes. Disassemble steering head and repack bearings (Chapter 6).

☐ Steering stem bent. Caused by a collision, hitting a pothole or by dropping the machine. Replace damaged part. Don't try to straighten the steering stem (Chapter 6).

☐ Front tire air pressure too low (Chapter 1).

Handlebar shakes or vibrates excessively

☐ Tires worn or out of balance (Chapter 7).

☐ Swingarm bearings worn. Replace worn bearings (Chapter 6).

☐ Wheel rim(s) warped or damaged. Inspect wheels for runout (Chapter 7).

☐ Wheel spokes loose (see Chapter 1).

☐ Wheel bearings worn. Worn front or rear wheel bearings can cause poor tracking. Worn front bearings will cause wobble (Chapter 7).

☐ Handlebar clamp bolts loose. Tighten them to the specified torque (Chapter 6).

☐ Triple clamp bolts loose. Tighten them to the specified torque (Chapter 6).

☐ Engine mounting bolts loose. Will cause excessive vibration with increased engine rpm (Chapter 2).

Handlebar pulls to one side

☐ Frame bent. Definitely suspect this if the machine has been dropped. May or may not be accompanied by cracking near the bend. Replace the frame (Chapter 8).

☐ Wheels out of alignment. Caused by improper location of axle spacers or from bent steering stem or frame (Chapters 6 and 8).

☐ Swingarm bent or twisted. Caused by age (metal fatigue) or impact damage. Replace the arm (Chapter 6).

☐ Steering stem bent. Caused by impact damage or by dropping the motorcycle. Replace the steering stem (Chapter 6).

☐ Fork tube bent. Disassemble the forks and replace the damaged parts (Chapter 6).

☐ Fork oil level uneven. Check and add or drain as necessary (Chapter 6).

Poor shock absorbing qualities

Too hard:
a) Fork oil level excessive (Chapter 6).
b) Fork oil viscosity too high. Use a lighter oil (see the Specifications in Chapter 1).
c) Fork tube bent. Causes a harsh, sticking feeling (Chapter 6).
d) Shock shaft or body bent or damaged (Chapter 6).
e) Fork internal damage (Chapter 6).
f) Shock internal damage (Chapter 6).
g) Tire pressure too high (Chapter 1).

Too soft:
a) Fork or shock oil insufficient and/or leaking (Chapters 1 and 6).
b) Fork oil level too low (Chapter 6).
c) Fork oil viscosity too light (Chapter 6).
d) Fork springs weak or broken (Chapter 6).
e) Shock internal damage or leakage (Chapter 6).

13 Braking problems

Brakes are spongy, don't hold

☐ Air in brake line. Caused by inattention to master cylinder fluid level or by leakage. Locate problem and bleed brakes (Chapter 7).
☐ Pad or disc worn (Chapters 1 and 7).
☐ Brake fluid leak. See paragraph 1.
☐ Contaminated pads. Caused by contamination with oil, grease, brake fluid, etc. Clean or replace pads. Clean disc thoroughly with brake cleaner (Chapter 7).
☐ Brake fluid deteriorated. Fluid is old or contaminated. Drain system, replenish with new fluid and bleed the system (Chapter 7).
☐ Master cylinder internal parts worn or damaged causing fluid to bypass (Chapter 7).
☐ Master cylinder bore scratched by foreign material or broken spring. Repair or replace master cylinder (Chapter 7).
☐ Disc warped. Replace disc (Chapter 7).

Brake lever or pedal pulsates

☐ Disc warped. Replace disc (Chapter 7).

☐ Axle bent. Replace axle (Chapter 7).
☐ Brake caliper bolts loose (Chapter 7).
☐ Wheel warped or otherwise damaged (Chapter 7).
☐ Wheel bearings damaged or worn (Chapter 7).

Brakes drag

☐ Master cylinder piston seized. Caused by wear or damage to piston or cylinder bore (Chapter 7).
☐ Lever binding. Check pivot and lubricate (Chapter 7).
☐ Brake caliper piston seized in bore. Caused by wear or ingestion of dirt past deteriorated seal (Chapter 7).
☐ Brake caliper mounting bracket pins corroded. Clean off corrosion and lubricate (Chapter 7).
☐ Brake pad damaged. Material separated from backing plate. Usually caused by faulty manufacturing process or from contact with chemicals. Replace pads (Chapter 7).
☐ Pads improperly installed (Chapter 7).

14 Electrical problems

Battery dead or weak

☐ Battery faulty. Caused by sulfated plates which are shorted through sedimentation. Also, broken battery terminal making only occasional contact (Chapter 5).
☐ Battery cables making poor contact (Chapter 5).
☐ Load excessive. Caused by addition of high wattage lights or other electrical accessories.
☐ Ignition (main) switch defective. Switch either grounds internally or fails to shut off system. Replace the switch (Chapter 5).
☐ Regulator/rectifier defective (Chapter 5).
☐ Alternator stator coil open or shorted (Chapter 5).
☐ Wiring faulty. Wiring grounded or connections loose in ignition, charging or lighting circuits (Chapter 5).

Battery overcharged

☐ Regulator/rectifier defective. Overcharging is noticed when battery gets excessively warm (Chapter 5).
☐ Battery defective. Replace battery with a new one (Chapter 5).
☐ Battery amperage too low, wrong type or size. Install manufacturer's specified amp-hour battery to handle charging load (Chapter 5).

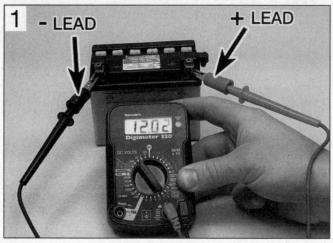

Measuring open-circuit battery voltage

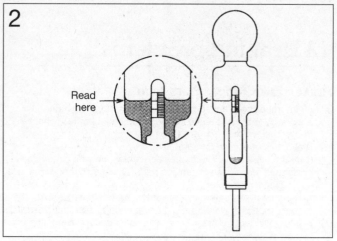

Read here

Float-type hydrometer for measuring battery specific gravity

Checking engine compression

● Low compression will result in exhaust smoke, heavy oil consumption, poor starting and poor performance. A compression test will provide useful information about an engine's condition and if performed regularly, can give warning of trouble before any other symptoms become apparent.

● A compression gauge will be required, along with an adapter to suit the spark plug hole thread size. Note that the screw-in type gauge/adapter set up is preferable to the rubber cone type.

● Before carrying out the test, first check the valve clearances as described in Chapter 1.

Checking battery open-circuit voltage

⚠ **Warning: The gases produced by the battery are explosive - never smoke or create any sparks in the vicinity of the battery. Never allow the electrolyte to contact your skin or clothing - if it does, wash it off and seek immediate medical attention.**

● Before any electrical fault is investigated the battery should be checked.

● You'll need a dc voltmeter or multimeter to check battery voltage. Check that the leads are inserted in the correct terminals on the meter, red lead to positive (+), black lead to negative (-). Incorrect connections can damage the meter.

● A sound, fully-charged 12 volt battery

should produce between 12.3 and 12.6 volts across its terminals (12.8 volts for a maintenance-free battery). On machines with a 6 volt battery, voltage should be between 6.1 and 6.3 volts.

1 Set a multimeter to the 0 to 20 volts dc range and connect its probes across the battery terminals. Connect the meter's positive (+) probe, usually red, to the battery positive (+) terminal, followed by the meter's negative (-) probe, usually black, to the battery negative terminal (-) **(see illustration 1)**.

2 If battery voltage is low (below 10 volts on a 12 volt battery or below 4 volts on a six volt battery), charge the battery and test the voltage again. If the battery repeatedly goes flat, investigate the motorcycle's charging system.

Checking battery specific gravity (SG)

⚠ **Warning: The gases produced by the battery are explosive - never smoke or create any sparks in the vicinity of the battery. Never allow the electrolyte to contact your skin or clothing - if it does, wash it off and seek immediate medical attention.**

● The specific gravity check gives an indication of a battery's state of charge.

● A hydrometer is used for measuring specific gravity. Make sure you purchase one which has a small enough hose to insert in the aperture of a motorcycle battery.

● Specific gravity is simply a measure of the electrolyte's density compared with that of water. Water has an SG of 1.000 and fully-charged battery electrolyte is about 26% heavier, at 1.260.

● Specific gravity checks are not possible on maintenance-free batteries. Testing the open-circuit voltage is the only means of determining their state of charge.

1 To measure SG, remove the battery from the motorcycle and remove the first cell cap. Draw some electrolyte into the hydrometer and note the reading **(see illustration 2)**. Return the electrolyte to the cell and install the cap.

2 The reading should be in the region of 1.260 to 1.280. If SG is below 1.200 the battery needs charging. Note that SG will vary with temperature; it should be measured at 20°C (68°F). Add 0.007 to the reading for every 10°C above 20°C, and subtract 0.007 from the reading for every 10°C below 20°C. Add 0.004 to the reading for every 10°F above 68°F, and subtract 0.004 from the reading for every 10°F below 68°F.

3 When the check is complete, rinse the hydrometer thoroughly with clean water.

Checking for continuity

● The term continuity describes the uninterrupted flow of electricity through an electrical circuit. A continuity check will determine whether an **open-circuit** situation exists.

● Continuity can be checked with an ohmmeter, multimeter, continuity tester or battery and bulb test circuit **(see illustrations 3, 4 and 5)**.

● All of these instruments are self-powered by a battery, therefore the checks are made with the ignition OFF.

● As a safety precaution, always disconnect the battery negative (-) lead before making checks, particularly if ignition switch checks are being made.

● If using a meter, select the appropriate

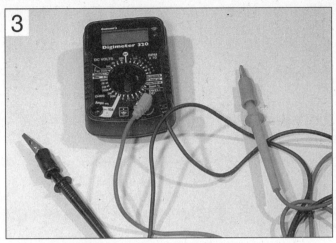

Digital multimeter can be used for all electrical tests

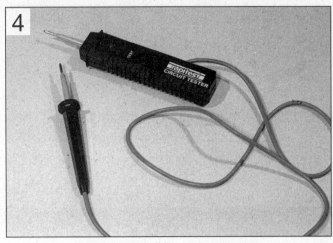

Battery-powered continuity tester

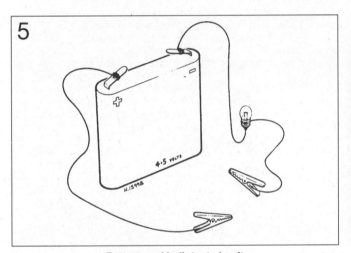

Battery and bulb test circuit

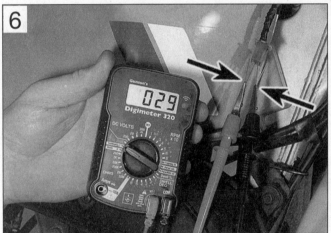

Continuity check of front brake light switch using a meter - note cotter pins used to access connector terminals

ohms scale and check that the meter reads infinity (∞). Touch the meter probes together and check that meter reads zero; where necessary adjust the meter so that it reads zero.

● After using a meter, always switch it OFF to conserve its battery.

Switch checks

1 If a switch is at fault, trace its wiring up to the wiring connectors. Separate the wire connectors and inspect them for security and condition. A build-up of dirt or corrosion here will most likely be the cause of the problem - clean up and apply a water dispersant such as WD40.

2 If using a test meter, set the meter to the ohms x 10 scale and connect its probes across the wires from the switch **(see illustration 6)**. Simple ON/OFF type switches, such as brake light switches, only have two wires whereas combination switches, like the ignition switch, have many internal links. Study the wiring diagram to ensure that you are connecting across the correct pair of wires. Continuity (low or no measurable resistance - 0 ohms) should be indicated with the switch ON and no continuity (high resistance) with it OFF.

3 Note that the polarity of the test probes doesn't matter for continuity checks, although care should be taken to follow specific test procedures if a diode or solid-state component is being checked.

4 A continuity tester or battery and bulb circuit can be used in the same way. Connect its probes as described above **(see illustration 7)**. The light should come on to indicate continuity in the ON switch position, but should extinguish in the OFF position.

Wiring checks

● Many electrical faults are caused by damaged wiring, often due to incorrect routing or chaffing on frame components.

● Loose, wet or corroded wire connectors

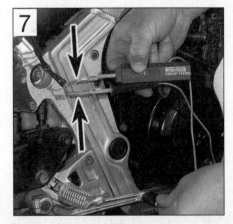

Continuity check of rear brake light switch using a continuity tester

can also be the cause of electrical problems, especially in exposed locations.

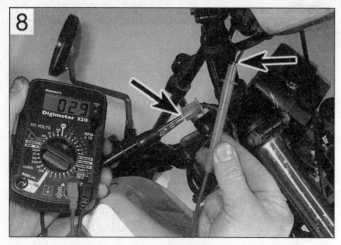

Continuity check of front brake light switch sub-harness

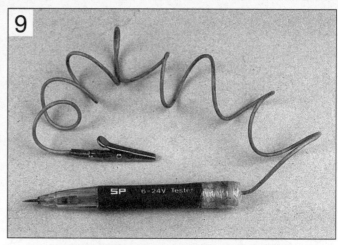

A simple test light can be used for voltage checks

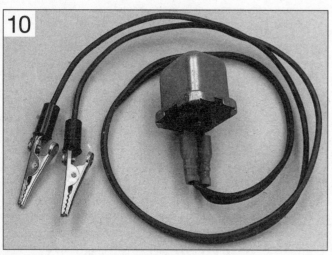

A buzzer is useful for voltage checks

Checking for voltage at the rear brake light power supply wire using a meter . . .

1 A continuity check can be made on a single length of wire by disconnecting it at each end and connecting a meter or continuity tester across both ends of the wire **(see illustration 8)**.

2 Continuity (low or no resistance - 0 ohms) should be indicated if the wire is good. If no continuity (high resistance) is shown, suspect a broken wire.

Checking for voltage

● A voltage check can determine whether current is reaching a component.

● Voltage can be checked with a dc voltmeter, multimeter set on the dc volts scale, test light or buzzer **(see illustrations 9 and 10)**. A meter has the advantage of being able to measure actual voltage.

● When using a meter, check that its leads are inserted in the correct terminals on the meter, red to positive (+), black to negative (-). Incorrect connections can damage the meter.

● A voltmeter (or multimeter set to the dc volts scale) should always be connected in parallel (across the load). Connecting it in series will destroy the meter.

● Voltage checks are made with the ignition ON.

1 First identify the relevant wiring circuit by referring to the wiring diagram at the end of this manual. If other electrical components share the same power supply (ie are fed from the same fuse), take note whether they are working correctly - this is useful information in deciding where to start checking the circuit.

2 If using a meter, check first that the meter leads are plugged into the correct terminals on the meter (see above). Set the meter to the dc volts function, at a range suitable for the battery voltage. Connect the meter red probe (+) to the power supply wire and the black probe to a good metal ground on the

motorcycle's frame or directly to the battery negative (-) terminal **(see illustration 11)**. Battery voltage should be shown on the meter with the ignition switched ON.

3 If using a test light or buzzer, connect its positive (+) probe to the power supply terminal and its negative (-) probe to a good ground on the motorcycle's frame or directly to the battery negative (-) terminal **(see illustration 12)**. With the ignition ON, the test light should illuminate or the buzzer sound.

4 If no voltage is indicated, work back towards the fuse continuing to check for voltage. When you reach a point where there is voltage, you know the problem lies between that point and your last check point.

Checking the ground

● Ground connections are made either

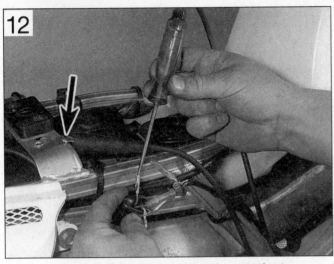

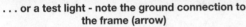

. . . or a test light - note the ground connection to the frame (arrow)

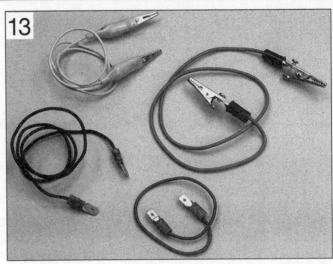

A selection of jumper wires for making ground checks

directly to the engine or frame (such as sensors, neutral switch etc. which only have a positive feed) or by a separate wire into the ground circuit of the wiring harness. Alternatively a short ground wire is sometimes run directly from the component to the motor-cycle's frame.

● Corrosion is often the cause of a poor ground connection.

● If total failure is experienced, check the security of the main ground lead from the negative (-) terminal of the battery and also the main ground point on the wiring harness. If corroded, dismantle the connection and clean all surfaces back to bare metal.

1 To check the ground on a component, use an insulated jumper wire to temporarily bypass its ground connection **(see illustration 13)**. Connect one end of the jumper wire between the ground terminal or metal body

of the component and the other end to the motorcycle's frame.

2 If the circuit works with the jumper wire installed, the original ground circuit is faulty. Check the wiring for open-circuits or poor connections. Clean up direct ground connections, removing all traces of corrosion and remake the joint. Apply petroleum jelly to the joint to prevent future corrosion.

Tracing a short-circuit

● A short-circuit occurs where current shorts to ground bypassing the circuit components. This usually results in a blown fuse.

● A short-circuit is most likely to occur where the insulation has worn through due to wiring chafing on a component, allowing a direct path to ground on the frame.

1 Remove any body panels necessary to access the circuit wiring.

2 Check that all electrical switches in the circuit are OFF, then remove the circuit fuse and connect a test light, buzzer or voltmeter (set to the dc scale) across the fuse terminals. No voltage should be shown.

3 Move the wiring from side to side while observing the test light or meter. When the test light comes on, buzzer sounds or meter shows voltage, you have found the cause of the short. It will usually shown up as damaged or burned insulation.

4 Note that the same test can be performed on each component in the circuit, even the switch.

Introduction

In less time than it takes to read this introduction, a thief could steal your motorcycle. Returning only to find your bike has gone is one of the worst feelings in the world. Even if the motorcycle is insured against theft, once you've gotten over the initial shock, you will have the inconvenience of dealing with the police and your insurance company.

The motorcycle is an easy target for the professional thief and the joyrider alike and the official figures on motorcycle theft make for depressing reading; on average a motor-cycle is stolen every 16 minutes in the UK!

Motorcycle thefts fall into two categories, those stolen 'to order' and those taken by opportunists. The thief stealing to order will be on the look out for a specific make and model and will go to extraordinary lengths to obtain that motorcycle. The opportunist thief on the other hand will look for easy targets which can be stolen with the minimum of effort and risk.

While it is never going to be possible to make your machine 100% secure, it is estimated that around half of all stolen motorcycles are taken by opportunist thieves. Remember that the opportunist thief is always on the look out for the easy option: if there are two similar motorcycles parked side-by-side, they will target the one with the lowest level of security. By taking a few precautions, you can reduce the chances of your motorcycle being stolen.

Security equipment

There are many specialized motorcycle security devices available and the following text summarizes their applications and their good and bad points.

Once you have decided on the type of security equipment which best suits your needs, we recommended that you read one of the many equipment tests regularly carried out by the motorcycle press. These tests compare the products from all the major manufacturers and give impartial ratings on their effectiveness, value-for-money and ease of use.

No one item of security equipment can provide complete protection. It is highly recommended that two or more of the items described below are combined to increase the security of your motorcycle (a lock and chain plus an alarm system is just about ideal). The more security measures installed on the bike, the less likely it is to be stolen.

Lock and chain

Pros: *Very flexible to use; can be used to secure the motorcycle to almost any immovable object. On some locks and chains, the lock can be used on its own as a disc lock (see below).*

Cons: *Can be very heavy and awkward to carry on the motorcycle, although some types*

will be supplied with a carry bag which can be strapped to the pillion seat.

● Heavy-duty chains and locks are an excellent security measure **(see illustration 1)**. Whenever the motorcycle is parked, use the lock and chain to secure the machine to a solid, immovable object such as a post or railings. This will prevent the machine from being ridden away or being lifted into the back of a van.

● When fitting the chain, always ensure the chain is routed around the motorcycle frame or swingarm **(see illustrations 2 and 3)**. Never merely pass the chain around one of the wheel rims; a thief may unbolt the wheel and lift the rest of the machine into a van, leaving you with just the wheel! Try to avoid having excess chain free, thus making it difficult to use cutting tools, and keep the chain and lock off the ground to prevent thieves attacking it with a cold chisel. Position the lock so that its lock barrel is facing downwards; this will make it harder for the thief to attack the lock mechanism.

Ensure the lock and chain you buy is of good quality and long enough to shackle your bike to a solid object

Pass the chain through the bike's frame, rather than just through a wheel . . .

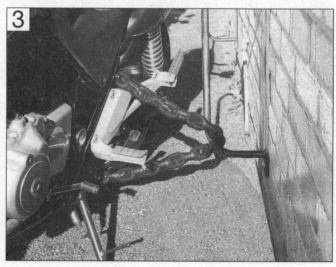

. . . and loop it around a solid object

U-locks

Pros: *Highly effective deterrent which can be used to secure the bike to a post or railings. Most U-locks come with a carrier which allows the lock to be easily carried on the bike.*

Cons: *Not as flexible to use as a lock and chain.*

● These are solid locks which are similar in use to a lock and chain. U-locks are lighter than a lock and chain but not so flexible to use. The length and shape of the lock shackle limit the objects to which the bike can be secured **(see illustration 4)**.

Disc locks

Pros: *Small, light and very easy to carry; most can be stored underneath the seat.*

Cons: *Does not prevent the motorcycle being lifted into a van. Can be very embarrassing if*

U-locks can be used to secure the bike to a solid object – ensure you purchase one which is long enough

you forget to remove the lock before attempting to ride off!

● Disc locks are designed to be attached to the front brake disc. The lock passes through one of the holes in the disc and prevents the wheel rotating by jamming against the fork/ brake caliper **(see illustration 5)**. Some are equipped with an alarm siren which sounds if the disc lock is moved; this not only acts as a theft deterrent but also as a handy reminder if you try to move the bike with the lock still fitted.

● Combining the disc lock with a length of cable which can be looped around a post or railings provides an additional measure of security **(see illustration 6)**.

Alarms and immobilizers

Pros: *Once installed it is completely hassle-free to use. If the system is 'Thatcham' or 'Sold Secure-approved', insurance companies may give you a discount.*

Cons: *Can be expensive to buy and complex to install. No system will prevent the motorcycle from being lifted into a van and taken away.*

● Electronic alarms and immobilizers are available to suit a variety of budgets. There are three different types of system available: pure alarms, pure immobilizers, and the more expensive systems which are combined alarm/immobilizers **(see illustration 7)**.
● An alarm system is designed to emit an audible warning if the motorcycle is being tampered with.
● An immobilizer prevents the motorcycle being started and ridden away by disabling its electrical systems.
● When purchasing an alarm/immobilizer system, check the cost of installing the system unless you are able to do it yourself. If the motorcycle is not used regularly, another consideration is the current drain of the system. All alarm/immobilizer systems are powered by the motorcycle's battery; purchasing a system with a very low current drain could prevent the battery losing its charge while the motorcycle is not being used.

A typical disc lock attached through one of the holes in the disc

A disc lock combined with a security cable provides additional protection

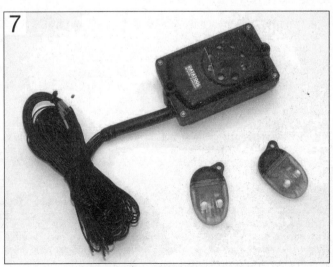

A typical alarm/immobilizer system

8

Indelible markings can be applied to most areas of the bike – always apply the manufacturer's sticker to warn off thieves

9

Chemically-etched code numbers can be applied to main body panels . . .

10

. . . again, always ensure that the kit manufacturer's sticker is applied in a prominent position

Security marking kits

Pros: *Very cheap and effective deterrent. Many insurance companies will give you a discount on your insurance premium if a recognized security marking kit is used on your motorcycle.*

Cons: *Does not prevent the motorcycle being stolen by joyriders.*

● There are many different types of security marking kits available. The idea is to mark as many parts of the motorcycle as possible with a unique security number **(see illustrations 8, 9 and 10)**. A form will be included with the kit to register your personal details and those of the motorcycle with the kit manufacturer. This register is made available to the police to help them trace the rightful owner of any motorcycle or components which they recover should all other forms of identification have been removed. Always apply the warning stickers provided with the kit to deter thieves.

Ground anchors, wheel clamps and security posts

Pros: *An excellent form of security which will deter all but the most determined of thieves.*

Cons: *Awkward to install and can be expensive.*

● While the motorcycle is at home, it is a good idea to attach it securely to the floor or a solid wall, even if it is kept in a securely locked garage. Various types of ground anchors, security posts and wheel clamps are available for this purpose **(see illustration 11)**. These security devices are either bolted to a solid concrete or brick structure or can be cemented into the ground.

11

Permanent ground anchors provide an excellent level of security when the bike is at home

Security at home

A high percentage of motorcycle thefts are from the owner's home. Here are some things to consider whenever your motorcycle is at home:

✔ Where possible, always keep the motorcycle in a securely locked garage. Never rely solely on the standard lock on the garage door; these are usual hopelessly inadequate. Fit an additional locking mechanism to the door and consider having the garage alarmed. A security light, activated by a movement sensor, is also a good investment.

✔ Always secure the motorcycle to the ground or a wall, even if it is inside a securely locked garage.
✔ Do not regularly leave the motorcycle outside your home; try to keep it out of sight wherever possible. If a garage is not available, fit a motorcycle cover over the bike to disguise its true identity.
✔ It is not uncommon for thieves to follow a motorcyclist home to find out where the bike is kept. They will then return at a later date. Be aware of this whenever you are returning

home on your motorcycle. If you suspect you are being followed, do not return home, instead ride to a garage or shop and stop as a precaution.
✔ When selling a motorcycle, do not provide your home address or the location where the bike is normally kept. Arrange to meet the buyer at a location away from your home. Thieves have been known to pose as potential buyers to find out where motorcycles are kept and then return later to steal them.

Security away from the home

As well as fitting security equipment to your motorcycle here are a few general rules to follow whenever you park your motorcycle.
✔ Park in a busy, public place.
✔ Use parking lots which incorporate security features, such as CCTV.

✔ At night, park in a well-lit area, preferably directly underneath a street light.
✔ Engage the steering lock.
✔ Secure the motorcycle to a solid, immovable object such as a post or railings with an additional lock. If this is not possible,

secure the bike to a friend's motorcycle. Some public parking places provide security loops for motorcycles.
✔ Never leave your helmet or luggage attached to the motorcycle. Take them with you at all times.

A

ABS (Anti-lock braking system) A system, usually electronically controlled, that senses incipient wheel lockup during braking and relieves hydraulic pressure at wheel which is about to skid.

Aftermarket Components suitable for the motorcycle, but not produced by the motorcycle manufacturer.

Allen key A hexagonal wrench which fits into a recessed hexagonal hole.

Alternating current (ac) Current produced by an alternator. Requires converting to direct current by a rectifier for charging purposes.

Alternator Converts mechanical energy from the engine into electrical energy to charge the battery and power the electrical system.

Ampere (amp) A unit of measurement for the flow of electrical current. Current = Volts ÷ Ohms.

Ampere-hour (Ah) Measure of battery capacity.

Angle-tightening A torque expressed in degrees. Often follows a conventional tightening torque for cylinder head or main bearing fasteners **(see illustration)**.

Angle-tightening cylinder head bolts

Antifreeze A substance (usually ethylene glycol) mixed with water, and added to the cooling system, to prevent freezing of the coolant in winter. Antifreeze also contains chemicals to inhibit corrosion and the formation of rust and other deposits that would tend to clog the radiator and coolant passages and reduce cooling efficiency.

Anti-dive System attached to the fork lower leg (slider) to prevent fork dive when braking hard.

Anti-seize compound A coating that reduces the risk of seizing on fasteners that are subjected to high temperatures, such as exhaust clamp bolts and nuts.

API American Petroleum Institute. A quality standard for 4-stroke motor oils.

Asbestos A natural fibrous mineral with great heat resistance, commonly used in the composition of brake friction materials. Asbestos is a health hazard and the dust created by brake systems should never be inhaled or ingested.

ATF Automatic Transmission Fluid. Often used in front forks.

ATU Automatic Timing Unit. Mechanical device for advancing the ignition timing on early engines.

ATV All Terrain Vehicle. Often called a Quad.

Axial play Side-to-side movement.

Axle A shaft on which a wheel revolves. Also known as a spindle.

B

Backlash The amount of movement between meshed components when one component is held still. Usually applies to gear teeth.

Ball bearing A bearing consisting of a hardened inner and outer race with hardened steel balls between the two races.

Bearings Used between two working surfaces to prevent wear of the components and a build-up of heat. Four types of bearing are commonly used on motorcycles: plain shell bearings, ball bearings, tapered roller bearings and needle roller bearings.

Bevel gears Used to turn the drive through 90°. Typical applications are shaft final drive and camshaft drive **(see illustration)**.

BHP Brake Horsepower. The British measurement for engine power output. Power output is now usually expressed in kilowatts (kW).

Bevel gears are used to turn the drive through 90°

Bias-belted tire Similar construction to radial tire, but with outer belt running at an angle to the wheel rim.

Big-end bearing The bearing in the end of the connecting rod that's attached to the crankshaft.

Bleeding The process of removing air from a hydraulic system via a bleed nipple or bleed screw.

Bottom-end A description of an engine's crankcase components and all components contained therein.

BTDC Before Top Dead Center in terms of piston position. Ignition timing is often expressed in terms of degrees or millimeters BTDC.

Bush A cylindrical metal or rubber component used between two moving parts.

Burr Rough edge left on a component after machining or as a result of excessive wear.

C

Cam chain The chain which takes drive from the crankshaft to the camshaft(s).

Canister The main component in an evaporative emission control system (California market only); contains activated charcoal granules to trap vapors from the fuel system rather than allowing them to vent to the atmosphere.

Castellated Resembling the parapets along the top of a castle wall. For example, a castellated wheel axle or spindle nut.

Catalytic converter A device in the exhaust system of some machines which

Cush drive rubber segments dampen out transmission shocks

converts certain pollutants in the exhaust gases into less harmful substances.

Charging system Description of the components which charge the battery, ie the alternator, rectifer and regulator.

Clearance The amount of space between two parts. For example, between a piston and a cylinder, between a bearing and a journal, etc.

Coil spring A spiral of elastic steel found in various sizes throughout a vehicle, for example as a springing medium in the suspension and in the valve train.

Compression Reduction in volume, and increase in pressure and temperature, of a gas, caused by squeezing it into a smaller space.

Compression damping Controls the speed the suspension compresses when hitting a bump.

Compression ratio The relationship between cylinder volume when the piston is at top dead center and cylinder volume when the piston is at bottom dead center.

Continuity The uninterrupted path in the flow of electricity. Little or no measurable resistance.

Continuity tester Self-powered bleeper or test light which indicates continuity.

Cp Candlepower. Bulb rating commonly found on US motorcycles.

Crossply tire Tire plies arranged in a criss-cross pattern. Usually four or six plies used, hence 4PR or 6PR in tire size codes.

Cush drive Rubber damper segments fitted between the rear wheel and final drive sprocket to absorb transmission shocks **(see illustration)**.

D

Degree disc Calibrated disc for measuring piston position. Expressed in degrees.

Dial gauge Clock-type gauge with adapters for measuring runout and piston position. Expressed in mm or inches.

Diaphragm The rubber membrane in a master cylinder or carburetor which seals the upper chamber.

Diaphragm spring A single sprung plate often used in clutches.

Direct current (dc) Current produced by a dc generator.

Decarbonization The process of removing carbon deposits - typically from the combustion chamber, valves and exhaust port/system.

Detonation Destructive and damaging explosion of fuel/air mixture in combustion chamber instead of controlled burning.

Diode An electrical valve which only allows current to flow in one direction. Commonly used in rectifiers and starter interlock systems.

Disc valve (or rotary valve) An induction system used on some two-stroke engines.

Double-overhead camshaft (DOHC) An engine that uses two overhead camshafts, one for the intake valves and one for the exhaust valves.

Drivebelt A toothed belt used to transmit drive to the rear wheel on some motorcycles. A drivebelt has also been used to drive the camshafts. Drivebelts are usually made of Kevlar.

Driveshaft Any shaft used to transmit motion. Commonly used when referring to the final driveshaft on shaft drive motorcycles.

E

ECU (Electronic Control Unit) A computer which controls (for instance) an ignition system, or an anti-lock braking system.

EGO Exhaust Gas Oxygen sensor. Some-times called a Lambda sensor.

Electrolyte The fluid in a lead-acid battery.

E0MS (Engine Management System) A computer controlled system which manages the fuel injection and the ignition systems in an integrated fashion.

Endfloat The amount of lengthways movement between two parts. As applied to a crankshaft, the distance that the crankshaft can move side-to-side in the crankcase.

Endless chain A chain having no joining link. Common use for cam chains and final drive chains.

EP (Extreme Pressure) Oil type used in locations where high loads are applied, such as between gear teeth.

Evaporative emission control system Describes a charcoal filled canister which stores fuel vapors from the tank rather than allowing them to vent to the atmosphere. Usually only fitted to California models and referred to as an EVAP system.

Expansion chamber Section of two-stroke engine exhaust system so designed to improve engine efficiency and boost power.

F

Feeler blade or gauge A thin strip or blade of hardened steel, ground to an exact thickness, used to check or measure clearances between parts.

Final drive Description of the drive from the transmission to the rear wheel. Usually by chain or shaft, but sometimes by belt.

Firing order The order in which the engine cylinders fire, or deliver their power strokes, beginning with the number one cylinder.

Flooding Term used to describe a high fuel level in the carburetor float chambers, leading to fuel overflow. Also refers to excess fuel in the combustion chamber due to incorrect starting technique.

Free length The no-load state of a component when measured. Clutch, valve and fork spring lengths are measured at rest, without any preload.

Freeplay The amount of travel before any action takes place. The looseness in a linkage, or an assembly of parts, between the initial application of force and actual movement. For example, the distance the rear brake pedal moves before the rear brake is actuated.

Fuel injection The fuel/air mixture is metered electronically and directed into the engine intake ports (indirect injection) or into the cylinders (direct injection). Sensors supply information on engine speed and conditions.

Fuel/air mixture The charge of fuel and air going into the engine. See **Stoichiometric ratio**.

Fuse An electrical device which protects a circuit against accidental overload. The typical fuse contains a soft piece of metal which is calibrated to melt at a predetermined current flow (expressed as amps) and break the circuit.

G

Gap The distance the spark must travel in jumping from the center electrode to the side electrode in a spark plug. Also refers to the distance between the ignition rotor and the pickup coil in an electronic ignition system.

Gasket Any thin, soft material - usually cork, cardboard, asbestos or soft metal - installed between two metal surfaces to ensure a good seal. For instance, the cylinder head gasket seals the joint between the block and the cylinder head.

Gauge An instrument panel display used to monitor engine conditions. A gauge with a movable pointer on a dial or a fixed scale is an analog gauge. A gauge with a numerical readout is called a digital gauge.

Gear ratios The drive ratio of a pair of gears in a gearbox, calculated on their number of teeth.

Glaze-busting see **Honing**

Grinding Process for renovating the valve face and valve seat contact area in the cylinder head.

Ground return The return path of an electrical circuit, utilizing the motorcycle's frame.

Gudgeon pin The shaft which connects the connecting rod small-end with the piston. Often called a piston pin or wrist pin.

H

Helical gears Gear teeth are slightly curved and produce less gear noise that straight-cut gears. Often used for primary drives.

Helicoil A thread insert repair system. Commonly used as a repair for stripped spark plug threads **(see illustration).**

Installing a Helicoil thread insert in a cylinder head

Honing A process used to break down the glaze on a cylinder bore (also called glaze-busting). Can also be carried out to roughen a rebored cylinder to aid ring bedding-in.

HT (High Tension) Description of the electrical circuit from the secondary winding of the ignition coil to the spark plug.

Hydraulic A liquid filled system used to transmit pressure from one component to another. Common uses on motorcycles are brakes and clutches.

Hydrometer An instrument for measuring the specific gravity of a lead-acid battery.

Hygroscopic Water absorbing. In motorcycle applications, braking efficiency will be reduced if DOT 3 or 4 hydraulic fluid absorbs water from the air - care must be taken to keep new brake fluid in tightly sealed containers.

I

lbf ft Pounds-force feet. A unit of torque. Sometimes written as ft-lbs.

lbf in Pound-force inch. A unit of torque, applied to components where a very low torque is required. Sometimes written as inch-lbs.

IC Abbreviation for Integrated Circuit.

Ignition advance Means of increasing the timing of the spark at higher engine speeds. Done by mechanical means (ATU) on early engines or electronically by the ignition control unit on later engines.

Ignition timing The moment at which the spark plug fires, expressed in the number of crankshaft degrees before the piston reaches the top of its stroke, or in the number of millimeters before the piston reaches the top of its stroke.

Infinity (∞) Description of an open-circuit electrical state, where no continuity exists.

Inverted forks (upside down forks) The sliders or lower legs are held in the yokes and the fork tubes or stanchions are connected to the wheel axle (spindle). Less unsprung weight and stiffer construction than conventional forks.

J

JASO Japan Automobile Standards Organization. JASO MA is a standard for motorcycle oil equivalent to API SJ, but designed to prevent problems with wet-type motorcycle clutches.

Joule The unit of electrical energy.

Journal The bearing surface of a shaft.

K

Kickstart Mechanical means of turning the engine over for starting purposes.

Only usually fitted to mopeds, small capacity motorcycles and off-road motorcycles.

Kill switch Handebar-mounted switch for emergency ignition cut-out. Cuts the ignition circuit on all models, and additionally prevent starter motor operation on others.

km Symbol for kilometer.

kmh Abbreviation for kilometers per hour.

L

Lambda sensor A sensor fitted in the exhaust system to measure the exhaust gas oxygen content (excess air factor). Also called oxygen sensor.

Lapping see **Grinding**.

LCD Abbreviation for Liquid Crystal Display.

LED Abbreviation for Light Emitting Diode.

Liner A steel cylinder liner inserted in an aluminum alloy cylinder block.

Locknut A nut used to lock an adjustment nut, or other threaded component, in place.

Lockstops The lugs on the lower triple clamp (yoke) which abut those on the frame, preventing handlebar-to-fuel tank contact.

Lockwasher A form of washer designed to prevent an attaching nut from working loose.

LT (Low Tension) Description of the electrical circuit from the power supply to the primary winding of the ignition coil.

M

Main bearings The bearings between the crankshaft and crankcase.

Maintenance-free (MF) battery A sealed battery which cannot be topped up.

Manometer Mercury-filled calibrated tubes used to measure intake tract vacuum. Used to synchronize carburetors on multi-cylinder engines.

Tappet shims are measured with a micrometer

Micrometer A precision measuring instrument that measures component outside diameters **(see illustration)**.

MON (Motor Octane Number) A measure of a fuel's resistance to knock.

Monograde oil An oil with a single viscosity, eg SAE80W.

Monoshock A single suspension unit linking the swingarm or suspension linkage to the frame.

mph Abbreviation for miles per hour.

Multigrade oil Having a wide viscosity range (eg 10W40). The W stands for Winter, thus the viscosity ranges from SAE10 when cold to SAE40 when hot.

Multimeter An electrical test instrument with the capability to measure voltage, current and resistance. Some meters also incorporate a continuity tester and buzzer.

N

Needle roller bearing Inner race of caged needle rollers and hardened outer race. Examples of uncaged needle rollers can be found on some engines. Commonly used in rear suspension applications and in two-stroke engines.

Nm Newton meters.

NOx Oxides of Nitrogen. A common toxic pollutant emitted by gasoline engines at higher temperatures.

O

Octane The measure of a fuel's resistance to knock.

OE (Original Equipment) Relates to components fitted to a motorcycle as standard or replacement parts supplied by the motorcycle manufacturer.

Ohm The unit of electrical resistance. Ohms = Volts ÷ Current.

Ohmmeter An instrument for measuring electrical resistance.

Oil cooler System for diverting engine oil outside of the engine to a radiator for cooling purposes.

Oil injection A system of two-stroke engine lubrication where oil is pump-fed to the engine in accordance with throttle position.

Open-circuit An electrical condition where there is a break in the flow of electricity - no continuity (high resistance).

O-ring A type of sealing ring made of a special rubber-like material; in use, the O-ring is compressed into a groove to provide the sealing action.

Oversize (OS) Term used for piston and ring size options fitted to a rebored cylinder.

Overhead cam (sohc) engine An engine with single camshaft located on top of the cylinder head.

Overhead valve (ohv) engine An engine with the valves located in the cylinder head, but with the camshaft located in the engine block or crankcase.

Oxygen sensor A device installed in the exhaust system which senses the oxygen content in the exhaust and converts this information into an electric current. Also called a Lambda sensor.

P

Plastigage A thin strip of plastic thread, available in different sizes, used for measuring clearances. For example, a strip of Plastigage is laid across a bearing journal. The parts are assembled and dismantled; the width of the crushed strip indicates the clearance between journal and bearing.

Polarity Either negative or positive ground, determined by which battery lead is connected to the frame (ground return). Modern motorcycles are usually negative ground.

Pre-ignition A situation where the fuel/air mixture ignites before the spark plug fires. Often due to a hot spot in the combustion chamber caused by carbon build-up. Engine has a tendency to 'run-on'.

Pre-load (suspension) The amount a spring is compressed when in the unloaded state. Preload can be applied by gas, spacer or mechanical adjuster.

Premix The method of engine lubrication on some gasoline two-stroke engines. Engine oil is mixed with the gasoline in the fuel tank in a specific ratio. The fuel/oil mix is sometimes referred to as "petrol".

Primary drive Description of the drive from the crankshaft to the clutch. Usually by gear or chain.

PS Pferdestärke - a German interpretation of BHP.

PSI Pounds-force per square inch. Imperial measurement of tire pressure and cylinder pressure measurement.

PTFE Polytetrafluroethylene. A low friction substance.

Pulse secondary air injection system A process of promoting the burning of excess fuel present in the exhaust gases by routing fresh air into the exhaust ports.

Q

Quartz halogen bulb Tungsten filament surrounded by a halogen gas. Typically used for the headlight **(see illustration)**.

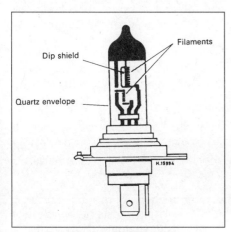

Quartz halogen headlight bulb construction

R

Rack-and-pinion A pinion gear on the end of a shaft that mates with a rack (think of a geared wheel opened up and laid flat). Sometimes used in clutch operating systems.

Radial play Up and down movement about a shaft.

Radial ply tires Tire plies run across the tire (from bead to bead) and around the circumference of the tire. Less resistant to tread distortion than other tire types.

Radiator A liquid-to-air heat transfer device designed to reduce the temperature of the coolant in a liquid cooled engine.

Rake A feature of steering geometry - the angle of the steering head in relation to the vertical **(see illustration)**.

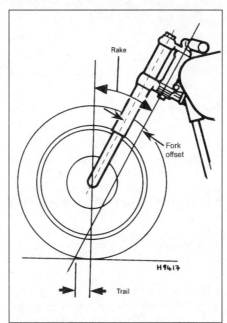

Steering geometry

Rebore Providing a new working surface to the cylinder bore by boring out the old surface. Necessitates the use of oversize piston and rings.

Rebound damping A means of controlling the oscillation of a suspension unit spring after it has been compressed. Resists the spring's natural tendency to bounce back after being compressed.

Rectifier Device for converting the ac output of an alternator into dc for battery charging.

Reed valve An induction system commonly used on two-stroke engines.

Regulator Device for maintaining the charging voltage from the generator or alternator within a specified range.

Relay A electrical device used to switch heavy current on and off by using a low current auxiliary circuit.

Resistance Measured in ohms. An electrical component's ability to pass electrical current.

RON (Research Octane Number) A measure of a fuel's resistance to knock.

rpm revolutions per minute.

Runout The amount of wobble (in-and-out movement) of a wheel or shaft as it's rotated. The amount a shaft rotates "out-of-true." The out-of-round condition of a rotating part.

S

SAE (Society of Automotive Engineers) A standard for the viscosity of a fluid.

Sealant A liquid or paste used to prevent leakage at a joint. Sometimes used in conjunction with a gasket.

Service limit Term for the point where a component is no longer useable and must be replaced.

Shaft drive A method of transmitting drive from the transmission to the rear wheel.

Shell bearings Plain bearings consisting of two shell halves. Most often used as big-end and main bearings in a four-stroke engine. Often called bearing inserts.

Shim Thin spacer, commonly used to adjust the clearance or relative positions between two parts. For example, shims inserted into or under tappets or followers to control valve clearances. Clearance is adjusted by changing the thickness of the shim.

Short-circuit An electrical condition where current shorts to ground bypassing the circuit components.

Skimming Process to correct warpage or repair a damaged surface, such as on brake discs or drums.

Slide-hammer A special puller that screws into or hooks onto a component such as a shaft or bearing; a heavy sliding handle on the shaft bottoms against the end of the shaft to knock the component free.

Small-end bearing The bearing in the upper end of the connecting rod at its joint with the gudgeon pin.

Snap-ring A ring-shaped clip used to prevent endwise movement of cylindrical parts and shafts. An internal snap-ring is installed in a groove in a housing; an external snap-ring fits into a groove on the outside of a cylindrical piece such as a shaft. Also known as a circlip.

Spalling Damage to camshaft lobes or bearing journals shown as pitting of the working surface.

Specific gravity (SG) The state of charge of the electrolyte in a lead-acid battery. A measure of the electrolyte's density compared with water.

Straight-cut gears Common type gear used on gearbox shafts and for oil pump and water pump drives.

Stanchion The inner sliding part of the front forks, held by the yokes. Often called a fork tube.

Stoichiometric ratio The optimum chemical air/fuel ratio for a gasoline engine, said to be 14.7 parts of air to 1 part of fuel.

Sulphuric acid The liquid (electrolyte) used in a lead-acid battery. Poisonous and extremely corrosive.

Surface grinding (lapping) Process to correct a warped gasket face, commonly used on cylinder heads.

T

Tapered-roller bearing Tapered inner race of caged needle rollers and separate tapered outer race. Examples of taper roller bearings can be found on steering heads.

Tappet A cylindrical component which transmits motion from the cam to the valve stem, either directly or via a pushrod and rocker arm. Also called a cam follower.

TCS Traction Control System. An electronically-controlled system which senses wheel spin and reduces engine speed accordingly.

TDC Top Dead Center denotes that the piston is at its highest point in the cylinder.

Thread-locking compound Solution applied to fastener threads to prevent loosening. Select type to suit application.

Thrust washer A washer positioned between two moving components on a shaft. For example, between gear pinions on gearshaft.

Timing chain See **Cam Chain**.

Timing light Stroboscopic lamp for carrying out ignition timing checks with the engine running.

Top-end A description of an engine's cylinder block, head and valve gear components.

Torque Turning or twisting force about a shaft.

Torque setting A prescribed tightness specified by the motorcycle manufacturer to ensure that the bolt or nut is secured correctly. Undertightening can result in the bolt or nut coming loose or a surface not being sealed. Overtightening can result in stripped threads, distortion or damage to the component being retained.

Torx key A six-point wrench.

Tracer A stripe of a second color applied to a wire insulator to distinguish that wire from another one with the same color insulator. For example, Br/W is often used to denote a brown insulator with a white tracer.

Trail A feature of steering geometry. Distance from the steering head axis to the tire's central contact point.

Triple clamps The cast components which extend from the steering head and support the fork stanchions or tubes. Often called fork yokes.

Turbocharger A centrifugal device, driven by exhaust gases, that pressurizes the intake air. Normally used to increase the power output from a given engine displacement.

TWI Abbreviation for Tire Wear Indicator. Indicates the location of the tread depth indicator bars on tires.

U

Universal joint or U-joint (UJ) A double-pivoted connection for transmitting power from a driving to a driven shaft through an angle. Typically found in shaft drive assemblies.

Unsprung weight Anything not supported by the bike's suspension (the wheel, tires, brakes, final drive and bottom [moving] part of the suspension).

V

Vacuum gauges Clock-type gauges for measuring intake tract vacuum. Used for carburetor synchronization on multi-cylinder engines.

Valve A device through which the flow of liquid, gas or vacuum may be stopped, started or regulated by a moveable part that opens, shuts or partially obstructs one or more ports or passageways. The intake and exhaust valves in the cylinder head are of the poppet type.

Valve clearance The clearance between the valve tip (the end of the valve stem) and the rocker arm or tappet/follower. The valve clearance is measured when the valve is closed. The correct clearance is important - if too small the valve won't close fully and will burn out, whereas if too large noisy operation will result.

Valve lift The amount a valve is lifted off its seat by the camshaft lobe.

Valve timing The exact setting for the opening and closing of the valves in relation to piston position.

Vernier caliper A precision measuring instrument that measures inside and outside dimensions. Not quite as accurate as a micrometer, but more convenient.

VIN Vehicle Identification Number. Term for the bike's engine and frame numbers.

Viscosity The thickness of a liquid or its resistance to flow.

Volt A unit for expressing electrical "pressure" in a circuit. Volts = current x ohms.

W

Water pump A mechanically-driven device for moving coolant around the engine.

Watt A unit for expressing electrical power. Watts = volts x current.

Wet liner arrangement

Wear limit see **Service limit**

Wet liner A liquid-cooled engine design where the pistons run in liners which are directly surrounded by coolant **(see illustration)**.

Wheelbase Distance from the center of the front wheel to the center of the rear wheel.

Wiring harness or loom Describes the electrical wires running the length of the motorcycle and enclosed in tape or plastic sheathing. Wiring coming off the main harness is usually referred to as a sub harness.

Woodruff key A key of semi-circular or square section used to locate a gear to a shaft. Often used to locate the alternator rotor on the crankshaft.

Wrist pin Another name for gudgeon or piston pin.

Trail rules

Just when you're ready to have some fun out in the dirt you get slapped with more rules. But by following these rules you'll ensure everyone's enjoyment, not just your own. It's important that all off-roaders follow these rules, as it will help to keep the trails open and keep us in good standing with other trail users. Really, these rules are no more than common sense and common courtesy.

• **Don't ride where you're not supposed to.** Stay off private property and obey all signs marking areas that are off limits to motorized vehicles. Also, as much fun as it might be, don't ride in State or Federal wilderness areas.

• **Leave the land as you found it.** When you've left the area, the only thing you should leave behind are your tire tracks. Stay on the trails, too. There are plenty of trails to ride on without blazing new ones. Be sure to carry out all litter that you create (and if you want to do a good deed, pick up any litter that you come across). Be sure to leave gates as you found them, or if the gate has a sign on it, comply with whatever the sign says (some people don't close gates after passing through them. Others may close gates when the landowner actually wants to keep them open).

• **Give other trail users the right-of-way.** There has been an ongoing dispute amongst trail users as to who belongs there and who doesn't. If the off-roading community shows respect and courtesy to hikers and equestrians, we stand a far better chance of being able to enjoy our sport in the years to come, and to keep the trails open for our children. When you ride up behind hikers or horses, give them plenty of room and pass slowly so as not to startle them. When you approach an equestrian from the opposite direction, stop your machine when the horse nears you so it won't get frightened and bolt.

• **Don't scare the animals!** Whether it be horses, cattle or wild animals like deer, rabbits or coyotes, leave them alone. Remember, you're visiting their home, so treat them with respect. Besides, startling animals can be dangerous. Loud noises or your sudden appearance can trigger an animal's defensive instinct, which could mean bad news for you.

• **Don't ride "over your head."** Sometimes the trails start to resemble ski runs, with a few irresponsible riders going so fast that they're barely able to maintain control of their bikes. They'd never be able to stop to avoid another trail user if they had to. Most collisions on the trail are caused by such individuals and the results are occasionally tragic. You should only ride fast in areas where you can clearly see a good distance ahead - never on trails with blind corners or rises high enough that prevent you from seeing what's on the other side.

• **Be prepared.** Carry everything you think you may need to make minor repairs should your machine break down. Know how to make basic repairs and keep your bike in good mechanical condition to minimize the chances of becoming stranded. Always let someone know where you're going, and ride with a friend whenever possible.

Note: *References throughout this index are in the form, "Chapter number"•"Page number"*